LETTER
OF
REPRISAL

JAMES H. MCGEE

ISBN: 979-8-9858142-0-0 Paperback
ISBN: 979-8-9858142-1-7 eBook

Cover design by Damonza

*Article I, Section 8, Clause 10 of the United States
Constitution authorizes the government of the United States:*

*"To define and punish Piracies and Felonies committed on
the high Seas, and Offences against the Law of Nations."*

Clause 11 of the same section authorizes the government:

*"To declare War, grant Letters of Marque and Reprisal, and
make Rules concerning Captures on Land and Water."*

**"People sleep peaceably in their beds at night only because
rough men stand ready to do violence on their behalf."**

Commonly attributed to George Orwell

CHAPTER 1

Somewhere in Central Africa, 2017

"Major," I heard Kip's voice in the headset of my Motorola Sabre tactical radio, "we're at the road." I knew he meant the dirt track leading up to the meadow that had featured so prominently in our original mission briefing, the meadow where our source had photographed the sad pile of murdered men, women, and children.

"Any sign of activity?" I asked.

"Negative."

Kip and Bobby's next checkpoint was at the top of the first ridge. We'd tried to set up the checkpoints so that they were in line-of-sight, since the little radios were operating in simplex mode. I sat alone in the troop compartment of the Mi-2 helicopter, the only light inside coming from the illuminated dials of the SATCOM radio and the faint red light that silhouetted the pilots sitting in the cockpit. Ten minutes passed, then eleven, then twelve—they'd gone overdue at ten. Finally, Kip checked in again.

"Problems?" I asked.

"Slow going," he replied. "The ridge's not all that steep, but the underbrush is really heavy. A lot heavier than most places around here."

"Push it harder," I said. "Five minutes here, five minutes there, and soon we're in deep shit."

I instantly regretted saying this. Kip Mwangi and Bobby Naburye were two of the best troopers I'd ever worked with; they didn't need me riding them. Still, we'd reached a critical juncture. Many hours ago, the Orion unmanned aircraft had been launched from Wideawake Airfield, a joint RAF/USAF base some 2500 miles away on Ascension Island in the South Atlantic; it would be overhead in another ten minutes, ready to fire its missile at the door of the poison gas facility. But the operator at the Wideawake ground station wouldn't fire the missile until we'd confirmed that we'd marked the door with the laser target designator. We'd been told that the Orion could loiter over the target for, maybe, thirty minutes, but we'd also been told not to count on it. Once the missile struck, it would take Kip and Bobby a half-hour to get back to the helicopter. Too much delay and we'd be flying out at dawn, when the superior night flying skills and equipment of our pilots would count for nothing. We could afford to be heard, but we couldn't afford to be clearly seen. With all this buzzing through my head, I gave mission command at Wideawake a sitrep on the SATCOM.

Ten minutes passed, then another ten. I wished that I still smoked, the combination of tension and inactivity was beginning to get to me. Another five minutes passed. Even though we had plenty of time, I didn't like the fact that Kip and Bobby hadn't called in. Maybe we had a radio problem. They would now be on a little down slope on the second ridge, which would affect my ability to receive them clearly. Finally, I heard Kip's voice in my headset.

"We've got big trouble, Major," he said.

"What kind of trouble?"

"There's a truck parked between us and the admin. building. It's taken away our line of sight to the target bunker. From where we are it's got the door completely blocked. There's no way we can mark the door from here."

"What about the missile? Will it clear the truck as it comes in?"

"The way we were briefed, it'll come from a high angle, should do just fine. The truck's maybe 50 meters from the door. It's just that we're down too low here."

"Can you back up the hillside and get high enough to aim over?"

"Tried that already. We just don't have enough slope or elevation behind us to make it work. Looks like our best chance is to work our way east. There should be a clear line to the door from there, shooting past the right-hand corner of the admin. building."

I pulled out the map we'd used in planning, gave it a quick scan.

"Should work. Just get the damned dot on the door."

"Take us about ten minutes or so to move around there."

"Then get going. The bird's not far out."

"I'll check in when we've got a set up."

"Roger."

I had no choice but to call this one back to Wideawake, hoping that the operators there were, in fact, wide awake; nobody had been expecting trouble and that kind of radio watch quickly becomes sleep inducing. Then I leaned forward into the cockpit and explained to our pilots what was going on. It didn't affect their job, but I've always believed that if someone's neck's in a noose, they deserve to know what might be tightening the rope.

Not for the first time, I wished that I understood more about the technology behind the mission. Our briefing back at Langley had been relatively superficial. We'd only been told that 'Friends' associated with the UN Peacekeeping Force in the DRC—the "Democratic Republic" of the Congo had received evidence that one of the competing militia groups in the region had gained a quantity of nerve gas and were showing obvious signs of willingness to use it. We were shown pictures of some of their "experiments," and while piles of bodies were scarcely new to anyone familiar with the border regions of the Congo and Rwanda, these had been especially sickening. The UN "friends" confessed that they lacked the assets to take down the facility; knowing the nature of "peacekeeping," I could only suspect that they were also afraid to even try.

The Air Force had jumped all over the opportunity to use its latest toy. The blue-suit briefer had proudly told us that the Orion had a longer range than any previous combat drone and that the missile's multi-function electro-optical targeting system would 'read' the identity of the nerve gas bunker, find the weak spot—the door— and target itself accordingly. We were there strictly as insurance, our laser targeting system a back-up in case something went wrong. Still, a lot of effort had gone into getting my team on the ground, too much effort to explain our supposedly ancillary role.

But soon Kip checked in again, right on time. "We're good to go. We can put the dot on the door about two feet down from the top, and we're actually closer by about 200 meters. Good enough?"

"Should be fine." I switched to the SATCOM, passed this along, and received a verbal 'thumbs up,' which I relayed to Kip.

Now it was just a matter of waiting. We'd get a heads up when the bird was overhead and ready to launch. You couldn't run the laser continuously for very long without draining the battery, and you didn't need to anyway. The final sixty seconds were what really counted. When the pre-launch warning came, I notified Kip, then told the pilots to put on their night vision goggles and told them to look north. I wished that I had goggles of my own, but the mission planners had only provided four sets.

The Orion was programmed to make its launch approach from the south-southeast, which meant it would come almost right over our heads, just a little to the left. It would also be coming in slow. Although faster than the original reconnaissance versions, the drone only flew at about 120 knots when programmed for a long-range mission. It would be flying high, too high for us to see or hear, but we would be able to see the missile launch. The missile would come in hot and fast, making quite a show.

Everything started to happen very fast. Kip reported that he'd marked the door. I reported this to Wideawake ground control, and immediately began scanning the sky through the portside window of the Mi-2, watching just above the tree line at the top of the ridge.

Then I saw it, a dim shadow trailing a brilliant white-hot light, the exhaust from the missile's engine. Not very loud, I thought, but then it was pretty far away. And just as suddenly it was gone, dipping low on its final trajectory, and then the horizon lit up in an immense and unearthly brightness, far brighter than I expected, far brighter than an explosion contained by a massive bunker should have been, and even in the scant moment between the flash of light and the sound of the explosion I knew that something had gone terribly wrong.

Chapter 2

Kip's first words confirmed the worst.

"We've got a class-A fuck up, Major. The missile flew right over the fucking bunker, right over the perimeter fence, right over the gorge and the river, and right into the side of the next ridge. Too high by about six feet. Six fucking feet."

"Did you have the laser on the door?"

"Right on, never even wavered. Hey, we can talk about that later. The whole compound down below us is going nutso. Bobby and me had better boogie on back to the chopper."

"Right. Pack up and move out. Get back here while they're still trying to figure out what the hell happened."

The pilots had been monitoring my traffic with Kip, but I took a moment to bring them up to speed on how I wanted to play things. This was critical since the exfil plan had just turned to shit, but it also gave me an excuse to put off the call back to base. Finally, I made myself key the SATCOM mike.

"Mirage Taxi to Winter City," I hate these computer-generated random code names.

"Winter City." The transmission delay with military satellite radios is minimal, unlike the lengthy pauses that characterize the commercial systems used by news reporters from places like Afghanistan.

"Total failure, I say again, total failure." Might as well be blunt.

There was a long silence, then "Please repeat your last."

"Total failure. The bird flew over the target. I'm extracting the team."

"What happened?" This was another voice breaking in, not the communicator I was accustomed to dealing with. A big boss of some sort.

"Your stupid missile overshot the damned target." I didn't have time for this shit, not until Kip and Bobby were out of the woods.

"Say again?"

I hesitated momentarily to collect myself. "Bird flew over the target. No further info at this time. Must concentrate on exfil. Out."

I switched off the satellite system. No point in getting into a command-level post mortem, not now anyway. I wished I had a radio set up to monitor the facility's security frequency. It would be good to know just exactly what was going on. But that, too, had been a detail left undone in our haste to mount the mission. Looking in the direction of the facility I could see a pillar of flame climbing above the ridgeline. Evidently the thermobaric warhead had started a forest fire.

The team radio crackled, Kip's voice saying, "Major, we've got big trouble."

"What trouble?"

"Climbing one of the steep bits, I lost my balance with the damned MULE, fell backward on Bobby, knocked him flat and landed on top of him. Good news is he's out cold. Bad news is, looks like maybe his leg's broke just above the ankle."

"Shit."

"Exactly."

"You all right?"

"Yeah, fine, knocked the wind out of me for a second. Thing is, I can tote him out, but I can't tote him and the MULE."

"Of course not."

"Only way I've got of destroying the MULE is the time charge."

This brought me up short. I hadn't been thinking about the need to destroy the laser device. The missile would destroy all traces of its origins—the thermobaric fireball would see to that—but we couldn't leave an obvious and highly sensitive item of U.S. military equipment laying around in the woods just a few hundred meters from the facility. It was precisely for this reason that we'd made a last-minute effort to rig the MULE with a C-4 charge. But we'd assumed that any need to destroy the MULE would not come so close to the facility. The time fuse was preset for sixty seconds, more than enough to retreat from the blast area, but not enough to give Kip much time to distance himself from an explosion that would no doubt draw the attention of every guard at the facility.

"You were trying to make it up a steep slope, right?"

"Yeah, only about fifteen feet up, but pulling ourselves up with our hands. After that there's rough patches, but nothing that bad."

"Get Bobby up the slope, then go back down and set the charge. That'll give you a little head start."

"Roger that. I'm starting now."

Nothing to do but wait. Aside from getting the helicopter ready to take off as soon as Kip and Bobby arrived, there were no positive actions to take. I debated making a further sitrep to Wideawake. It was certainly what I was expected to do, but I just couldn't bring myself to do it. I felt helpless and hopeless, a useless old man in the midst of a situation where he no longer belonged.

Kip came back up on the radio. "I've set the charge, Major, and I'm back with Bobby, moving your way. Should take maybe twenty minutes to get to you. I'm going for speed, not stealth."

I stepped outside of the helicopter, scanning the tree line to the northwest. In a matter of seconds, I saw a flash of light, followed almost immediately by the sound of the demolition charge. There would be no overlooking the fact of an explosion, and no mistaking its location. Now it would be a foot race. Five minutes passed uneasily, then ten, and then I heard a sound that told me that the race was about to be over. From below and to the left, the direction of the dirt road that led up into the test meadow, I heard the sound of a large truck grinding its way uphill in low gear. Then it stopped, and I heard shouts, too far away to understand, but the tone of command was clear. Then the truck started up again, and, after about a minute, stopped further along the road. More shouts. A lifetime of soldiering told me all I needed to know. Someone at the target facility had gathered up a truckload of troops and was now spreading them along the dirt road and the meadow, cordoning off all escape to the east, pinning whoever was responsible for the explosion inside a rectangle formed by the river to the north, the lab compound to the west, the hard surface road to the south, and the line of troops now spreading just past the trees in front of me.

I called Kip and told him to hold up at the first tree line; under no circumstances was he to break back across the road until he'd heard from me again. I hurriedly organized the equipment I had, which wasn't the equipment I needed, since I had virtually none of the things I really needed for the task at hand. I looked at the radio in my hand and then reached for my rain jacket, thankful that, despite our civilian cover, I'd had sense enough to buy one colored olive green rather than the bright yellow yachtsman's version hanging next to it in the sporting goods store back in Virginia. I didn't need protection from the rain, but since I didn't have a tactical vest to carry gear, I needed something with big pockets. My radio went into the jacket's left side cargo pocket. My next problem was the radio headset, not a sturdy tactical model with headset, but a simple ear piece and throat mike, connected to the radio by a fragile wire, an executive protection kit designed to be worn, Secret Service-style, under a suit coat. The damned thing would rip away at the first hint of underbrush. I grabbed a roll of "hundred mile an hour tape"—"duct tape" to civilians—and hastily taped the wire to the outside of my jacket, leaving enough slack inside my jacket pocket so that a sudden extreme movement wouldn't jerk the ear piece out of my ear. The Velcro closure on the flap of my jacket pocket would, I hoped, keep the radio from falling out. I reached into my gear bag, pulled out a black watch cap, and stretched it down over my ears. This would help anchor the ear piece in place and cover my too-bright white hair.

Having attended to the commo issue, I popped the latch of the equipment locker that was bolted against the back wall of the helicopter's passenger compartment. In addition to the various tools, the locker contained what our geological survey cover story would've identified as "wilderness survival items." One of these was a Remington 870 12-gauge shotgun, the one made for boaters, with the rustproof electroless nickel plating and a black fiberglass stock. This was clearly the better close-range weapon, but I already had a Makarov pocket pistol for that purpose. Besides, the shiny nickel plating might just give me away. So instead I reached for the little Sako, a bolt-action, full-stock carbine with an 18½ barrel, chambered for the Swedish 6.5mm round.

I lifted the rifle out, along with a box of Norma 156 grain soft points, a long bullet with a generous amount of soft lead exposed at the tip. These were hunting bullets, designed to mushroom on hitting flesh. Hunters regard such bullets as the perfect tool for making humane "one-shot" kills on big bucks, but, perversely, the Geneva Convention forbids their use on humans as unnecessarily cruel. For my purposes, this hardly mattered. If the bullet expanded quickly on impact, it would kill more quickly, and I had no objection to quick kills. What did matter was that the soft lead point would translate into reduced effectiveness against body armor. I could only hope the bad guys weren't wearing any.

I drew four cartridges out of the plastic carrier inside the ammunition box, pulled back the rifle bolt, and pressed them through the open action into the internal box magazine. I closed the bolt, chambering the top round, reflecting that I had come full circle, after a lifetime of automatic assault rifles I was back to the simple Mauser-style bolt action I'd first learned to shoot as a ten-year-old in 1961. But this was no time for reverie. I dropped the empty cardboard cartridge box on the compartment floor, shoving the plastic cartridge carrier with the remaining sixteen rounds into the free pocket of my jacket alongside the Makarov pistol. I pressed the flap of this pocket inside so that the Velcro wouldn't fasten. Unlike the other pocket with the radio, I needed ready access to the cartridges and the pistol, needed it enough to risk leaving them unsecured. Besides, Velcro makes a distinctive noise when opened. That was it. For better or worse, I was as well-equipped as I was going to be. I stepped down out of the helicopter and headed west into the darkness.

Actually, the semi-darkness, for the moon was up, bright and full. Since we'd only had a small red light on in the helicopter, my eyes were already night-adapted. I quickly traversed the open space of the LZ and crossed the tree line, working toward the continuing sound of shouted commands. Fortunately, at this particular point the trees were widely spaced and the undergrowth sparse. I could make good time without undue effort. Still, by the time I'd covered the hundred meters to the lip of the little ridge above the edge of the road, my breathing had become ragged and heavy, and sweat poured from my forehead. I knelt behind the trunk of a tree, and paused long enough, maybe a minute, for my chest to stop heaving. Time was critical, but I'd be worthless if I couldn't hold the little Sako steady and control my breathing. It's hell being old.

With my body back under control, I inched forward across the ten meters that separated me from a view of the road. Good tactical movement means being either very deliberate or very sudden, not the same thing as simply being slow or fast. When someone may be hunting you, you take a few careful steps, never jerky, and very quiet, then you stop, look, and listen, being very, very still. Then you move again, the same way. But if you have to move across an open space, you pick your destination carefully, and then you dart like a deer across the space. The trick, of course, is in knowing when to be deliberate and when to be sudden. In my case, the decision was easy. I didn't think I was capable of darting like a deer.

I could tell that the trees stopped abruptly just above the road. I dropped into a low crawl and edged up to where I could see. But just as I reached the point where the ground fell away, I heard a sharp 'pop,' below and to my left, and a small white dot of fire arced steeply into the night sky above the road, then burst brightly and started to flicker downward, suspended from a tiny parachute. A slap flare, or maybe—more likely from the sound—a flare fired from a grenade launcher, maybe one of the little Chinese 35mm jobs that have been spreading across Africa. I looked over the rim of the embankment and saw the truck, maybe thirty meters up the road to my right. Behind it stood perhaps a half dozen armed militiamen, made spectral by the strobe light effect of the descending flare. Directly below me I could see another soldier kneeling in the ditch at the roadside, and, as I scanned from right to left, others spaced at similar intervals.

The radio crackled in my ear.

"Major, are you okay."

"I'm okay, Kip. You?"

"I'm at the edge of the trees, looking down on the road. There's troopers moving below me, spreading out. They're cordoning us off, I think."

That's exactly what they were doing. "Can you see the truck?" I asked.

"No. The road curves just below me. I can't see round the bend."

The flare died out, and then another was fired by someone in the little group standing at the back of the truck. They weren't practiced enough to keep illumination in the air all the time once they started. One wants either continuous light or none at all. It confirmed my impression that these weren't very good troops, an impression formed first by all the yelling I'd heard—no individual radios—and now, in my first glimpse, by the ragged appearance of the few I'd glimpsed by the flare light. Still, there were a lot of them.

"You're just up the road from me. The curve—it has to be the one you're seeing from the other end—starts about fifty meters past where the truck's parked. There's a wide spot just before it, a turn out, and the road gets steeper. It's a good ambush spot, the guy in charge must've not wanted to risk the truck any further up."

"Roger."

"Listen up, here's what we'll do. After I sign off, wait one and then get Bobby up on your back, get ready to run. You'll hear shots from down here, and that should bring your guys this way. I don't think they're disciplined enough to hold position. When you've got a clear crossing, move fast, and don't stop til you get to the helicopter. I'll meet you there."

"Not much of a plan, Major."

"Best we've got."

"Roger that."

Kip was right. It wasn't much of a plan. It was a desperate hope, born of the silliness of assuming that nothing would go wrong, that we'd slip in quietly and then slip out again in the confusion after the missile blew up the facility. But I was also right. We didn't have time for a better one.

A third flare went up, and I trained my carbine on the men gathered at the back of the truck. I was assuming that this was some kind of command group, and, by way of confirmation, I heard across the night air the sound of a voice from a radio speaker. Probably the commander's radio link back to the facility, since none of his soldiers seemed to have radios. I moved the scope slowly across the group, stopping when I glimpsed a radio sitting on the tailgate of the truck. One man hunched over it, another stood next to him. The commander? Probably. I centered the scope between his shoulders. Now, while I still had good light.

I took up the slack in the trigger, controlling my breathing in precisely the manner that had been drilled into me so long ago. The rifle bucked against my shoulder, and almost automatically I brought it back down, the scope covering the man I'd hit even as he staggered and then slumped out of view. I worked the bolt as I adjusted to the right and down, picking up the man who'd been kneeling over the radio, and was now lying prone below the tailgate, putting a second round into either his shoulders or buttocks. The way he was twisted it was hard to tell, but either would do just fine as the big hunting round plowed through flesh. Then the flare went out, and this time there wouldn't be another, not until they collected their wits. It was a good time for sudden movement, since, after the flares, everyone's night vision would've turned to shit.

I hurried back into the trees, and then curved to my left. The two shots I'd taken wouldn't be quite enough. I emerged again from the tree line at a point that was only a few feet above the road on a relatively gentle slope. I couldn't see anyone in the ditch below, but I could see the truck very clearly in the moonlight. So, I shot the truck, knowing that my round would go over the head of anyone in the ditch, knowing too that, with a moment to collect themselves, all of them would be better able to key upon the direction of a gunshot. Once again it was a time for rapid movement. I dashed back into the trees, running as hard as I could as AK rounds cracked high overhead, snapping branches above me, confirming yet again the hard-earned insight that startled men usually fire high. There were at least a dozen firing now, a drum roll of small arms fire, but that was a good thing. They couldn't shoot worth a damn, but any one of them could probably outrun me. After about thirty meters I allowed myself to slow to a walk, catching my breath again, the continued shooting chewing up the trees behind me. When I could speak again, I keyed my radio.

"Kip?"

"Major."

"Across the road?"

"Yeah, and into the trees. Blew right across while all the shooting was going on."

His words were interspersed by heavy sharp intakes of breath. Kip, I knew, was in superb physical condition, but he was also carrying a 170-pound man slung across his shoulder.

"I'm maybe 10 minutes from the helicopter," I said, aware that, though the distance wasn't great, I was too winded to run anymore. "You?"

"Less than that, a little."

"Good. Out."

"Stew, ears on?" I called on the radio to the pilot.

"Go ahead, Harry."

"Start warming up."

"Lotta noise. You sure?"

"Fuck the noise. Start winding the damned rubber band!"

I pressed through the last underbrush and out into the clearing, ducking under the slowly turning rotor blades, glancing up at the black letters on the yellow and blue livery of the Mi-2. "Gorilla Country Adventure Tours," they read, the name of the civilian cover outfit for our helicopter operation. Well, we'd just had the motherfucker of all adventure tours, I thought as I climbed through the door. I saw Kip kneeling bent over, tending to Bobby who was stretched on the floor, still unconscious. By the sound of things, the soldiers back at the road were still shooting up trees. Perhaps I had killed the commander with that first shot. They were certainly acting more and more like a leaderless mob than an organized unit, but then again, this was a Congolese militia. As long as they kept their frantic fusillade, the gunfire would drown out the sound of the Mi-2. But a deliciously good feeling came over me when I heard the pitch of the rotors change and felt the aircraft go light on its skids, and an even better feeling when we lurched forward and started to gain momentum and altitude.

I relaxed against the back wall of the compartment, glancing out the open door at the flare and tracer show to our left. Sensing motion to my right, I turned to see Bobby raise his head slightly before settling back at Kip's knees. I looked past them out the right-side window, watching the moonlit horizon open up as we cleared the trees. We gained another hundred feet as our forward momentum carried us close to the road, still trying to gaining airspeed before turning away. I looked back at the door as a flare popped just to our left, felt the increasing rate of turn, and gave Kip a grin and a high sign just as a 7.62mm round pierced the aluminum floor of the helicopter cabin and entered Bobby's head just behind the ear, blowing out the right side of his face as it exited, and spraying Kip from chin to belt buckle with brains, bone, and miscellaneous gore.

CHAPTER 3

I STRIPPED OFF my rain jacket, emptied the pockets, and wrapped it around Bobby's shattered head, the best I could do until we reached the little private airfield at Fort Portal, just across the border in Uganda, the base for our central African cover activities, Gorilla Adventure tours and Ruwenzori Geological Surveys. So much for the Agency's future ops in the region; both companies would likely be irretrievably blown within the next twenty-four hours. But someone would come out from Kampala to clean up the mess. Our job was to get clear of the area, and fast. We rolled our fixed-wing aircraft, an old Cessna Caravan light cargo plane, out of the hangar and rolled the Mi-2 inside. Now our pilots reversed roles. The helicopter co-pilot, Alan Nakuru, was the lead fixed-wing pilot, and he took the left seat while Stew Williams switched to the right. We bundled Bobby's body in a couple of blankets and took off, heading northeast. Our "bugout" location, just barely within the Caravan's ferry range, was Camp Lemonier, a U.S. Navy base in Djibouti. Six long hours, six hours marked by exhaustion and might have beens—six miserable hours.

A Marine security team met us when we stopped rolling, preventing us from checking in at the small Agency office on the base. Instead they took Bobby's remains from us and consigned us immediately to a waiting C-40 transport, all the while treating us like lepers. Similar treatment awaited us during the refueling stops at Sigonella in Sicily and again Lajes Field in the Azores. Finally, when we landed at Andrews, we received a moment of civility when my boss, Betty Foster, met us at the plane and gave each of us a brief hug. But this gave way immediately to the icicle treatment when two strangers in suits loaded us into the back seats of a Suburban and drove us out to Langley. The two suits subjected us to a perfunctory group debriefing, with Betty sitting in, watching and listening without contributing more than a few words, her manner decidedly somber.

After about four hours, the suits called things to an abrupt halt. We were told to say nothing to anyone about the mission and then we were dismissed, with Stew and Alan given the clear message that their services would no longer be needed—they were both contractors and thus easily dumped. I felt badly for Stew Williams, but knew he'd quickly find his feet. I felt worse for Alan, who was Kenyan, and whose combination of language and flying skills would likely find little appreciation if he couldn't operate any more in central Africa. So, I wrote him a personal check for $10,000 and told him to stay in touch, that I'd soon find him something. I felt worst of all for Kip, who, apparently, was being consigned to limbo. When they dropped Kip and me at our respective homes in Herndon and Alexandria, they gave us explicit orders not to contact Bobby Naburje's wife in Annandale or his parents in Kinshasa, and they told us not to show up at the office until called. They clearly implied, in Kip's case at least, that the call might be a long time coming.

My call, however, came the following evening. A meeting of 'principals,' I was told, to take place at 0800 the following morning at a classified conference facility located in an office complex near Dulles Airport. The following morning, I drove west along I-66, cruising at the speed limit as I watched the heavy east-bound traffic creeping toward the District. I turned north on 28, following the signs toward the airport, but turning short near the Westfields shopping center. I wound around through a series of bland modern office buildings, eventually finding one with a guard at the entrance to the parking lot. I identified myself to the guard, who checked my name against a visitor list and gave me directions to the conference location. I found a parking place in front of a gray stone building and went inside and downstairs to the basement, where a bored looking guard checked my ID against an access roster, made me sign the visitor's log, and then admitted me through a vault-type door.

I'd arrived early because I wanted to be able to observe all the others as they walked through the door. Instead I discovered that all but one of the seats around the small conference table were already taken. Evidently there'd been matters to discuss before my arrival.

"Hi, Harry," said Betty Foster from her place next to the empty chair. She motioned, unnecessarily, for me to take the seat and gave me a moment before introducing me around the table. "You know Bob Barnhart, of course." Barnhart was Betty's boss, a long-time Agency careerist whose chief talent had always seemed to be his ability to avoid giving offense. Barnhart sat at the end of the table to my left. "The two gentlemen across from us are Kevin Sykes and Colonel Mac Baldwin of the Air Force." Sykes I knew by name, though I'd never met him. He was a horse holder for the Deputy Director and thus, by proxy at least, the most potent Agency representative present. He looked the part of a major player, in direct contrast to Colonel Baldwin, who uniform enhanced, rather than masked, his essential geekiness.

"And I am General Rivers Rickman," said the officer sitting at the end of the table to my right. At first glance he appeared the total opposite of Baldwin, slim, youthful-looking, with just a hint of gray at the temples. His voice matched the look, resonant and commanding. He seemed every inch a general, a fighter jock general. Reflexively I checked his ribbons. No Air Force Cross, no DFC, no Air Medal— from the top line down a Distinguished Service Medal, some kind of joint DoD senior level service medal, a Legion of Merit with several Oak Leaf clusters, a similarly festooned MSM, and two rows of Air

Force "mystery medals," a mix of low-level commendation and "been there" ribbons. No pilot's wings, but the badge of a missileer, someone who'd spent his military formative years sitting at the bottom of a Minuteman silo in North Dakota, waiting for orders to blow the world away. It's said that you can read a serviceman's biography by the colors on his chest, and Rickman's colors identified him as nothing more than a more august version of Baldwin's military techno-weenie. But a general for all that.

"Now that Major York has joined us," began Sykes, making it sound as if I had arrived late," let me tee things up for everyone. We had a chance the other night, a real chance, our best chance in a very long time, to strike a major blow against a terrorist cell in central Africa, one that has directly threatened the UN peacekeeping mission, using nerve gas that they have from a Syrian connection. All the pieces were in place. The fix was in with the Congolese government, first-rate local intel, a rock-solid technical package. We had it all just the way we wanted it, the result of a lot of hard work by a very good team, a closely-coordinated Agency-Air Force team. We had a big one in the palm of our hands, and now we've got jack shit. There are a lot of good people who are very unhappy today."

"And there's one very good young man who's dead today," I interjected. I hadn't liked what I'd just heard.

"Quite," said Sykes. "A good mission that turned into a failure and a tragedy as well."

"A failure," said Rickman, "that demands an accounting."

He caught his next words at the sound of the door opening. The young Staff Sergeant stuck her head in and said, "There's a lady out here, a Dr. Sandra Sawyer, Congressional staff ID, says she's here for the meeting. Her name's not on the authorization list."

"Who the hell invited Sandy Sawyer?" asked Sykes.

"I did," said Rickman, "I did, with the Deputy Assistant Secretary's blessing. The Sub-Committee's been deeply involved in the missile project from the beginning. She's got the right clearance and the right tickets. She needs to be here."

"Where's the coordination on this thing?" asked Sykes. He sounded seriously unhappy.

"No time. I only got the word late last night." Since he'd obviously had ample opportunity to bring this up while they were together prior to my arrival, this clearly had the tone of a 'screw you, I can do what I want' challenge. Sykes considered this, appeared to be pondering a counter challenge, then opted for surrender. "Send her in," he said to the Staff Sergeant.

At first, I didn't know what to make of the woman who strode through the door. She was slightly built, dressed in a suit coat over a tee-shirt and tight designer blue jeans. Her complexion was unbelievably pale, her hair coal black—unquestionably dyed—and her earlobes were pierced for a row of six small silver earrings. She looked less like a Congressional aide than the lead singer for some MTV Euro-trash rock band. But, then, I freely confess that I know very little of Congressional staffers, or, come to that, rock bands. Her first words confirmed the visual impression.

"Is somebody going to get me a fucking chair?"

This produced a flurry of activity, ending when a chair was retrieved from an adjacent room and squeezed in at the corner of the table next to Rickman. As Sawyer took her seat she placed her hand on Rickman's forearm and leaned over to whisper something in his ear. Then she addressed the room.

"When General Rickman called me last night it was too late to call Congressman Royall, so I went around to see him this morning before coming out here. Why the hell did you guys choose to have this meeting out in the boonies anyway? It's not like there's not ten thousand fucking secure conference rooms closer to civilization." More contrast—her crude language was expressed with exquisite diction. Maybe she was a Harvard Ph.D. "Just the same," she continued, "Congressman Royall is pissed and the other members of the committee are not going to be happy campers when he tells them."

"We had hoped," said Sykes, "to keep this fairly close hold."

"C'mon, Kevin, give me a fucking break. I'm not talking about the

Post here, or Anderson fucking Cooper. I'm not even talking about the membership as a whole, maybe not even the Speaker. I'm just talking the Sub-Committee on Military Special Technologies. In this town that's about as close hold as a clenched asshole." She paused to take a breath. "But we went out on a fucking limb for you clowns, let you use project research dollars to finance an actual operation. In case you've forgotten, that's mixing pots of money, crossing over budget authorization boundaries, and that's not just forbidden by Congressional rules, but by public law."

"Yes, I know," said Sykes, whose buttoned-down composure seemed to be wilting under Sawyer's verbal assault.

"Look, Kevin," she said, "nobody wants a leak on this thing. If it had worked as planned, we'd have had major kudos for all hands, and nobody would've griped that a few laws got bent. But instead we've got this shit sandwich on the table. Nobody, but nobody, wants it to get out, but if it does, the sub-committee chairman has to have protection. Otherwise, the media's going to bend him over and butt-fuck him so hard that snot'll shoot out of his nose." She settled back in her chair, glaring around the table. I confess that I was impressed. My best friend is a retired Marine gunny with what I'd thought was an Olympic command of raw invective, but now I'd have to view him as merely a silver medalist. The awed silence continued until finally Sawyer spoke once again. "Kevin," she said, her tone emphatic but now almost gentle, "we've got to have accountability. You know what I mean, don't you?"

"Just what I was saying before," added Rickman.

"Precisely," said Sykes. "An accounting. What went wrong?"

"Who screwed up?" said Rickman.

Sykes met his eye. "Let's stay with 'what went wrong' for now," he replied evenly. I'd already begun to doubt that Sykes would step forward as my defender, but it was his meeting, and, after his pounding from Sawyer, he clearly wished to regain control of the agenda. He paused just long enough to make sure he had everyone's full attention. "Colonel Baldwin," he said, "let's begin with you. Please review the technical capabilities of the various systems, the UAV and the missile, and the preparation for this mission."

What ensued was an ostensibly impromptu dissertation, made informally and without notes, but delivered with a practiced fluency that only comes from careful preparation and rehearsal. I tried to resist the confidence-inspiring allure of the endless technical detail, but I could see very clearly that I was the only one. Even Betty Foster, the closest I had to a real ally in the room, seemed hypnotized by Baldwin's presentation. And it was convincing. The Orion drone was a special "one-off" development, basically a prototype, optimized for stealth and very long range, a major step up from the MQ-9 attack platform. As Baldwin noted, the MQ-9 had been used in Yemen in 2002 to carry Hellfire missiles in action for the first time, firing a missile successfully at a truck load of al Qaeda operatives. Since then it had proven itself repeatedly, in multiple theaters. The big deal with the Orion was range. I'd heard rumors that the Air Force had actually flown one of the original Predator unmanned aircraft from California to Australia, just to prove it could be done. But now, as our mission had demonstrated, the long-range capability was not just a stunt. I'm no big fan of high tech, but flying an unmanned aircraft from an island in the South Atlantic halfway across Africa and back by remote control from a ground station in thousands of miles away impressed me. And the Orion, at least, had worked perfectly, finding the right location above the poison gas storage bunker, that was a real accomplishment. Baldwin and his team had every reason to be proud.

Similarly, there was no good reason why the Maverick shouldn't have worked as advertised. The Maverick guidance system, according to Baldwin, had been nothing more than the adaptation of two proven designs, the laser-guided system of the Maverick E and the electro-optical system of the Maverick K, coupled with a GPS referencing system. The only really novel aspect of the design had been the combination of the hard target penetrator with a thermobaric secondary warhead. But that had gone 'boom,' at the very least, and we'd never know if it would've taken out the bunker, since it hit half a klick away. No, the issue was the guidance system for the Maverick adaptation. Baldwin was Rickman's boy, and Rickman had put together a closely-held 'black' operation that combined the developed of the combined Predator and Maverick systems, with a raft of special tweaks, all designed to enable this country to strike deep into hostile territory without placing any ground troops in harms' way, at least not once the system was proven and the laser back-up was no longer needed. This, I gathered had been meant to be a great thing for the Air Force, which wanted to raise its game now that we were back in the business of dealing with "near peer" adversaries like the Chinese and Russians, either directly or by virtue of their willingness to support Third World movements. And it was also clearly meant to be a great thing for General Rivers Rickman, for it was now crystal clear that the whole thing, from design to delivery, belonged to Rickman and, at a higher level, to Sandy Sawyer, her congressman, and whatever defense contractor was in bed with all of them.

As I pondered all of this I'd partly tuned out Baldwin's techno-monotone. He was spending far too much time on the two-stage thermobaric warhead, and no one had, as yet, bothered to point out that the efficacy of the warhead was not at issue. The real issue was the reliability of the guidance system, but this he glided over rather quickly—too quickly.

"So, as you can see," he concluded, "there's absolutely no basis for believing that the missile was at fault."

Since no one else chose to speak, I decided that I had to.

"Colonel Baldwin, I will grant you that the missile represents a very impressive system, and one that has a solid track record. But what about the mission set up? The guidance computers have to be programmed, and this opens up the possibility of error."

Baldwin hesitated, and Rickman spoke in his place.

"The programming was performed by Colonel Baldwin himself, and he has more hands-on experience with these guidance systems than anyone else in the entire world. The chances that a programming error took place are infinitesimal."

"So, the missile should have been right on target, right on the door of the underground lab. Am I right?"

Barnhart, surprisingly, spoke up. "That's right, Harry. That's what we were all told back when the mission was first planned."

"You are absolutely correct," added Rickman. I glanced across the table, noticed that Colonel Baldwin was carefully studying his fingernails.

"So, again, if properly programmed, there's no way that the missile shouldn't have been right on target?" I knew that I was on to something; I just didn't know precisely what. But Rickman didn't like the direction of my question and moved to head me off.

"There's no way that the missile could have gone off target unless it was interfered with in some way."

"And what might have interfered with it? Something external? Electromagnetic pulse?"

"Not possible," said Colonel Baldwin. "The guidance system is shielded, and the shielding has been tested numerous times out at Sandia National Laboratories. There's just no way. Besides, what would have been the EMP source?"

"I have no idea," I said. This was true. Most of the little I knew about EMP came from reading *Popular Mechanics*.

"I should have thought the problem was obvious," said Rickman.

"Yes?"

"Your man Mwangi pulled the missile off course with the laser."

"Now we had come to the point of the whole charade, namely laying the failure on Kip.

"How?"

"It's obvious, I should think. He didn't have the laser properly aligned on the door. You and he both reported that he had to take up an alternate position, one that was offset sharply from the one identified for you in the plan."

"Yeah, but he still had direct line of sight to the door, and he had the dot planted right in the center."

"How do you know?"

"Because he said so."

"And your faith in Mwangi is absolute?"

"Exactly. He wouldn't have reported what he hadn't done. I have no doubt whatsoever on that score. Besides, Kip Mwangi was a Marine sniper before I recruited him. He's had years of training and experience with precise targeting, and he's done laser targeting under fire, in situations far worse than this one, and he never screwed up."

"As an officer I understand the importance of standing up for one's subordinates. But I fail to see how you can be so sure. You must understand, it cannot possibly be a problem with the missile, and that means that the only possible source is human error."

"Maybe so, General," I answered and then paused, choosing my next words carefully. "But if I grant you the fact that the only possible source is human error, then I ask you to grant that Kip Mwangi was not the human who erred. If Kip says he had the laser on the target, then he had the laser on the target."

Rickman glared at me, started to speak, then caught himself.

"Wait a minute?" injected Betty. "When we were originally briefed about this mission, the whole business of the laser targeting system was presented as, what was it, I think it was called a 'supplement' to the missile's guidance system. Wasn't that right, Bob?" she said, turning to Barnhart.

"Yes, exactly. I think it was called an insurance policy. The missile would go right to the target, using its own guidance system, and the laser just provided a confirmation, so to speak."

"Colonel Baldwin," I said, "what would've happened if there had been no laser in the first place?"

"The system would have followed its programmed course to the target."

"And what would've happened if the laser-designated course disagreed with the course and target profile information programmed into the guidance system?"

Rickman came half out of his chair. "Baldwin, do not answer any more questions about the guidance system. That's a direct order.

Mr. Sykes, we need to draw a line under this and get on with the purpose of this meeting. These people have no need-to-know concerning the technicalities of the missile's guidance system."

"General," I spoke up, "I'd say I have all the need to know in the world. Because your missile failed, one of my men got killed, and I damned near got killed myself. If this meeting is, in effect, some kind of informal court of inquiry, then I'd say I have every right—I'd say everyone around the table has the right—to know exactly how your missile works."

"Sykes," said Rickman, "this meeting was your fucking idea. You'd better get the goddamned thing back in the box, or I'll pull the plug right now and take the whole thing to the SecDef's people. And you, York, you better get one goddamned thing perfectly fucking straight. My missile did not fail. My people did not fail. No fucking way. And I am not going to sit here and let some superannuated semi-Kraut jumped up NCO—some 'special fucking operator,' pardon my fucking French—suggest anything to the contrary."

Rickman's tone of voice matched his choice of words, and his complexion had turned a mottled purplish-red. He looked like a man halfway to a heart attack. And at this point, I didn't care if he had one.

"Listen up and listen good, you two-star piece of shit," I said, "I was shedding my foreign by-God blood for this country when your mommy was still putting band-aids on your scratches. And you can get one thing perfectly straight yourself." By this point I was also out of my chair, with Betty tugging at the sleeve of my jacket. "Kip Mwangi is as reliable in the field as any piece of hardware the air farce—excuse me, the Air Force—has ever produced. So, you can take your perfect missile and you can shove it...."

"Harry, please!" said Betty.

"That will just about do, Dr. York," said Sykes.

I put my hand up, palm outstretched. "Okay, okay, fine." It wouldn't do Kip any good if I let things get completely out of hand. I took a moment to gather my thoughts. "Okay, what about this? If you grant the general's point that his hardware and his people didn't screw up, and if you grant my point that Kip wouldn't have reported the laser on target if he didn't genuinely believe—if he didn't have a positive indication—that the laser was lined up on the door, then there is a third possibility. Maybe there was something wrong with the laser designator."

"How wrong?" asked Colonel Baldwin. "What kind of wrong?"

"I don't know," I said. "All I know is that we were stuck using an old piece of shit MULE, when every Agency or SF team in Afghanistan and Iraq has a SOFLAM."

"A what?" asked Sykes.

"A SOFLAM—a Special Operations Forces Laser Aiming Module, an AN/PEQ-1. Only weighs about 15 pounds, not much bigger than a large pair of binoculars, a pair of Navy night glasses maybe. That's what we needed, not a hundred pounds of old junk."

"Harry, it's what we had available," said Betty. "The Middle East has had the priority. You know that. There hasn't been any need for your team, for a team designated for the Russian Far East, to even think about laser targeting. If General Rickman hadn't had a MULE to loan us from his missile test project, we wouldn't have had anything for you."

"You mean to say that Rickman supplied the MULE that we used."

"Well, yes, Harry. I mean, the mission came to us almost overnight...."

"Which raises another question," I said. "Why did we have so little prep time?" I could see that Rickman was still very angry, but, if the meeting had diverged far from his original agenda, at least it had turned away from consideration of the reliability of his missile. For my part, I could've cared less about the missile, so long as no one wanted to hang this thing on Kip. Right now, it worked for me just to raise as many questions as I could get away with, until someone, Sykes or Rickman, decided to pull the plug.

For the first time since the meeting started Bob Barnhart decided to become involved, maybe because the lack of prep time impinged on his role as the direct line supervisor. He started on a long-winded explanation that revealed, in the end, nothing more than the fact that neither he nor Betty really had any idea why the mission, our end, at least, if not the Air Force's, had been launched so hastily. And if Sykes or Rickman knew, they weren't saying. Predictably, Sandy Sawyer couldn't take more than a few minutes of Barnhart's bureaucratic monotone.

"This is bullshit!" she exploded. "You idiots may have nothing better to do than sit around here yanking your cranks, but I can assure you that my time is a lot more fucking valuable." To underscore this, she made an ostentatious point of checking her lady's gold Rolex. "I'm due back in the big world in an hour because the congressman wants some answers, he wants them this morning, and he's not going to sit around in some fucking soundproof closet just so I can call him on a fucking STU phone. So, you can just cut the shit and get to the bottom line. The missile didn't fail, there's no fucking way our missile failed, so you've got two choices: either York's little buddy Gilligan screwed up with the laser thingy or the laser thingy itself was fucked."

I was shaking with anger when I finally found my voice.

"I thought I'd made one thing absolutely goddamned clear. My colleague, Mr. Mwangi, did not screw up. He damned near died trying to carry out this half-assed mission, and my other colleague, Mr. Naburje, was killed. Neither deserves some snide 'Gilligan' crack from a jumped-up grad student, and I don't give a shit who you work for, either. As for the 'laser thingy,' well maybe it failed, and just maybe there's a third possibility. Maybe General Rickman's 'missile thingy' failed. Or maybe Colonel Baldwin screwed up when he programmed the 'missile thingy.' Just because your committee is invested in the damned missile system doesn't make it immune from failure. At this point, I could give a shit about what went wrong, but I'll tell you one thing right now. If you bastards try to set Kip Mwangi up for this, then you'll have to come through me. I'm not afraid of you, lady, or your precious goddamned congressman." That was rank heresy, and she tried to interrupt, but I cut her off. "Let me put this in your language, just so you can't misunderstand. If you," I looked around the table, "if any of you decides that fucking Kip over is the solution to your problem here, then I will personally take you one by one and ram you up the congressman's ass, in front of God, Wolf Blitzer, and everybody! Since you seem determined to lay the blame on a black man with a first-class record of service to this country, then I'll make sure that you're all tagged as a bunch of racists." That brought a deep frown to Sawyer's face. "And when I'm done with you bastards, the SecDef and the DCI can take turns kissing my ass!"

Faced with that turd in their punchbowl, Sykes and Rickman quickly concluded that the outdated laser aiming module must have been the source of the problem. To provide additional bureaucratic cover for Rickman and the hapless Bob Barnhart, they further decided that reliance on the MULE hadn't been an error of managerial judgment, but instead yet another resource issue for organizations stretched too thin by the global war on terrorism, something they could all use to browbeat the congressional finance committees in support of their next budget submissions. So, a nice political solution had replaced the attempt to destroy a good man's reputation. If anyone cared about what had really gone wrong, or about the dangers that the undamaged poison gas lab continued to pose, then I sure as hell couldn't see it. Sandy Sawyer hurried out the door, followed closely by Rickman and Baldwin. Sykes ordered Bob Barnhart and a somewhat shell-shocked Betty Foster to leave, but insisted that I stay behind.

"I'm sorry it's come down to this," he said, not actually looking sorry at all.

"Sorry? How so, sorry?"

You've had a good career with us, Dr. York. You've done many good things for the Agency, just like you did for the Army before. But this has got to be the end. There are layers in this thing that I can't go into, but the only way to clear the decks and get on with things is to take you off the table. We need to work something out. I hope you understand the harm that would come from going public with this thing, going to some of your old friends, using your military reputation or your money. Yes, I'm aware of your money. I hope that you know how damaging that would be, damaging to a lot of things you yourself have sacrificed for, damaging for the country, for the Agency, for the war effort."

"I didn't see much sign of concern for the country or the war against terrorism in that little kangaroo court you all were trying to stage."

"I didn't mean for it to go the way it started. Rickman, I think, was using Sawyer to try and take it away from me."

I felt like I was being manipulated, but I was also starting to cool down and, as I did, I realized that, however insincere the source, the words he'd spoken were true. I really didn't want to take this public, it would damage all manner of things I'd come to hold dear. When you reach your late sixties, you begin to think a lot about the meaning of the contributions you've made.

"So, what's the deal?" I asked.

"Keep this quiet and then step aside. No one messes with you, no one messes with Mwangi. Fair enough?"

It wasn't fair, not really, but the whole business had suddenly turned very sour for me.

"Personally, I've had it. I'll go. Maybe it's time I finally sat down to write my memoirs." He grimaced. "No—I haven't forgotten my submission agreement," all CIA employees, regular and contract, sign an agreement that anything they propose to publish must first be vetted by the security and CI types, "and I'm not going after anyone about this business as long as you treat Kip right."

"What's your definition of that?"

"What would really be fair would be to give him a commendation and a promotion. Never mind the result; he did one helluva job for you out there. But you won't do that. So, the bottom line is, give him a fair chance to continue his career. This is what he loves doing."

"What, specifically, would you suggest?"

"Give him paid leave of absence for a month or two. Then park him down at the Farm or the Point or out at Marana for a while. Make him an instructor. Once this blows over, bring him back into ops.

He's a very good man. He gave the Marines ten very good years, and he's given us another ten. He doesn't deserve to be made a scapegoat."

"I'm sure that Mr. Mwangi is a very good man," said Sykes, but his tone wasn't encouraging. "I'm not sure that this hasn't gone well beyond the question of his competence, or yours."

"I take your point. Look. I was the man in charge on the ground, after all," I said, "if I go out the door, you can claim credit for firing me and that ought to work for Rickman, and Sawyer, and her precious congressman, and whoever."

"Perhaps,"

I was finally and completely tired of all this. "Listen," I said. "I just don't care anymore. I'm out the door. And I'll go away quietly, and I won't make waves, as long as it's just me. Okay? But if anyone comes after Kip, all bets are off. Deal?"

"I'm not here to do deals,"

"You were here to seal the deal with Rickman, weren't you? I mean, that's what this little charade was all about, wasn't it?"

"Get out."

I stood my ground. "Deal?"

"Yeah, York, sure—deal. Now get the fuck out of my sight."

I pondered a rejoinder, but decided it wasn't worth the waste of breath.

CHAPTER 4

Summer, 2020

FROM THE BALCONY of my ninth-floor condominium overlooking the ocean front at Virginia Beach I can watch the world go by, or at least the world consisting of naval vessels, tankers, massively stacked container vessels, and cruise ships as they lined up approaching Hampton Roads and the port of Norfolk. Before the previous March I could enjoy a sampling of each when, like I was doing, I enjoyed my morning coffee and fresh-baked croissants from the coffee shop on the ground floor. The Covid-19 pandemic, of course, had dropped cruise ships from my morning visual menu, and the traffic overall had slowed. I was tracking a Nimitz-class aircraft carrier in the distance, wondering if it carried a stricken crew, when my iPhone trilled. I hesitated at the absence of a caller ID—these days I tend to screen my calls carefully—but then decided to take a chance.

The caller gave me a long-outdated code word, a date, a time, and a location, then asked me to repeat it back. Then she hung up, leaving me both irritated and profoundly intrigued.

The next morning found me still puzzling over the whole business as I powered my Porsche northward along I-64 and I-95, marveling at the extent to which the pandemic had diminished the traffic along these normally congested routes. Past D. C., I turned northwest toward Frederick and then west across gorgeous Maryland farm country, eventually reaching the little community of Sharpsburg. I followed the signs to the Antietam National Battlefield Park. I arrived about an hour early, thinking that maybe I should scout the setup before committing myself, standard tradecraft for a covert meeting. I knew from the Park Service website that the visitor center was closed, but the roads and trails were open. Playing the simple tourist, I followed the markers for the Park Service's vehicle tour, looping north to just below the Dunker Church, then back through the Cornfield, nearly-forgotten names that once resonated like "Omaha Beach," or "Khe Sanh." Turning back from the Confederate left flank I followed the battle line in the other direction, parallel to Antietam Creek and the Sunken Road. Directly above this notorious killing ground loomed the great stone observation tower. I pulled into a parking space next to the only other vehicle near the tower, a glistening dark green Range Rover. I opened the car door and stepped out of the air conditioning into the June heat, my sunglasses fogging with the humidity. I cleared them with my handkerchief, fitted my natty black mask over my nose and mouth, then walked over to the tower. Ignoring the sign that said that the tower was closed, I began climbing the stairs, pausing at each landing to look out windows that had been modeled after firing slits.

Mounting the steps, I could feel my pulse quickening with anticipation. Just before I reached the top, I paused for a moment to collect myself, to get my thoughts in order and catch my breath. As I cleared the final steps I first saw a man's legs, then his back, then gray-flecked reddish-blond hair. The man wore green knit shirt and bone-colored slacks, and very much looked the part of someone dressed for a round of golf. Incongruously, this leisure outfit was complemented by a padlocked aluminum-shell briefcase resting at the man's feet. Although he must have heard my footsteps, he remained with his back toward me, looking out along the line of the Sunken Road. He turned slowly and recognition dawned as his profile gave way to that famous face, the square jaw, the rakish mustache. The Right Honorable Congressman Toby Parks, the man who the newsmagazines apostrophized as the "Robert Redford of the House of Representatives." What the magazines didn't say, and the pictures didn't really show, was that acne had left his face as pitted as the surface of the moon. Perhaps no one cared, not the journalists, not the famous actresses he regularly squired around Washington and L.A. and New York City. Perhaps power and charisma had done for his complexion what they had once done for Henry Kissinger's waistline. He smiled, not the thousand-watt smile he saved for the Sunday morning political talk shows, but instead a gentler and more genuine grin.

"Hi, Harry—it's been a while, hasn't it?"

"I guess we just don't move in the same circles anymore."

"It has been a long time? Still, you've settled down in the old neighborhood down at Norfolk. Do you ever hang out at Chick's? Maybe see any of the gang from Dam Neck?"

Chick's is a Virginia Beach bar and seafood joint. Dam Neck is an annex to the Norfolk naval complex, home to a very special group of Navy SEALs. Before ruining his left knee in an assault on an offshore oil platform during the first Iraq war, Parks had been a member of this elite group.

"No, not a soul—not that I know anybody much from the Teams anymore. They're all young enough now to be my children, if I had any—hell, my grandchildren. Besides, they were always more your family—my guys were either up the road at the farm or down in North Carolina."

"Just as well. If you were still part of the in crowd, you'd be no good to me right now. By the way, why don't you lose that silly looking mask. I guarantee that I'm not spreading Covid and I know that you aren't either."

"Oh? How so?"

"Did a little checking before I reached out to you. It wouldn't do to have you out of commission just now." I wondered how he had ascertained my health status, but I'd only just had the test performed and come back negative. Still, this was Toby Parks.

"By the way, I see that you and your buddy Kip have been doing some good work in Africa. Nice to see how you've both recovered from being on the Agency's shit list."

I didn't bother to ask how Parks had come to know about a mission that had been closely held and tightly compartmented. He sits on one of the intelligence committees, and he has all manner of friends throughout the special operations community. The greater surprise would have his not knowing.

"Yeah, Harry, it's not everyone who can piss off the Agency, the DNI crowd, the Air Force, a billion-dollar defense contractor, and a powerful Congressman, and come out as nicely as you and Kip. Rickman and Sawyer really wanted your ass, and it really torqued them to discover how bulletproof you actually were. After the missile fiasco, they had you sized up as the perfect scapegoat, and then they discovered that you didn't really need your little piddly contract with Christians in Action, that you're rich enough maybe even to buy a whole sub-committee full of Congressmen off your back, and that, once upon a time, you were the Audie fucking Murphy of the spec ops world. He didn't find out who you really were until after you told Sandy Sawyer to go piss up a rope. God, Harry, I'd have loved to have been a fly on the wall that morning."

I was momentarily dumbstruck. Finally, I said, "You might as well have been a fly on the wall. You might as well have been sitting there."

"Sandy Sawyer can't keep her mouth from running, especially when she's burned up about something. Apparently, she went back to her boss and got her pretty little butt chewed."

"Pretty little butt?"

"What can I say, Harry, I'm an ass man, I notice these things. She couldn't understand why you weren't afraid of her. She started asking around, and along the way she must have pumped maybe a dozen of her staff buddies around the Hill. One of 'em used to work for me, and he gave me a call.

"So much for secrecy."

"Now don't get me wrong, I like being where I am these days, and I think I get some things done, but the Hill isn't like the Teams or your Green Beanies. The only secrets most of them respect up there are their own. But make no mistake. Three years on, both Rickman and Sawyer would still like to have your balls. Now Rickman's a pussy, but Sawyer's a fucking killer. She makes Tony Soprano look like Mother Teresa."

"I get your drift."

"Still, no harm, no foul. The missile may have missed, but it scared the Chinese sufficiently to make them rethink putting a nerve gas facility into the hands of their Congolese militia buddies. Rickman still got the funding he wanted for his toy, which was really what the whole thing was about in the first place. So you could look back and count the mission a success."

"Not exactly no harm, Toby. Bobby Naburje came home in a body bag."

"Sorry, Harry—I shouldn't have put it that way." We paused over that for a moment.

"Why'd you call me, Toby? Not for a walk down nightmare lane."

He apparently needed a moment to digest this. When he spoke again it was almost a whisper.

"Would you do it again?"

"Go back in time, minus the stupid hi-tech wizardry, minus the 'Golden BB' that killed Bobby. What the fuck, Toby? What the hell are you actually asking me? Have you got a time machine hidden in that briefcase?"

He turned away from me, looking out over the battlefield below. After a long silence he spoke. "I really can't picture it."

I stepped up beside him, followed his gesture. "What can't you picture?"

"The way it must have been when the battle was fought. Bright, like today, but the end of the summer, hot and sticky, and masses of men crammed together, sort of like a rock concert or a football game. But there," he pointed to his left, where the Union attack on Lee's center had developed, "in that field, men marching shoulder to shoulder, and then other men rising up from that ditch below us," he pointed to the vestigial traces of the Sunken Road, "and pouring bullets into them."

"That was war. Still is, in a way."

"The job had to be done. The South couldn't be allowed to walk out on the Union, and slavery had to end."

I recalled that Parks came from an old and wealthy Long Island family. His inherited sympathies would, of course, be with the Union. I wasn't a Southerner or even an American by birth, but my own eastern European background compelled some measure of understanding for lost causes, even morally dubious lost causes. Without ever having considered it before, I realized that, on this battlefield, I identified with the Confederates.

Parks looked back at me.

"If you were going to do the job over again, how would you do it?"

"A team on the ground. Take the facility away from them, and blow open the doors, set charges inside the production line, and blow it properly."

"That's a lot of troops."

"Maybe, maybe not. Depends who's guarding the place. Why are you asking me? What are you asking?"

He gave me a long hard look. "Okay, Harry, here's the deal. The Chinese are at it again, this time with a bioweapon, this time in Wiangara, the breakaway bit. They're playing with something that makes Covid look like hay fever, and they've got 10,000 square miles of bush country and a small army of screaming assholes surrounding it."

Wiangara I knew from my recent work in Africa, a territory in the wilds of the northeastern Democratic Republic of Congo, snug against the border with Uganda and the Sudan, a place of great beauty and unspeakable tragedy, devastated first by the infamous Lord's Resistance Army and then by a succession of equally nasty so-called "militias." The writ of the Congolese government stopped well shy of the former provincial boundary and the UN peacekeeping forces no longer attempted to operate there.

"The details are in the briefcase," Parks continued, "but, briefly, the Chinese have taken a lesson from the Covid pandemic. First, make sure this time that the source can't be traced back to them. Central Africa is perfect as a source location, it's just the kind of place where the world expects nasty viruses to emerge. Second, make it easy to spread, and just deadly enough to overload the treatment capabilities of even the most advanced western countries. Third, just when you've driven everyone to the breaking point, step forward and save the day with a vaccine, one you're prepared to make available worldwide. Distribute it in a manner designed to earn maximum influence while discrediting the U.S., and, not incidentally, at least temporarily crippling the U.S. military. Want to take Taiwan? Yours for the doing. Want to take 'Belt and Road' and wrap it around our geopolitical necks? No problem. All it takes is the virus, the vaccine, and buying enough influence in an out of the way hellhole to hide your source lab."

"How do we know this isn't just some intel analyst's fever dream?"

"There's a long answer for a later time, but the bottom line is that we have a source, an absolute gold-plated source, a woman who's one of the lab scientists, but lost her stomach for what they were planning. Once she ran up the red flag, we targeted some overhead imagery and some SIGINT, stuff we don't normally run in that part of the world. Trust me, this is the real deal."

It took me a long quiet moment just to take this in. "Okay, Toby, but where do I come in?" I was beginning to have an odd feeling, part dread, part the excitement of an old-fashioned trumpet call. "Why isn't this a job for the teams, or, God help us, one of that bastard Rickman's funny missiles?"

"We're in the midst of an election year, Harry, and worse, the folks who are in the know don't even want to take it to the man in charge. Nor do they dare take it to the other guy. Try to work this through the usual channels risks leaks and then a political circus—everything turns to shit, the "fake news" arguments go into hyperdrive, the Chinese pretend that it's a disinformation campaign and then just bide their time. You've been on the outside for three years now—you've no fucking idea just how silly and stupid things have gotten in D.C."

"So, again, Toby, where do I come in?"

"The source lab in Wiangara has to be taken out, cleanly and quietly, but sending an unmistakable message to the Chinese that we are not to be fucked with. I've just explained to you why using national assets is off the table. We are asking," he paused to let the "we" sink in, letting me know that this was no longer just Toby speaking, "we are asking you to do it as a private venture."

"Private venture? Are you out of your mind?"

By way of answer he knelt to the briefcase at his feet and manipulated the lock. From the briefcase he withdrew a manila folder, and from the folder a heavy piece of parchment paper. This he handed to me. Although the words were typed, the language was oddly stilted, as if it were a translation of something foreign, and old. As I continued to read, I realized that this was partly true—not foreign, but old enough.

"Letter of Marque and Reprisal," I read aloud. "You really can't be serious."

"On the contrary. The Constitution provides for it, and, even though there was an international declaration in the 19th century that proscribed the issue of Letters of Marque, the United States never ratified it."

"But surely...."

"Why not? It's a means of commissioning private citizens to go after enemies of the state on the high seas. And the term 'Reprisal,' so I'm told, extends its reach to enemies on land. There are a couple of good constitutional scholars in Congress who've been interested in this since 9/11, and we've had a couple of the top academics looking at it since then, too. Plus, a Supreme Court justice, believe it or not. It's an idea that's been cooking for years. The particular interest recently has been as providing color of law arming merchant ship crews to defend themselves against pirates off the Horn of Africa. One of my House colleagues has even introduced legislation to support doing it. Didn't go anywhere, but still. Anyway, if you Google it and you'll be amazed at what you find."

"Well I'll be damned."

He gave a short, tight chuckle. "No, actually you won't, that's the whole point. We can't actually do a properly executed Letter of Reprisal without an act of Congress, but what we have in mind mimics the whole thing complete with some heavy-duty signatures on it, tying the whole thing back to some very big players in the government. They'll be putting their whole careers on the line. The point is that they know that they are asking someone else to put big money behind this, and that, down the line, there'll be some people putting their lives on the line. Yeah, it may be constitutional bullshit, but it elevates the responsibility. The man with the letter doesn't wind up living out his days in Leavenworth, or being pilloried on the nightly news. He gets to say that he had an official authorization, that the country was behind him, regardless of who wants to argue the political point after the fact. The letter lays that all on much bigger fish, the ones who signed on the bottom line."

"Then why? Why me?"

"Because you're perfect. You know the lie of the land. You've been working the general area for the last three years with the charity you set up in honor of Bobby Naburje. More, your name still counts for something in the spec ops community, and there's a lot of people who'll do things for you who wouldn't give the time of day to someone else. Plus, you're sitting on, what is it, maybe 50 million bucks that you've never seemed interested in spending, and you've got nobody obvious to leave it to. That's key. We can give you a piece of paper, we can say we're with you, we can keep it close hold, but when we start trying to move money around, the whole fucking world will find out. We don't have the kind of money it needs. I mean, some of us are pretty well-heeled, and nobody expects you to carry it alone. I can assemble about four or five million that different folks are ready to pony up for you. But none of us has any access to any 'black' funds, and if we start trying to play around with some appropriations somewhere, we're back on Sandy Sawyer's turf. These days, she's the 'Black Queen' of moving appropriations around. Be nice to put something over on her, wouldn't it?" He gave me that look again. "Besides, your last mission left a sour taste didn't it? I don't have a time machine, but I'm offering you a do-over—how many times does life give you one of those.

"I don't know. I really am too old for this shit."

"True enough, but we're not asking you to lead the team in, just plan things, build the team, and pay most of the freight. That's all we're asking, that you take it on and give it your best shot. If you can't put it together, we're no worse off than we are now. It's time to step up to it. I mean, I've got all the respect in the world for you, but look at yourself. If you'd really wanted to stop being a player, you'd have walked away from it when you retired from the army, been a college professor like you played at doing for a while. But you invited yourself back into the secret world and then let yourself spend the last twenty years as a minor league contract player. Harry, you're a fucking legend to the operators, to the shooters, but with your brains, when that pot of money fell in your lap, you could've made yourself a heavy-hitter. You could've had a place at the top table. But instead you tried to stay in the field, running and gunning with the boys, the spec ops world's very own Peter fucking Pan. You're what, now, seventy years-old? Don't you want to grow up before you die?"

I wanted to argue with this, but the arguments died unspoken. He'd read me like a street sign.

"Okay, Toby. I'll give it a shot."

The look he gave me said volumes.

"All right, then," he said. "In the briefcase, I've got something for you. The intel we've gotten since your hit went down, and a clean intel point of contact you can use going forward. You'll have to use your own Naburje foundation points of contact where you can, just keep it clean if you do, and stay away from the buddies you've made in the

UN force in the area—I don't have to tell you why. Once you have a plan, we'll link you directly to our inside source."

"Fair enough. Next thing, you're going to need gear, there's some reliable equipment and weapons suppliers I can get you hooked up with. I know you know the turf still, but I figured that you might need help to move fast. Plus, these guys don't have any Agency or FBI or ATF tripwires attached. These days, you start promoting weapons and you may wind up on some terrorist watch list. We don't want that. You need something big, you come straight to me."

"You're sure?"

"I'm sure. Look, we're not setting this up to hide behind you, if we can help, we will. Okay, then? You can take all the stuff in the briefcase and study it when you get home, but there's one thing in there I want you to look at right now." He reached into the briefcase, took out another sheet of parchment, identical at first glance to the "Letter of Marque and Reprisal" he'd shown me before. "The other was an unsigned draft, just to introduce the idea to you. This one is the real deal. Look at the signatures."

I scanned down to the bottom of the page, to a signature block with three names. One was a senior member of the House, another a senior member of the Senate, names that would resonate throughout the country. It was the third name, however, that truly astonished me, a stalwart of the national security community over multiple generations, someone whose name was a byword for international respect.

"You've got to be kidding?" I said. "This is not real. Not this man."

"It's real. If you don't believe it, I can give you a time, and a phone number, and the man himself will confirm it. We've been talking this whole process with him almost from the time the idea of the 'Letters' first came up. He feels like if something like this is going to be used, it's his duty to play a role. You know what he said when I brought him this one. He said, 'Tell Dr. York that he will be in my thoughts and in my prayers.' And then he took a little piece of note paper out of his desk and handed it to me, said it was something he'd kept with him since he was young. He said give it to you, if I needed to persuade you. I guess I don't need to persuade you, but here it is anyway."

He took a slightly crumpled slip of paper from his wallet and passed it to me. I straightened the sheet of paper and saw that it contained a single sentence, a quotation from Confucius, copied carefully in longhand. The sentence read: "To see the right and not do it is cowardice." I carefully folded the paper and placed it in my wallet, shook Parks's hand, and departed for home with my thoughts in turmoil and my heart racing.

CHAPTER 5

DRIVING HOME TO Virginia Beach, I struggled to keep my mind from racing. Stopping along the way for dinner, I forced myself to leave the briefcase unopened in the locked car, parked where I could see it from my booth in the restaurant. This was an obvious security measure, but it also prevented me from yielding to the temptation to start reviewing its contents while I ate. Still, I couldn't keep myself from mentally reviewing all that I knew about Wiangara. First, "Wiangara" doesn't actually exist, at least not in the sense of a country on a map. Instead, it consisted of the better part of the three northeastern provinces of the DRC, the ironically-named "Democratic Republic of the Congo." Most Westerners don't appreciate how big the DRC itself actually is—it stretches across an area roughly the size of the U.S. east of the Mississippi. And Wiangara covered a space roughly the size of Florida or Wisconsin. I'd not been on the ground there in several years, but I could readily recall the open savannas to the north along the border with Sudan, the rain forests in the higher plateau, and the wild mountains in the east that cascaded down to Lake Albert and the border with Uganda. A beautiful place, but also tremendously afflicted. A succession of "militias" had roiled the area for decades, murdering each other and the hapless farmers and miners who lived in the area, living off the spoils of war and trading on the abundant mineral riches to bargain for influence with outsiders. For the last several years, however, a kind of peace had descended over the area, a peace imposed by the dominance of one militia group, headed by the self-designated "General-President" of Wiangara. More murderous than any of his predecessors—and far better organized—he'd ended, at least for the present, the repeated orgies of massacre and rape, except when it served his own purposes to turn his followers loose on the people. He imposed his will through fear, and he'd struck a bargain with a Chinese conglomerate eager to exploit the area's abundant resources. I suspected that when I opened up the briefcase, I'd find that this had opened the door for the Chinese plan. I wondered if the "General-President" was in on the scheme, and was already preparing himself for a rich, safe, and comfortable exile before the virus was released. Or, equally likely, he would soon find himself just the latest to be duped and then destroyed.

When I arrived home, I brewed myself a cup of coffee and settled down at my desk to work. First, I read every item in the briefcase, slowly and carefully, making longhand notes on a legal pad as I went along. Then I made more coffee and went through it a second time, resisting the temptation to pour a long stiff drink as I contemplated what lay before me. For sheer unmitigated ugliness—and I've seen more than my share of such—it couldn't be beat. The Chinese Communist regime seemingly planned to murder thousands upon thousands of Africans in one of the poorest and most destitute regions of the world, all as a first step in propelling an international health and economic catastrophe. I knew of their contempt for Africans, the thoughtless racism that lay hidden behind a decade's worth of investment in the sub-Saharan region. More, I couldn't help but recall that a similar logic had informed their plans for the poison gas facility that our 2017 mission had failed to destroy. Evil isn't a word I use lightly, but this was the darkest of evils.

Still, Parks hadn't reached out to me for my dubious credentials as a moral philosopher. The clock, after all, was ticking. My highest priority was to quickly think through the operational and tactical problems, and determine, at the very least, if they were solvable. My planning tools combined old and new, my recently-acquired Mac-Book for Internet data, a stack of maps of the region accumulated for my Naburje foundation activities, and a very old set of navigator's dividers for distances. By 10:00 p.m. my eyes were so tired that I could no longer focus on the computer screen, and my legs ached from the nervous tension and the pacing. Like Horatio Hornblower, I can't sit still when I'm really thinking. I didn't yet have a plan—I hadn't expected to have one—but I had a list of names and a list of questions, out of which I hoped to distill a plan.

I sat back and pondered simply going to bed. Instead, I turned off the computer, switched off my desk lamp, and went into the kitchen. I made myself one last mug of coffee, but instead of going back to my office, I took it out to the living room. I took a brandy snifter and a bottle of Bushmills from a small cabinet and poured myself a generous measure, and took both the coffee and the whiskey out to the balcony. I don't like Irish coffee. I think pouring whiskey into coffee ruins both. But I do like coffee and I do like Irish whiskey, the latter a taste I'd acquired from my former father-in-law. I find that they are aids to contemplation, and I had some things to think about.

I'd taken Toby's fancy piece of paper, his 'Letter of Marque and Reprisal,' and I'd just spent eight hours convincing myself that, from an operational standpoint, the whole idea wasn't completely crazy. But to have any hope of meeting the deadline, the next steps would have to start with the dawn's early light. And those next steps would mean real actions and real commitments with real people, people whose respect and trust I valued more than anything in this world. People who trusted me. Like Kip had trusted me. Like Bobby Naburje.

I turned seventy not quite a year ago. I've reached that time in life when looking backward becomes second nature, when, without really thinking about it, one measures the days by things done rather than things planned. I like to think that my accomplishments are, if not great, then at least respectable and that my place in the tight little world of special operations is honored and secure. I've "been there and done that" again and again, and what I've done, I've done well. I've fought on three continents, in jungles and in deserts, in villages and in great cities. I've won and kept the respect of my peers, the members of the most exclusive club in all the world. This had been my armor against those intimations of failure that creep up on all of us as the years accumulate, and it had served me well enough.

Yet Toby Parks had pierced that armor with a few well-chosen words. Composure under fire is a gift as much as an accomplishment, and it is a gift that comes to boys as well as men. It had come to me, fortunately, at nineteen, in Vietnam, and in the years since, whenever I'd had call for it. But for Bobby's death and the mission's failure, I'd have once again known the quiet satisfaction of finding the magic within myself. Still, any reasonably good thirty-year-old SF staff sergeant could have done it as well as I'd done that night, probably better. Parks had been crushingly penetrating with his "Peter Pan" remark. For all its seriousness of purpose, the world of the career special operator has an "Island of Lost Boys" quality. Like professional athletes, we hate to let go of the life. Once or twice I'd ventured a toe into life's greater ocean, once, for a short while, I'd even managed to go wading, but each time I'd fled back to the island, reaching for the "Pixie Dust." Even my most recent—and arguably most grown-up endeavor—the work in central Africa that Kip and I had done to honor Bobby's memory—had partaken, in a small way, of the old special ops mission, helping farmers and refugees to learn how to protect themselves from the depredations of the marauding militias. "De opresso liber," as the motto goes.

I went back inside, poured myself another measure of Bushmills and took the glass into my office. I sat down at my desk once again and, ignoring the spread of maps and papers, took a small picture album from the right-hand desk drawer. I opened it to the middle, to the one photograph I have of my father. It's not a formal portrait or an intimate family snapshot, but a print from a newsreel negative, capturing him in the midst of addressing a political rally. My grandfather had been a war hero in his youth, first as a lieutenant in the Tsar's army, then, and more notably, as a leader in Estonia's struggle to throw out the Bolsheviks at the end of World War One. But he hadn't stopped there. Instead he'd gone on as an historian, helping define the character of our newly independent nation, then as a respected political leader, and finally as a source of national inspiration when Stalin stole our freedom in 1940. When his father disappeared into the gulags, my dad, a mere student, had taken up the cause. His curse had been his later association with our erstwhile German "allies," but, given a fresh start after war, he'd dedicated his life, and had given his life, to "free the oppressed," working for the CIA as one of the Estonian "Forest Brethren," the partisans still holding out against Stalin's rule after the end of the war. From there he went on to become an original and then legendary member of the U.S. Special Forces. By their standards, my own achievements had been petty, merely a fortunate combination of skill and circumstance. If the true measure of manhood lies in shaping the larger world, rather than drifting along with the tide, then Parks was absolutely right. After all these years, it still remained for me to grow up.

I turned from my father's picture to the adjacent one of my mother and me and my sisters, one older and the other a tiny baby in my mother's arms. We were sitting on the steps of our tiny family quarters at Fort Bragg, not long before we learned that a husband and father wouldn't be coming home. I took a sip of whiskey and allowed my finger to trace the outlines of my mother's face. I was struck as always by the fact that my older sister, as she reached the age of my mother in this picture, had briefly mirrored this frozen final image.

I looked once again at the two pictures, lying before me on facing pages of the album. Unlike my sister, my face had mixed the features of both parents, my father's high forehead and slightly hooded green eyes, my mother's straight nose and full lips. As a boy I'd been too-frequently taunted with the phrase "lips like a girl." My gaze rested on the little bundle in my mother's arms. What would she have looked like? Which parent would she have resembled? What would she have become? With Parks's words inside my head, I could only remark on the unfairness of it all, for if life had dealt generously with me, it had been cruelly parsimonious with her.

I finished the last of my glass of whiskey and turned to the back of the album, to three pages filled with pictures of a very beautiful young woman, through whom fate had brought me a great deal of money, more than enough, as Parks had noted, to finance out of pocket an operation against the biological facility in Wiangara. When I retired from the Army in 1992, I was a forty-two-year-old major, a very odd fish, way outside all of the age-in-grade parameters, but kept on, first because I'd spent a long time as an NCO and company grade officer in Special Forces, then because I'd been detailed to the CIA for special projects. Letting go of the Army was hard, doubly so since it encompassed my entire identity as a person.

At first, I struggled finding a path to follow, even a sense of place to call home. Astonishingly, my notably pragmatic sister had sold off the business she'd created with her late husband and moved to newly-independent Estonia; I briefly contemplated joining her, but hesitated to embrace that closely our gigantic family legacy. I'd done enjoyable exchange tours with both the SAS and the French Foreign Legion, but couldn't see myself as a Brit or a Frenchman. I had spent substantial time with SF Detachment A in Berlin, but I wasn't a German.

I was, for better or worse, an American, and so, in keeping with a fine old American tradition, I went to college in search of myself, in search of my own private vision of America. Of course, I didn't see it quite that way then. I'd picked up enough credits in the service for a bachelor's degree in history, and the idea of being a soldier scholar was not alien to me—my grandfather's example, once again. So, going to graduate school seemed both natural and practical, a means to a new career, a respectable coda to my gypsy years.

I fell in love with the school. An Agency friend had steered me in the direction of Indiana University, which in those years was wondrously challenging and exciting, cosmopolitan as a good university should be and yet wondrously American. What, after all, could be more all-American than a Hoosier? I loved Bloomington, which had all the virtues of a traditional college town. I loved the color and noise of football games on a Saturday afternoon, and wasn't yet quite American enough to be downcast when the home team lost, as it always did, to Michigan and Ohio State. I discovered the mad passions of basketball, Indiana-style. I was entranced by the charms of nearby Brown County, whose wooded hills reminded me of the Black Forest while at the same time fulfilling my vision of a righteous American landscape.

After a lifetime of military discipline, even the very eccentric and creative Special Forces variety, I luxuriated in the indulgences of student life, above all the indulgence of following newly awakened intellectual obsessions wherever they led. But I also enjoyed the less arid indulgences as well. I spent long, lazy Sunday afternoons making love to the young women I met in my graduate classes, intellectually earnest twenty-five-year-olds, with names like Tammy and Tracy, Julie and Jennifer, who came from towns like Huntington or Wabash or Evansville, who argued about Camille Paglia and earnestly pondered the lyrics of Morrissey records. I loved how they found me "mature," even "exotic," but never "old." I sat until late at night writing papers in the library, and stayed up later still arguing political and historical issues in coffee shops and bars. Most of all, two years after I started, I met, fell in love with, and married Patti.

And Patti became my true America, my new world, my promised land. She sparkled in seminars, charmed in everyday conversation, and looked as if she had sprung, full-grown, from Hugh Hefner's brow. She glided effortlessly from the *Federalist Papers* to the funny papers, from Zubin Mehta to ZZ Top, from Willie Wonka to Willie Nelson. She would jog two miles and then light up a Marlboro, insisted on church every Sunday morning and raunchy sex every Sunday afternoon. She initiated me into the mysteries of cartoons and soap operas, the "Simpsons" and "General Hospital." She ordered cap-snafflers, bamboo steamers, and Ginzu knives. She was pleased to have introduced me to Gilligan and the Skipper, and delighted when, over pizza, in the midst of a typical beer-fueled student debate, I had stood up for the transcendent sexiness of Ginger against a table filled with Mary Ann supporters. She said that this proved that I was truly, decadently European. She was foursquare for decadence and Europeanness. But her real impact was to take me in entirely the opposite direction. With her, through her, I came home to America.

Admittedly, an acculturation that combined the influences of the U.S. Army, particularly its snake-eating sub-culture, and a twenty-seven-year-old woman left me a somewhat disjointed American, at least in terms of my relationship with the popular culture and with my own generation of Americans. The real surprise in our marriage, I suppose, was that it lasted two years. She was eagerly seeking life's challenges; I was looking for a little tranquility. If we were united, despite our age difference, in a common quest for our respective selves, then she was looking outward while my focus was within. When we met, she was researching a dissertation on the role of women in the Protestant Reformation. A year after we married, she suddenly dropped her doctoral studies and undertook an MBA in marketing, a very late-'90s' thing to do. When she left me, it was on the arm of a bright young financier from Chicago, who, having apprenticed in pork belly futures and then stopped off at Indiana for an MBA of his own, was heading off to New York and currency arbitrage. But I kept our Schnauzer, and most of the books, and the Ginzu knives, and, once the pain receded, I knew that I had no cause for regret. What Patti took with her was a tiresome and frenetic future, but what she left me with was a homeland.

And she also left me with a vast pile of dollars, albeit not exactly intentionally. When it came time to divide our assets, she took our cash savings and talked me into accepting a thousand shares of a small company that her father and his friends, a group of computer mavens and engineering professors at Purdue, had recently established. The shares were valued at ten thousand dollars and were worth that, or maybe nothing, depending on your view of the company's future prospects. But her young commodities trader took a dim view of the prospects for her dad's company, and I didn't much care. I just wanted a clean break. I kept the shares partly out of regard for her father, a good and gentle man whom I'd always enjoyed, but mainly because I didn't know what else to do with them. I tried being a college professor, then drifted back into the secret world as a contract player. Then came a time when miniaturization and micro-processors became the next "big thing," and it turned out that the little company owned the rights to a process essential to achieving this. Unlike other nice computer guys who were chewed up and spit out by other not so nice computer guys, they had the wisdom to find some nasty lawyers who were willing to fight an apparently unending series of patent wars in return for a stake in the company, and when these wars were finally done at the turn of the new Millenium, they were unspeakably rich and I was only a little less so. It's an odd thing about big money. There's a certain threshold that you cross, and then it just goes on getting bigger and bigger. I diversified before the technology bubble burst a few years later and emerged with even more, more than enough to invest in my sister's varied business interests in Estonia, more than enough to gratify any conceivable material whim. More than enough, I thought ruefully, to have taken my windfall and done something more meaningful than indulge my desire to go on living in special operations Neverland.

I gave the pictures of Patti once last lingering look, and then started to close the album. But instead I turned back to the picture of my father and set the album down on my desk, leaving it open at that page. I went back into the living room, refreshed my snifter of whisky, and returned to the desk. I don't normally drink all that much anymore, and I realized as I walked back that I'd taken on the beginnings of a buzz. I carefully placed the snifter alongside the album, sat down again, and took a shoe box from the desk drawer that had held the album. I'd created the family album in a brief burst of nostalgia and longing many years ago, but most of the rest of my personal photos, the ones from Vietnam to the present, still rested haphazardly in the shoe box. I took off the lid and began to poke around, eventually surfacing a little red booklet of shapshots, bound with plastic rings, the kind of thing that photo development companies provided back in the days before the whole country graduated from Brownie Starmites to 35mm SLRs, when photos were still taken to preserve the likeness of loved ones or favorite places and not as an expression of one's inner artist. Patti's parents had had stacks of these little booklets, Patti and her sisters bundled up around a snowman, or dancing through the spray of a garden hose.

The pictures in my little red book were less domestic, but just as personal. All were pictures of soldiers, caught against the back drop of the Headquarters of the 10th SF Group in Bad Tolz. The date stamp inside the cover of the booklet said 1959, but any knowledgeable observer would have pegged the time frame from two significant features. First, all of the soldiers, if not bareheaded, wore the old-fashioned Army fatigue cap, not the Green Beret, which came years later. Second, everyone wore the distinctive Alpine hiking boot, locally made, that 10th Group favored over any other footwear, including jump boots. I lingered momentarily over each of the group pictures, stopping finally at the last picture and laid the open booklet alongside the album on the desk.

There were two men in the picture, one who had anglicized his family name to "York," without realizing the sardonic jibes this would occasion when he first sewed on sergeant's stripes. The other, somewhat older, with his arm across the younger man's shoulder, was Master Sergeant Lem Lauristen, my father's half-Finnish cousin, mentor in all things military, and, in a very real sense, the man who'd opened the door to my present life.

In the 1950s, Special Forces was something of a foreign legion, filled with former soldiers from virtually the gamut of nations now under Stalin's rule, selected for their potential for conducting guerilla warfare in the event that the Soviets came rolling across the Elbe. They came in, like my father, under the auspices of something called the Lodge Act, which provided American citizenship to selected individuals who chose to earn it through service in the U.S. Army. Lem was one of the first Lodge Act veterans, one of that famous cadre of Finns known as "Marttinnen's Men," from the man who recruited his compatriots into Special Forces. My dad had been one of the last. They'd served together at Bad Tolz, and in Laos and from the very beginnings of Vietnam. In late 1964 my dad got on a helicopter with a team of "Yards" and disappeared, this time forever, into the mists of Laos and SF legend. It was Lem who came to us at Bragg, full of shared grief and consolation, and, for me, a life's inspiration.

I went to Vietnam as an 18-year-old, an ordinary grunt with the 5th Mech. One day, back with our tracks at a firebase, a helicopter landed and a grizzled master sergeant emerged. He sought out my own rather awestruck platoon sergeant, and soon I was sitting on a stack of sandbags next to my godfather, trying hopelessly to match his beer consumption, sharing private memories in the foreign language we shared.

"You're learning how to kill Reds," he said, and then, with a small smile, "When you've gotten better at it, you will come to me and become the best." He paused. "We're where we are now to kill Reds for the Americans." By this time in his life he'd have killed most any man who suggested that Lem Lauristen was anything less than 100% American, but this was a conversation among family, in Estonian. "But the real reason we kill Reds is that someday, if we kill enough of them, our homeland will be free."

Fifty-two years later, I sat at my desk with my empty glass in front of me, my thoughts full of the intervening years. I thought about the gift that Patti's money represented, I thought about my family, and I thought about Lem's challenge. In the end Estonia had regained its freedom, without obvious reference to the number of Reds I'd killed down through the years. In countering the world's evils, I'd offered little more than pinpricks. I'd spent little of my magic fortune, denied myself all but a few self-indulgences, telling myself that I didn't deserve to live higher than I'd earned. Until tonight, I'd thought this a way of being virtuous, but, until tonight, I'd never tried to look at it from my father's point of view. Oh, what he could have done with such a windfall, what he would have done for our little country. When I was very small he had said to me, "Dream big dreams—let them fill our little world to the brim, and then spill out into the great wide world beyond." Another challenge I'd dodged.

Well, I'd done nothing for the little country of my birth, and precious little for my adopted homeland, or the great wide world beyond. But, starting the next morning, that would change. Leaving the pictures lying open on my desk, I turned off my desk lamp, walked down the hall to the kitchen, and rinsed my glass in the kitchen sink. I went to bed and slept soundly, more peacefully, in fact, than I'd slept in years.

CHAPTER 6

THREE MORNINGS LATER I left my apartment at "oh-dark-thirty," driving north, then west. As I crossed the West Virginia state line, I noticed that the sky behind me had become more gray than black. In another half-hour the sun was visible in my rearview mirror. A few minutes later I passed the sign saying "Singing Creek, population 257." I followed the road to the blinking yellow light at the intersection in the center of town, Singing Creek's recently-acquired concession to traffic control. I turned right, tracking north along the narrow county road that follows the creek that gives the town its name. Just past the ruins of an old saw mill I turned right again, this time onto a graveled road that, despite twisting and turning to follow the contour of the terrain, climbed steeply enough to require downshifting into a lower gear. As the road rose I passed mailboxes and driveways I hadn't seen the last time I visited. Clearly Singing Creek was developing its own version of suburban sprawl. Finally, nearly at the top of the ridge, I turned down a short driveway leading to a rambling two-story cedar cabin. Lights were on upstairs and in the kitchen. I parked, got out, and walked around the side of the house to the kitchen door. There was a slight chill in the air, enough to remind me that I had gained two thousand feet in altitude since leaving Virginia Beach, enough to make me grateful that I'd worn a light jacket. I was fumbling with my face mask when the door opened to my second knock.

"Come on in, Harry," said a maskless Mary Anne Dawkins. Despite the early hour, she was dressed in a nice floral print blouse and a trim navy-blue skirt, the only clue to her current task a bright yellow apron. "Take off your coat and hang it on that hook over there. Grady's out fussing around with the dogs, but he'll be back in a minute. I don't think you need bother with that mask, do you? We could hardly be more socially-distanced out here. Have a seat, breakfast is almost ready."

Her last comment had been superfluous, since the kitchen was filled with enticing aromas, freshly brewed coffee, steaks sizzling in a big cast iron skillet, and diced potatoes with green peppers and onions in another.

"You really didn't have to do steak," I said.

"It's no big deal. They're venison steaks, which we've got coming out our ears. We've got a freezer full of venison steaks and venison sausage and venison everything else. We have 'em all the time. We wouldn't do anything company-like for you Harry. You know that. You're just family around here."

Being just family in the Dawkins household was far superior to being company almost anywhere else. She asked me how I wanted my eggs, then walked over past the big kitchen table to the foot of the stairs and shouted for Abby to hurry down and set the table. A moment later Abby came bounding down wearing blue jeans and a red tee shirt. The tee shirt bore a picture of a skull wearing a green beret, with a dagger between its teeth. Under the picture was a slogan that read: "Join Special Forces, visit exotic places, meet interesting people—and kill them!" I'd given her the shirt some years before, mainly to get a rise out of her father. At that time the tee shirt had been much too big for her, but not anymore.

"Morning, Uncle Harry." She looked amazingly like her mother, more so now that she had matured into a young woman. She gave me a quick hug, stepped back, composed a solemn face.

"Unca Hawwy," she said, mimicking a small child's voice. I knew what was coming. "Unca Hawwy, green beanies eat—."

"That will just about do, Abby Dawkins," interrupted her mother. "It was cute, once, a long time ago, but I'm tired of it and I'm sure Harry is too."

To understand, you needed to go back a few years. In late 1990, during the run-up to Desert Storm, I'd been in charge of a small composite team probing into northern Iraq from a base in Jordan. The team consisted mainly of Army operators, with a Jordanian liaison, but, because we'd been pulled, of all places, from a training assignment in northern Norway, we also had two exchange operators with us, Peter Rudd, a member of the Royal Marines' Special Boat Service, and Grady Dawkins, a Force Recon Marine. Between missions we were based in a small village. Almost immediately we noticed the fatherly interest Grady seemed to have taken in the gang of street urchins who hung around the entrance to our compound. But we didn't think much about it. Then one afternoon, as several of us were leaving to go into the ville, the children gathered around us while smiling broadly, and began chanting: "Green beanies eat shit." Grady Dawkins, our token Marine, had made his presence felt.

Years later, not long after Grady retired back home to the hills of West Virginia, he invited me to come and meet his wife and daughter. I made the trek up to Singing Creek. The cabin was smaller then, and the deer would actually come right up to the back porch. And Abby was a heartbreakingly beautiful five-year-old. Her mother introduced me to her, while Grady mysteriously absented himself. After introductions were made, Abby looked up at me and fixed me with a quite serious blue-eyed stare.

"Unca Hawwy," she said, "gween beanies eat shit."

Tradition thus honored, the now-teenaged Abby turned to the task of setting the table. Mary Anne pronounced the steaks and the potatoes done and turned them down to a low heat. She started the eggs, remarking that she wasn't going to wait any longer, and if Grady hadn't arrived by the time everything was ready, he could just eat a cold breakfast. I was reasonably certain that such a threat had been uttered before, and that Grady had suffered through a few cold breakfasts. When the eggs were done we sat down at the table. Mary Anne bowed her head and blessed the food, then we began to eat.

"This isn't just a social visit, is it?" asked Mary Anne. "You've got a job in your pocket, right?"

"Well, yes, but I'm not sure that it's the kind of thing he'll want to take. It would tie him up pretty thoroughly for several months."

Abby chimed in. "Where would you and Daddy go this time?"

"We have to wait and see if your father is even interested. It's been a long time since we've done anything together," I replied. "And, after that, I'm not sure about some of the places we'd be going." It was almost an honest answer.

"Oh, he'll want to go, all right," said Mary Anne. "Grady 'Go' Dawkins—it should've been his middle name. But it's a good thing you've come up with something. The fishing around here's not enough to keep him busy, and this Covid thing has kept him away from his police training jobs. I've got to get him out from underfoot until deer season starts."

"Underfoot's not usually a problem, is it? I mean, he's got his wildlife photography these days."

She gave me one of those tolerant smiles, the kind that women use to gently suggest to men that they're in fact clueless about the way life really works. But I also caught a hint that things were perhaps a bit out of sync.

Conversation lagged as we settled into our breakfasts. The food was delicious, made all the more so by my early start; I'd been up long enough to have a really powerful appetite. I finished one piece of venison and took another from the platter. Mary Anne and Abby were lagging behind, eating at a more ladylike pace. I was in the midst of buttering a second biscuit when we heard, from the back door, the sounds of mud being kicked and scraped from a pair of boots. And then the door opened and the man himself walked in.

If you could picture Karl Marx as a cowboy, then you have the image of Grady Dawkins. He had the big face, the full beard spread broadly over his collar, and the high forehead. His hair had the look of steel wool, although he usually stuffed it under a much-battered and discolored gray Stetson. The remainder of his uniform consisted of a plaid flannel shirt, either red, green, or blue, an old green fatigue jacket, blue jeans, and a pair of Tony Lama boots, as dilapidated as the Stetson.

In really warm weather he exchanged his flannels for colored tee shirts. In really cold weather he traded the Stetson for a black watch cap and the fatigue jacket for a fur-lined air force flight line parka. For dress occasions, which Grady defined as happening at most only once or twice a year, he invariably wore a Doc-Holliday black suit, a second Stetson as pristine as the regular one is ratty, and gray-and-black ostrich-hide dress cowboy boots, spit-shined to perfection. His scrupulous cleanliness, his erect posture, and the globe-and-anchor tattoo on his right bicep were the only visual clues attesting to Gunnery Sergeant (ret.) Grady Dawkins's twenty-two years in the Marine Corps.

This morning he wore a light blue flannel and the fatigue jacket, testimony that he considered the weather less than brutal. He poured himself a cup of coffee and sat down with his plate of steak and eggs. Only the coffee showed any sign of warmth, but Grady seemed not to mind, or even to notice.

"Hi, there," he said to me, "you rolled out kind of early this morning—this must be a big deal." He cut a piece of venison, speared it with his fork, and smeared it around in egg yolk before putting it in his mouth. Mary Anne got up and went upstairs to finish getting ready for work—evidently, in this corner of West Virginia, being a bank teller qualified as an essential service. Abby stacked the dishes in the sink, ran enough hot water for them to soak, and then went upstairs to her room. Grady stayed at the table to finish his breakfast.

"Always tastes like shit when it's cold, don't it?" he said. "But it's my own damn fault, so there's not much I can say. Mary Anne always gets pissed off with me for being late, but I didn't mean to be. One of my bird dogs is bad sick, and I was tending to her."

He took his last bite, put his plate and coffee cup in the sink, as Mary Anne made her goodbye, and drove away. In deference to Abby's continued presence, we got up from the table and, freshly-refilled coffee cups in hand, took the stairs to the basement. At the foot of the basement stairs we entered a large room, which accommodated the furnace and a hot-water heater, a washer and a dryer, a big table for folding laundry, and rows of metal shelves filled with the usual family junk. Off to one side was a wooden door. Carved into the wood were the words "Do Not Disturb." We opened the door and stepped into what was scarcely more than a glorified closet. Here Grady had squeezed in two armchairs, a small end table, a lamp, and a bookshelf.

"Never brought you back here before, have I?" he said. "I cleaned this place out not long ago, brought the chairs and the other stuff in. My place. I'll be damned if I'm gonna be like most men, going off to the shitter whenever they want a little peace and quiet. That's just fucking stupid. So now I come back here. This's about as private as it gets around here, so tell me what you've got for me."

I paused to gather my thoughts. I had to get this right. I'd spent the better part of five days putting together a plan I could sell, but if I couldn't sell it here, the plan would die. Grady was the only one I could ask to lead this mission. If he said 'no,' there was no mission.

"How does Africa sound to you? Not training, not security exercises, not helping me and Kip provide protection for some humanitarian crowd, but a real mission."

"You're shitting me! Africa? A real mission, no farting around?"

"Northeastern Congo, a place called Wiangara, to be a bit more precise."

"Never heard of it."

So, I began at the beginning, starting with my meeting with Toby Parks, and ending with the basics I'd gleaned from the files he'd given me.

"That's about the damnedest story I've ever heard, Harry. At your age, how the hell do you get yourself into that kind of shit? Damn, if those AARP motherfuckers get wind of what you've been up to, they'll tear up your membership card, break your cane in two, and drum your skinny old ass right out of the senior citizen corps. They'd think you got your *Modern Maturity* subscription mixed up with *Soldier of* fucking *Fortune*. He paused for a second before continuing, and when he did, the banter was gone from his voice. "I'm sorry, partner. I didn't mean that the way it came out. I mean, I'm not exactly a kid anymore, either. But hell—neither one of us has any business running around playing commandos anymore."

"Is that why you were trolling last year for some contract security work in Afghanistan last year?" He gave me a dirty look. "Yeah, I heard about it from Homer Pate."

"Yeah, I tried, all right. They said I was too old, that they had a long waiting list of guys who wanted to go over, younger guys, guys who they said had 'fresher skills,' whatever the fuck that means. Shit, Harry, maybe they're right. I just had my fifty-seventh birthday and that's getting pretty goddamn old."

"No, but you're a lot younger than I am, and much more fit. But if this thing goes the way I've been thinking, it won't need any marathon men, any super-troopers. Even an old man like me might manage it. No, this one's about balance, and good sense, and keeping your head when things don't go according to plan." I hesitated, knowing I'd come to the critical point. Before I could continue I saw the light go on in his eyes.

"Jesus H. Christ! You didn't come here just to get my two cents' worth. You want me to go in on this deal, don't you?"

"I want you to lead it."

"You're shittin' me."

"Who else? I'd love to think I could still do it, but, honestly I know better. Anyway, I need to concentrate on setting the thing up, putting things together, getting the gear in place, managing the money. It's too big for me to do all that and be the tactical lead as well. I don't know anybody better for that than you."

"And you think I'm not too old? You really think I can do this?"

"If I thought you were too old, I wouldn't be asking you. When Parks asked me and I said 'yes,' I was thinking to myself that, if you'd do it, it might just come off. It needs someone like you to lead it, and it needs someone like you to get the troops."

"How so?"

"Mostly, it's a generational thing. In my circle these days, you're one of the young guys. "There's Kip, of course, and he's already in this thing with me neck deep. But I need him at my side to help me with the logistics, and if we have to put someone on the ground early for any reason, he's the only one who could do it. But you've been working with people who might be just right." Since leaving the service Grady had padded his retirement income as a contract trainer, teaching tactics and close quarter combat to local law enforcement SWAT-types and security guards at places like nuclear power plants. Many of them were ex-Rangers and Marines. Some of them, I was hoping, might sign up for the mission if Grady was leading it.

He thought about this for a second. "Yeah, I know some kids who'd give their right nut to go on something like this, good guys, got out of service because they were going back for a second or third tour, their marriages were falling apart, and the job was turning into just sitting behind Hesco barriers in some God-forsaken outpost waiting to get lit up." He got out of his chair, paced in a tight circle around the tiny room. "There's a bunch of 'em. Hell, the best of the lot, believe it or not, there's this girl down in Kentucky, sheriff's deputy now, ex-Air Force security police. If she ever found out I'd aced her out of a deal like this by turning it down, she'd shove a stick up my ass, run it out my mouth, and roast me over a fire. Yeah, I could maybe turn up a half dozen. That enough?"

"Not really. But Kip's in, like I said. He's got two guys on line for the team, he thinks, one French, one Dutch guy, knows them from his Legion time and they both have worked with us on the Foundation. Kip's pretty sure they'll go for it." In fact, Kip had called me the night before, sounding very enthusiastic about both.

"French guy, huh. You sure you trust some French bastard?"

"Why not, if Kip believes in him and he believes in Kip. Besides, I know them both, at least a little, and while working the villages down there hasn't been this kind of job, I've liked what I've seen."

"Okay. It'll be like French toast and French fries. We'll call him 'Freedom Guy."

"If it works for you, Grady."

"How many did you have in mind?"

"At a rough estimate, sixteen."

"Hard to snoop and poop with that many bodies. Why not go with three, maybe four guys? Sneak 'em aboard the site. Bring in just enough explosives to do the dirty deed, then sneak out again, and by the time the charges go up, they're way the fuck outta Dodge. Quick in, quick out—before you know it we're sitting around the old fireplace at home, drinking coffee, and picking our noses."

I explained about the close-in guards, drawn from the Chinese "Leishen" commando team and the select group of Wiangara militiamen based just down the road from the site. I described the alarmed fences and the interlocking doors to the laboratory, how we would have to simultaneously take down the alarm-monitoring station and the control room at the gatehouse.

"That's three teams," I continued, "two men each, having to hit three widely separated locations. Two of those teams taking on three or four guards each, in hardened guard posts, just to get at the controls for the interlock system. And that many locations means two or three times the chance that somebody may get off a duress alarm. If that happens you've got at least a dozen screaming Chinese commandos pouring out of that guard barracks on site, and a couple of dozen more African guys riding "technicals" with 12.7s mounted on the truck beds."

"Okay, I get your point. Forty versus four or five is lousy odds, even if it's forty fucking Mary Kay ladies."

"Exactly. If you go in with only four guys then, yes, you might have more chance of a stealthy success, but if something goes wrong, you've got no hope, no backup, no Plan B."

"It's gonna be hard to shake that many fleas out of the mattress. I mean, like I said, there's people I know, they'd love to take this on, but not that many, not without taking some of the wannabes and the losers. Sixteen's a steeper mountain than this mule can climb."

"It may not take sixteen. I might be able to make it work with a couple less, but a dozen is the minimum, I think. I get your point about smaller making it easier to get in and out cleanly, but still, I don't know. It's not much more than a week that I've been trying to come up with a plan, I still have a lot of details to work out, but I need you to find some good troops for the team."

"What about weapons and gear?"

"Parks gave me a name, says the guy can make all our wishes come true, given enough money. I'm fixing Kip with a line of credit and he goes off on a buying spree."

"Okay, Harry, run it by me again. Not the whole deal, just the barracks for the off-duty guards."

Recounting the details was not hard. I'd pored over most of the details during the past week, and stayed up late the night before going over the updates in the folder Parks had given me. The off-duty guards slept in a building with six small rooms, two beds to each room. Individually assigned weapons were kept by each man. I'd hoped that they turned them into a central armory off shift, which would've made my task much easier, but such was not the case. At one end of the building two squad rooms had been turned into a single large bay, which served as a day room. At the other end of the building were toilets and showers. Actually, quite luxurious for that part of the world. Outside doors permitted entry at the bathroom end or the day-room end, so an assault team could clear the building along its longitudinal axis, which again was what I wanted. Silence and speed were essential. I explained all this to Grady.

"Hell," he said, "it's like one of those word problems in Abby's math books at school. 'A dozen men are sleeping in six rooms, two per room. It takes two seconds for a single steely-eyed killer to murder one man in his sleep and move on to the next sleeping man. It takes six seconds to move from one room to the next. How many steely-eyed killers are required to murder all the sleeping men in less than ninety seconds?' And you figured two, with two more to cover them. Right? Plus, more steely-eyed killers to deal with the on -duty guards, and the lab workers."

"Exactly right."

"Course it is. You taught me this shit, a lot of it anyway. But, you know what, I think maybe there's a better way."

"I'm always open to suggestions."

"Think about it. There's a lot of risks your way. You got your suppressed weapons, there's still some noise from the escaping gases, and the mechanical noise when the action cycles a new round. That wakes up some guy who's sleeping light. You shoot somebody in his sleep, there's no promise he dies quietly. Maybe your team's going from room to room and they run into some guy coming back from the head. Or maybe there's some poor bastard curled up under the covers beating his meat, hoping his buddy won't hear him. Any little thing like that, and even with four guys you are well and truly fucked. But not if you just blow up the whole goddamn building to start with!"

He was right. It was so obvious that I kicked myself mentally for not having seen it immediately. With some well-placed explosive charges, the building itself could be dropped on their heads, taking out the lot of them wholesale. The same approach could be employed at the building where the scientists and technicians slept. From the very beginning these 'civilians,' some of them women, had posed a special problem. On the one hand, they had to be taken out. On the other, executing them room-by-room would have taken very strong stomachs. Blowing the building, if nothing else, took things out of the face-to-face category.

"I agree with you, it's a safer way of taking out the guards in the barracks, but it still requires four men, probably, to get the charges set quickly."

"You'll need some specialists anyway, say a corpsman, for example. I don't know any of those, but one of the kids I've worked with was a civilian EMT and a fireman before he got righteous and became a SWAT cop."

"That would be great. If we do it right, we should be in and out before we get a strong reaction, but we can't count on not having any casualties."

"Still, I can't get you anywhere near sixteen bodies, sixteen good ones anyway. There's just no fucking way. You said you have some other people in mind?"

"Besides Kip and the guys he thinks he can get. Then, Peter Rudd, from our time in Jordan, and Colin Graham, the alarm system guy on that CIA job we did together back in 2014. Peter, I know how to find, and he should be able to find Colin. That's a start."

"Still hard to come up with sixteen, Harry."

"And impossible if I don't have you. Are you in or out?"

He sat back down again, looked at me for a moment, then looked down at his big calloused hands, examining them as if they contained the secrets of the universe. "Look, Harry, I know this is important to you, and I always thought I'd follow you anywhere. Parks is a good guy. Hard for me to say about a politician who used to be a sailor, even a SEAL. Remember when he first showed up down at A.P. Hill, when we were going out to Norway that time back in '89, wearing his ice-cream sailor suit, sounding like some la-di-da Harvard asshole. All I could think was wondering why we'd got stuck with him, but he turned out solid, didn't he? Not faggoty, like most squids. Then, again, the Teams aren't really the Navy, are they? So, I respect you, and I respect him, and God knows, that's a real soldier's name you mentioned being at the bottom of your fancy legal piece of paper. And, yeah, I'd like my crack at those assholes as well, and maybe if we don't do it, they'll come over here and kill everybody in New York or L.A. with their damned virus. But I still don't know."

"Why not?"

"I don't know 'xactly why not. Back before the bug kinda shut us all down, I had to drive up to Morgantown to get some reloading equipment. Spent the afternoon doing my business, got me a steak at the Golden Corral, it was getting dark when I was ready to head home. Stopped at a Seven-Eleven to get some gas. There was this girl standing there, leaning up against the side of a van, big blond hair, tight little black mini-skirt, red top stretched across her big titties like sausage skin. Looked like a blowjob just waiting to happen. But I just walked right on by, got in the Cherokee, and drove away. I didn't need what she was selling. For a minute there I wanted it real bad, but it just didn't feel right, and I went with the feeling. I think about this, and part of me wants it badder than I wanted to climb right into that van with her, badder than I've wanted anything since I got out of the Corps. But when I married Mary Anne, she said that I'd done enough fucking around before I met her and my fucking around days were behind me, and she was right. And when I retired she said that I'd done enough fighting and that my fighting days were behind me, too. What she'll say to me is, I'm thinking, there's others around to protect New York and L.A., and that I need to stay home now and take care of her and Abby."

I'd played things badly, made my pitch the wrong way. I'd come at this too much like the high-end operational entrepreneur I'd resolved to become, not the asshole buddy Grady knew and respected.

"You know what, Grady," I began, "that's a nice story, but you know what else? I think you're full of shit." That got his attention big time. "I don't know about the fucking around part, and I don't much fucking care." I may be the only ex-NCO who struggles to use 'fuck' as the universal modifier. Patti taught me to appreciate the word as a breathy feminine urge to carnal exertion, but it never exactly trips off my tongue. But right now, I badly needed to get through to Grady. "I know about the security contractor thing, remember? We just talked about it not ten minutes ago. But going to Kabul's not a trip to the ATM. Those are nasty fuckers over there. They blow your butt to bits with roadside bombs, or maybe they snatch you and cut your head off. You want Mary Anne and Abby watching that one on Headline News. And for what? Dignitary protection? When did you ever give a shit about dignitaries? Convoy security? You want your tombstone to read, 'he died for a truckload of MREs?' Protecting a bunch of aid workers? The only 'aid workers' you ever cared about were aiding a load out of your dick in an Olangapo whorehouse. We're talking nurses giving shots, not strippers blowing smoke rings out their pussies."

He was looking at me like I'd suddenly grown two heads, but I finally, truly, had him focused.

"Now all of that dignitary and convoy and aid worker protection is well and good, Kip and I have been doing it for three years with the Bobby foundation, but I never thought to ask you in on it. Not because you couldn't do it, but because I knew you'd be bored out of your gourd. But why contract security now—why you? The big bucks?" He flinched, and suddenly I understood. "How bad is it? How much do you need?"

He turned away from me, refusing to answer.

"There's money, too," I said softly, "enough money to help you take care of Mary Anne and Abby in a very big way."

"Fuck you, Harry."

"I was thinking a half-million dollars, just for you, for leading the team."

He caught his breath, then exhaled slowly.

"You can't just fucking buy me, you son-of-a-bitch?"

"Grady, I don't want to buy you, God knows, but this thing won't go without you. I want it to go, worse than I've ever wanted anything in my whole life. Parks told me I was seventy years old, and it was time I finally grew up. So, I'm being a grown up. I've got money, and I'm laying it on the line. You want to go, I know you do. You don't really want to run around guarding mess halls or pipelines or raghead politicians. You want the big one you never got to do. You want Makin with Carlson's Raiders, just like your dad. You want Son Tay with Bull and Bud and Dick. You want it so bad you still wake up with a hard on just dreaming about it." Suddenly I ran out of passion. "Look, Grady, I'm not taking shots at you, and I'm really, truly not trying to buy you, but I need you for this. Maybe you're right, maybe you're not as young as you once were, and maybe not as hot shit tactically. But I've turned this thing inside out, I've thought about everyone I know, and you're the only one I've got who's got even a ghost of a chance of finding the right kind of people and building a team in time. And I know you want it, the same way I want it. But I really am too fucking old, and I've got to do other stuff now. The money? I wasn't even thinking about buying you. I was just trying to make it feel right to you."

He sat for a long time staring down at his big hands.

"Buys my little girl a lot of college, don't it?"

I allowed that it did.

"It's a neat deal, Harry, but you and I both know that it adds up to a lot of different ways of getting screwed, some of them terminally. But I've gotta be honest with you. I need the bucks. I need 'em really bad. You had deer steak for breakfast. We eat venison a lot, not because it's a treat, but because in season I can bring it in cheaper than buying meat in the store. I haven't done too well since I left the Corps. Never had the knack for being a civilian. I mean, I do okay sometimes in that cop-training job, those jobs for you overseas helped a bunch, then I had that stint with Fish & Wildlife, then I was a deputy before I pissed off the sheriff. But right now, I don't have much of anything going, especially now with this Covid thing. Most of what we're living on right now is what Mary Anne brings in, and the bank isn't really doing too good either. But Abby's gonna be ready for college in another year, and we've got nothing put by. My ex gets all my Corps retirement."

"I'm not trying to buy you, I'm really not. You know that."

"I do know that, and I'm sorry I got pissed at you. How soon do you need an answer?"

"We don't have a whole lot of time to launch this thing, and if you say 'no,' I'm back to square one."

"Give me two hours. You can stay here, I'll go into town to talk to Mary Anne. That okay?"

"Of course. Tell her you'll be gone for a while, tell her it may be dangerous, don't tell her exactly what it is."

"I'll tell her it's maybe a little dangerous, but she'll kill me if I tell her how fucking insane it is. Tell her about the money?"

I thought about this. The money would be a dead giveaway that this was something very big. On the other hand, my fancy letter didn't give me the power to send anyone to Leavenworth if they spoke out of turn. This whole thing depended on trust, a lot of trust.

"Go ahead, tell her what you need to, just don't do the where and when."

"It matters, Harry, it really does. I mean, maybe it doesn't show, but we're a little unhappy these days, she works all days with these banker guys, and they don't hurt for bucks, and I think it's gotten to her some. I think sometimes, maybe she's wondering if she made the right choice with me. Maybe, too, maybe she's right to wonder. Sometimes I think that my fire's been just slowly going out, ever since I left the Crotch. I mean all that 'once a Marine, always a Marine' shit works at reunions, but a lot of days it's just memories and no one cares what became of you. And you were right, Harry, right about the other thing."

"Which other thing?"

"The big mission. The big fight. Look, I'm not a cherry. I know a big fight's just a bunch of little ones rolled together, and I've had my share of the little ones. But I grew up on my daddy's Raider stories, and I always wanted to be Sandy Bonnyman or Manila John Basilone. I mean, shit, Harry, the whole fucking Corps is a bunch of fucking romantics when it comes to shit like that. You just never can say so out loud."

There's not much you can add after goading someone into baring his soul. "Go on, then, Grady, go talk to Mary Anne, and you guys kick it around. I'll see you in two hours."

I followed him back upstairs, and watched from the kitchen window as he drove away in the Cherokee. Then I took a can of Coke from the refrigerator and went outside on the back deck to watch for the deer and to wait for his return. I was dozing in the morning sun when I heard the sound of the Cherokee, straining its way in low gear up the steep driveway. I got up and met Grady as he came through the kitchen door. He had a troubled expression on his face.

"What did she say?"

"Not much. She just said, 'Do it, if that's what you want to do.' It was kind of like…," he paused for a moment, "it was kind of like she really didn't care one way or the other."

"Did you tell her about the money?"

"Yeah," he said. "I started not to, it didn't seem to matter, but I guess I just wanted to get some kind of reaction. So, I told her and she said, 'Well, if Harry has that kind of money to give away, then why doesn't he just give it to you, period.' Just like that."

"You never told her, did you?" Years ago, right after the stock started to skyrocket, I'd offered Grady some shares, not a lot, but enough to tide him over at another time when I knew his finances were tight. He'd responded by saying that he didn't 'need any fucking charity.'

"Tell her I'm so fucking stiff-necked I'd pissed away a chance to give her all the things she wanted? C'mon, Harry, give me a break."

"So, you're in?"

He straightened his shoulders and gave me a salute.

"Reporting for duty, sir."

I returned the salute and then extended my hand.

"We probably ought to have a drink on it."

"You know I'm not a big drinker, but this time I won't say no."

"Bar's in the den, Harry. Let's go."

After pouring the drinks, Grady turned to me with a big smile. "I can just see it, Harry. Picture this. The job's over, and somehow some TV announcer is right there, in my face with a big microphone, and he's saying 'Grady Dawkins—you've just saved the whole fucking world from being virused to death. What're you going to do now?' And I'm jumping up and down like some Super Bowl asshole with my arms waving, and I shout back at him: 'I'm going to fucking Disney World.'"

And, on that note, the mission really began.

CHAPTER 7

ABOUT THIRTY HOURS later I was standing on the tarmac at the private aviation terminal at San Francisco International Airport, drinking machine coffee from a paper cup, watching the mere handful of commercial flights taking off and landing. I continued to watch and found my thoughts drifting to our final approach over the bay. I'd been sitting on the right-hand side of the executive charter, looking north toward the city itself, noticing the sharply diminished city lights, and thinking about what cities like San Francisco and Seattle and New York were already enduring, thinking about the creeping, spreading fear, and thinking about what I knew might be coming if I couldn't stop it. We'd been shaken by a bunch of guys with box cutters and were now shaking in fear of an invisible killer. Now, well, failure didn't bear thinking about. Having Grady sign on had given me hope, but the whole thing still hung in the balance, waiting for another special someone.

I tossed the dregs, dropped the cup in a nearby receptacle, then went back inside to wait some more by the drive-up door on the other side of the building. The two attendants, resplendent in masks bearing the colors of the private aviation service, were chatting softly behind the counter. Most of the chairs inside were empty, only a few other business travelers either waiting for their ride or waiting for a flight, awkwardly maintaining their distance from one another. None of the usual bustle, none of the usual buzz of conversation. I was just about to start a second cup of coffee—don't ask me why, when Moira walked in. She stood in the door, scanned the area briefly, then caught my beckoning wave, smiled, and came over—no mask for her. As she threaded her way between tables, the clerks and the businessmen all turned to follow her progress. Dark blonde hair, dark eyes framed by high cheekbones, not tall but seeming so with her erect posture and three-inch heels, and very much on display in her form-fitting slacks of lavender-colored suede and nicely-filled matching silk blouse. She walked with attitude—not a girl, but a woman, proud of her years and her looks. And it gave my ego a nice boost when her appreciative audience saw her drop her jacket and purse on the table and lean over and brush my forehead with her lips before sitting down beside me.

"May I offer you a drink?" I gestured toward the coffee machine.

"Give me a break, Harry," she replied. "Let's get out of here."

She seemed a tad preoccupied as we walked out to her car, and I asked if something was wrong.

"No, no, I'm fine. I just need a little space. I've just come from an ugly meeting. I probably should've scheduled it for another time, but the meeting was near here, over on the private aviation side, in fact, and it just seemed sensible to combine the meeting with picking you up. The client wanted face-to-face, or, God help us, mask-to-mask, and I've not been having much luck with Zoom lately."

"What happened?"

"Standard silliness. One of my corporate clients has a marketing VP who thinks sex with the pilot is part of the service. I had to, shall we say, 'clarify' the issue with the chairman of the board. I mean, looking good is part of the business, and if I like someone, well, whatever. But it's my call what I give away. All I'm selling is flying the airplane." She paused, shook her head in irritation. "Worked out all right, but it's just hateful to have to fool with such idiocy, especially with this damned virus—who wants to have sex with strangers these days? The damnable thing is having to try and be nice to assholes, but I have to be careful. Business is off, and I need to keep up the lease on my Beechcraft Baron. Don't worry. I'll be myself by the time we get home."

In the private service parking lot, we found Moira's big red Dodge Ram pickup with the vanity plates that read 'AV8TRIX.' She unlocked the doors, and we got in. I studied her expression before the dome light went out, decided that she was still not fit for conversation. We drove north on 101, through the heart of San Francisco and across the Golden Gate Bridge to Sausalito.

We left the truck in the driveway. The garage, I knew from previous visits, was filled with everything from gardening tools to dusty stacks of old *Life* magazines, plus a space squeezed out for a big Yamaha YZF-R1 sport bike—motorcycles, in recent years, had come to compete with airplanes for Moira's affections. Although the garage was level with the street, the house, a 1950's-vintage bungalow in blue-gray stucco, was sufficiently down slope that, from the street, one could only see roof tiles. I got my bag from the truck and followed Moira down the stair-stepped footpath that led to the front door. From the outside the house looked slightly run down. But inside it was a real home, warm, comfortable, artful and yet jumbled all together in perfect reflection of the woman herself.

Moira took my coat and hung it alongside her jacket in a narrow closet just inside the door. "Make yourself comfortable, Harry."

I settled in on the couch. She went down the hall, bustled about in the back of the house. When she came out she had changed into a white flannel nightgown with blue roses that covered her from neck to ankle. She had scrubbed the make-up from her face, revealing youthful freckles across her cheeks and age wrinkles around her eyes and at the corners of her mouth. She sat down in an armchair across from me.

"Harry, love, I know that you have tons that you want to talk about, and I can't wait to hear it. But you've been traveling for hours; you're on East Coast time. I know it must feel like the middle of the night for you."

"I'm all right, really."

"Okay, then, why don't I fix us a pot of coffee and we'll get to it. Guest bedroom's down the hall, on the left."

I picked up my bag and took it to the guest bedroom, which evidently doubled as Moira's study. Bookshelves lined two walls, a single bed the third, under the only window. A computer stand took up the remaining space. I paused for a moment to consider the books. Most were paperbacks, and all looked well-read yet well-cared for. They were neatly organized by subject matter and, within each subject, by author's last name. The bottom shelves were designed to accommodate oversized books, with several editions of *Jane's All the World's Aircraft* sharing space with Janson's *History of Art*, which was accompanied by several other art books, ranging from a work on the Impressionists to a collection of Boris Viejo illustrations. The paperbacks ran heavily to war books, adventure stories, and mysteries.

Hearing the high-pitched buzzing of an electric coffee grinder, I started for the kitchen, but as I reached for the light switch I happened to glance down at Moira's desk. The face that stared back at me from the gilt-framed black-and-white photograph on the desk was that of Larry Beale, younger than when I had seen him last, probably taken shortly after he and Moira had first met. Indiscreet—she shouldn't even have the picture, much less display it, but understandable that she would want to do so.

"Are you ready for some coffee?" Moira asked as I entered the kitchen. "The pot's just about done. I've got some doughnuts, too. Fresh baked this morning. Well, I guess yesterday morning now."

"That's fine. Sounds good."

She opened a cabinet, considered a bright array of souvenir mugs.

"What's your pleasure, Harry?' You can have your coffee in a Forty-Niners mug, red and gold. No, it's slightly chipped, that won't do for company, will it? How about a Smith & Wesson mug, dark blue with white letters, just the thing for a man like you? I've got a Bart Simpson, but I can't picture it in your hand."

"It really doesn't matter, believe me."

She took down a dark blue mug, not the Smith & Wesson, but a souvenir of the play "Les Miserables." For herself she selected a bright red mug with a black "Miss Saigon" logo. She poured coffee into the mugs.

"There's sugar on the counter, some sweetener, too. You're right there, could you get the half-and-half out of the refrigerator, please."

I took the mugs of coffee, and Moira followed me into the living room with a plate of doughnuts. We sat down together on the couch, not touching, but close enough to make me uncomfortably aware of the woman underneath the flannel shroud.

"Check out the needlepoint," she said, gesturing to a spot above the television and to the right side of a framed poster of "Xena, the Warrior Princess."

"'If there are no titty-dancers in heaven,'" I read aloud, "'then I don't want to go.'"

"Just finished that one a few weeks ago, and every time I look at it I think of you."

I first met Moira in 2002, at a little airport just outside Gulfport, Mississippi. I'd gone back to work for the CIA after 9/11, and I had come to hit up my old friend Larry Beale for a Central America project, not having run the proper background first, not realizing how, after straightening up after his air cowboy period in the Eighties, he'd run off the rails once again. We were sitting in his shabby cramped office, a small space partitioned off within a corrugated metal hangar, drinking Dixie beer, and swapping lies about the old days. A young woman walked in, stunning in spite of her baggy coveralls and the dark smudge of grease along her forehead. She sat down in the only vacant chair, put her feet up on the desk, and gave Larry a quick, pungently-worded review of the status of the engine she was working on. When she finally paused to catch her breath, Larry turned to me and made an introduction. In those days her name wasn't Moira Finnegan. It doesn't matter anymore what her name was then. I turned to her and asked if she was an aircraft mechanic. Larry answered for her.

"Why sure Harry, she's a mechanic, I taught her that, but mainly she's the best copilot I've ever had." His tone suggested that she was much more to him than a copilot.

"So, then," I said to her, "you're a professional pilot."

"No, Mister York, I'm an amateur pilot, in the old sense of amateur. I fly airplanes because I love doing it, and, if I make a little money at it sometimes, then that's just fine. Professionally," she paused for emphasis, "professionally, I am a titty dancer."

Her words just hung in the air. And then I said, "Well, if there are no titty dancers in heaven, then I don't want to go."

Nearly twenty years had passed, but I still smiled at the recollection.

"You know, Harry, from that moment on I knew you were really all right. I mean, even before you showed up that day, Larry had talked about you, he thought very highly of you, but I wasn't sure how you'd take me. I mean, men can be so narrow-minded and so judgmental."

"I saw his picture in the bedroom."

"It's the only picture I have of him. I got rid of all the others, just like they told me to, but I put that one away in a safety-deposit box. I finally decided a few months ago that, no matter what, I was going to get him out again. I'm glad I did."

She stood up, got a cigarette, lit it from a table lighter on the coffee table, and curled up on the couch once again. "It doesn't hurt like it used to, but sometimes I miss him so badly."

"He was quite a character." I couldn't give her more than that. Larry had been an otherwise hardheaded woman's one great illusion— or delusion—largely, I think, because between wheeling and dealing with the CIA, the DEA, and the drug cartels, he taught her to fly and gave her entrée into his 'Terry and the Pirates' existence.

"It was so ugly, the way it ended. So ugly."

"Remember the good times."

Easy for me to say, harder for her to do. I noticed that her eyes had moistened.

I took a bite of doughnut and waited to see where she wanted to take the conversation.

"Tell me about our mission," she finally said.

Just like that. The surprise must have shown in my face.

"Honestly, Harry, saying 'yes' is just a no-brainer for me. Really it is. You told me on the phone that it was the real thing, a live mission. I trust you that it isn't something stupid or trivial. And I trust you on the money side. You've always been straight up with me, after all. So, I'm in. Now tell me what I'm in for. Where? When? You told me on the phone 'three thousand miles, un-refueled round trip, mountainous country, lots of lakes and rivers.' I broke part of the code immediately. You didn't say a word about a seaplane, but I knew that's what you were thinking. But where?"

"Central Africa, the worst corner of the Congo. Maybe staging from alongside a freighter somewhere in international waters."

She pursed her lips, whistled softly. "Not bad, not bad at all. I was thinking maybe Africa from what you said on the phone, I mean, I know that's where you've been working for a while, but, hey, I like it. But why the remote launch?" She was really asking why I needed one of the few pilots left in the world with genuine seaplane expertise, but I let it hang for a moment.

"It's pretty Wild West, and there's no good place for us to stage in-country without possibly compromising security."

"Real "Heart of Darkness," kinda? We're going after Mr. Kurtz?"

"Not really, but that's a good enough way of thinking about it."

"Why are we going there?"

I told her exactly what I had told Grady.

"Oh, my God, oh my ever-loving God. That's playing at the top table," she responded. "That's our whole world on the knife edge. Why us? Why not Delta or the SEALs?" For a moment, I feared that the sheer magnitude of the mission might change her mind about signing on. Then she smiled that 1,000-watt smile. "Okay, then. Larry and I never played for stakes like that. How do you see it working?"

"The bioweapon lab sits on a steep bluff at the bend of a river.

The river empties into a good-sized lake only a few miles downstream. We fly into the area the night before the hit, have the team parachute in to a nearby drop-zone and lie in, while you fly onto the lake. You land there and then camouflage the aircraft and wait for the team. The team takes out the facility, rafts down the river to where you are, and then you fly them out. That's the outline. But you're the lead pilot. You'll have to work out the details."

"It's clean and simple. I love it. I'll need a copilot for sure, both to help me handle the plane I have in mind and while we're on the water. It'll be like a big boat, too big for me to handle by myself. I know a guy, in fact the perfect guy. Okay, let me go get a map."

She returned shortly with a thick world atlas and compass. She sat down beside me and spread the atlas across her lap, opening it to a double-page representation of sub-Saharan Africa. I pointed to a spot on the map. "Wiangara. That's the target location. Figure for the sake of preliminary planning a launch point somewhere in the Indian Ocean off the coast of Kenya."

She fished around in the desk drawer, came up with a protractor, took a measurement.

"Roughly eleven hundred miles, as the crow flies. Say twenty-two hundred round trip."

"But we don't want to make a straight round trip."

"No, of course not. The range itself is not a big deal. The plane I have in mind can carry your dozen people easily and it might stretch to the sixteen you're hoping for. We should be good for 2800, maybe more. I'll have to work out a fuel consumption projection down to the gallon to be sure. But then we get into the tricky parts. Air-defense environment. Are we going to have to dodge some things? Back in the days when Larry and I were going in and out of Florida, he had this guy at Homestead, some air force major with a gambling problem, we kept him on the payroll just to make sure what we were up against each time."

"I can get detailed data, but what I already know is that Kenya has a decent little air force, but the resources are all concentrated against al Shabab, well away from us. I don't think they have anything resembling a real early warning network, not like getting into this country along the southern border. Tanzania, if our path starts that far south, again, no problem, same with overflying Rwanda or Uganda. Congolese airspace security isn't even a joke. What isn't funny is that the Chinese may have installed a mobile tactical air defense radar at the airport—the only serious airport—in Wiangara. The other not funny detail is that apparently, they've slipped in a pair of Hongdu JL-8 training jets, probably armed, my source doesn't know for sure. But we have a pretty good idea of why they're there."

"Fair enough. And I'm not really worried. I know how to beat the kind of radar you're talking about, but doing it may lengthen the route in and out. Plus, we're going to be flying really low, right on the deck. That's not optimum for fuel economy. And if we take off and land a couple of times, that burns a bunch more fuel too."

"We can likely launch just a short distance offshore, though we buy more security if we're further out. Top off fuel from the ship, then two takeoffs and two landings if everything goes according to plan."

"Well, we probably have enough range anyway, but shortening things wouldn't hurt. Still, a ship means other problems, like sea state. That's no big deal on the outbound, we should have some choice on the weather, but we also need decent conditions on the return. That's a pretty big weather window. Seaplanes really don't like anything more than glassy smooth waters. Moderate we can deal with. Heavy seas, that's a big roll of the dice. Can you really get a ship?"

"I can get a ship. Better put, I have one." From her tone I could tell that, while laying hands on the right airplane left Moira undaunted, arranging for a mother ship appeared to be a major challenge. In fact, it was just the opposite. My sister and her husband had built up a small shipping company in the Eighties, and she had carried on with it after his death in 1991. When my cash windfall had occurred, I'd funneled a useful portion of it to her, and, at the same time as her relocation to Estonia, she had taken her operation worldwide. I'd spoken to her already, and knew that she had a vessel in Tallinn that had been loading up for Spain before Covid had idled the recipient business in Barcelona. She was ready to place the ship at my disposal and had already started to implement the cover story—the making of an action-adventure movie—with the crew. Years ago, for another project, I'd prepared a plan for refueling helicopters from an improvised base on a freighter, using fuel bladders as deck cargo and rigging a refueling boom to a cargo mast. I was sure that this could be adapted to present purposes.

"Well then." said Moira, "When do we go?"

"Three-four weeks, six at the outside. The smart kids working with Toby Parks think that the Chinese will wait to pull the trigger until Covid subsides, but before any real recovery occurs; that way they maximize the psychological and economic impact. Just when the world thinks it's coming out of lockdowns and the hospitals start to manage the first surge, the whole thing starts again, only worse. But that's guesswork, and the inside source apparently has no idea. The point is, we can't delay this and get caught flatfooted. The weather should be with us. We're past the heaviest monsoon, I gather, and the shipping forecasts look okay to me, but I'm no expert. Six weeks from now looks like the best it could possibly be."

"Okay, then, we'll have to have a lot of weather info, and a good source for local updates, not just for the launch site, but over the landward portion as well. You'd need that anyway for your parachute jump. Anyway, any kind of reasonable sea state, all we have to do is have a freighter waiting for us in international waters, right? We could go in the way you indicated, then come out this way," she pointed," further up the coast of Kenya? And the freighter meets us out here, your team gets back on the freighter, we refuel and then fly out. I hope you aren't thinking about hoisting the airplane on and off the freighter."

"No, but why?"

"Well, back in the day, seaplane tenders sometimes lifted the planes onboard, but these were large, dedicated ships with special lifting cranes. No way you can recreate that on your freighter. So, we will need a relatively nearby land base, and credible story for a flight plan to get there."

"Working on that," I remarked. "Hoping to line up something on a place called Reunion, it's an island territory of France, and then, as a potential way station, Mayotte, another French controlled island between Madagascar," I pointed to a spot on her atlas map, "and the mainland coast of Africa." As she reached for her protractor, I continued, "I've already checked—it's about six hundred miles from there to the Kenya coast."

Moira frowned and said, "Wish it were three hundred miles."

"Why?"

"Three hundred miles and we might just dispense with the ship, at least from a refueling standpoint. But not six, not if we want a comfortable reserve."

She studied the map for a few minutes more. "Get me the air-defense stuff, such as it is, and this part won't be a problem. I've managed harder."

"What about detailed charts. Should I send you some?"

"Charts I don't need, not right now anyway. I can get charts. You can get everything on line or on disc these days. Street maps of every city in the United States. Telephone numbers for every residence. Or, airline-quality flying charts for every place in the world with regularly scheduled air service. That'll do for initial planning. By the end of the week, though, we'll probably need some satellite mapping data, military quality, and a tie-in to the military GPS network. You can do that?"

"I can do it," I said, hoping that Parks would come through as promised.

"Now, that still doesn't solve the problem of places to land for the pickup. I like your lake idea, and we can go with that for planning. The locations you've highlighted on your map give it to us in theory, but just because its wet doesn't mean I can land on it. I have to have a landing area, say, at least 200 feet wide. That's still awfully tight, since our wingspan will be 104 feet. And, ideally, we need a good five thousand-feet for takeoff, less for landing, but where you land, you've got to take off again, so it comes to the same thing. There are tricks to beat that length requirement, but we don't want to rely on them. Depth of the water isn't that big a deal. The plane I have in mind, somebody once landed one by mistake on a mudflat covered with about a foot of water, and they managed to fly it out again. But we don't want to do that. The worse thing is underwater obstructions, a rock or something that at landing speed could just rip up the belly of the plane like a can opener. I like the lake, cause it's big and wide, big enough even in the little cove where your river empties into it. But it's not a lock, not until we know what's under the water. Can you get that kind of information?"

"Probably, but not in the next few days. Let me think about it." The lake I had in mind sat right in the middle of Wiangara, in a relatively isolated mountain valley, conveniently so for the Chinese, but also for us, since we meant to land on the lake. But this made it harder to get someone in to the area without using a plane. I had hoped to avoid using my Naburje foundation network for any part of this mission, but I had a guy who would ask no questions, someone for whom I could arrange a little boat and a depth sounder, and have him run the area where the river dumped into the lake. "If I solve that, where does that leave us?"

"If you solve it, makes us golden. In the meantime, still leaves us okay. We can still come up with the outline of a plan. The lake'll work. There can't be underwater crap everywhere, we just have to make sure there's not any where we want to land. Once we take off from the lake, it's only about ninety minutes before we're flying over Lake Albert," she put a finger on the map, "and over Uganda. If it's like you told me, we're safe there, even though the plan is to avoid putting down in Ugandan territory. And the ocean landing on the way out—I didn't mean to get you worried. Ocean landing's a piece of cake if the weather's even halfway with us. Don't forget. I didn't just do things with Larry in the Caribbean. And I've done Canada, Scandinavia, much more challenging weather and ocean, and I've done aerial firefighting in nasty places. I can deal with the Indian Ocean, and I can deal with marginal weather, don't you worry. Half my business these days is up to Alaska anyway."

Without meaning to she'd just underscored, in no uncertain terms, why I had to have her fly the mission. I knew no end of helicopter pilots, but I'd ruled out a helicopter insertion early on, for all the reasons that had made the Iranian hostage rescue in 1980 a catastrophe. And I knew a good few bush pilots who could do anything imaginable with a typical fixed wing aircraft. But Moira flew amphibians, virtually a lost art.

"You're the master," I said.

"No, the mistress," she countered, smiling. "That's that, then. Do you want to see my miracle plane, the one that solves all your problems?"

"I certainly do."

"Come back to the study with me."

She sat down at her computer, made a few quick entries. In about forty seconds she had pulled up a black-and-white picture of a twin-engine amphibian with military markings.

"The Catalina, officially the PBY-6A. Last of a whole series, manufactured from the 1930s until almost the end of World War II. My grandfather flew an earlier version when he was in the navy back then. Granpa saved a bunch of Dutchmen by picking them up right in the middle of the Japanese fleet, right after the battle of the Java Sea. He won a Navy Cross and some big Dutch medal, almost like a knighthood. Anyway, it was the best all-around amphibian ever built. Length sixty-three feet and six inches, wingspan 104 feet. Maximum speed about 180 knots, maximum range about 2300 miles. Don't dwell too much on the range, just like any other aircraft that's a function of a whole bunch of other variables. Best for you to simply say 'Range—enough'."

"Moira, we're talking about a fifty-year-old aircraft."

"Not to worry." She started tapping the keyboard again. "This is a great data base," she said over her shoulder "Larry started it years ago, kept everything on index cards and notebooks. I've added to it, found a program to manage it, and entered it all in the computer, plus I've scanned in a lot of pictures and diagrams and what not."

"I can see that."

"Now, look here. This is some stuff I've compiled from aircraft registries and recent advertisements for sale. I like to keep track, even though I've been away from the business for a while. Anyway, what you have to understand is that an awful lot of Catalinas stayed in service for many years after the war. Some air forces were still running them in the early Sixties. Larry and I had one in 1993. Believe it or not, that was my idea, although most people thought it was Larry's. Anyway, you can probably find at least twenty Catalinas around, still in pretty good flying condition. Three I've identified as currently for sale, going price about a million per. We can swing that, can't we Harry? And, for more money, we could probably get someone to part with a plane that he hadn't planned to sell. But we don't have to. Look at this."

She brought up another picture. At first, I thought the aircraft in the picture was identical to the one she had already showed me. But as I looked closer, I realized that there were some changes to the nose, but the big difference was four engines instead of two.

"That's not the same plane."

"Well, not exactly. It's the latest rendition of something called a Bird Conversion."

"Explain."

"Well, after the war there were hundreds of surplus Catalinas around. They're big enough for cargo, or with a redone interior, even for passenger service, at least by the standards of the time, before everything was jets. But they're underpowered. What some people did was swap out the Pratt & Whitney engines for a pair of Wright Cyclones taken off of surplus B-25s, which gained a bunch of horsepower for not much increase in weight. They called those 'Super Cats.' The other idea came in the early Fifties. Take two small Lycoming turboprops, which don't weigh all that much, install one on each wing outboard of the main engines. You get fifty per cent more power, plus, with the turboprop you can reverse props, which helps handling when you're on the water, among other things. They built one prototype, it tested out with a 3,500-mile ferry range at 200 knots, with 16 passengers, rest rooms, air conditioning. What do the Brits say, all mod cons. But they couldn't compete with the new airliners, and the plane was a one-off."

"So, you have a line on that plane? Is that it?"

"No, that plane went away a long time ago. When they added the Lycomings and the nice passenger fittings, they took it up above the weight certified for water landings. Made it all kind of pointless, since the whole idea was to have an air yacht that could take charter customers into all sorts of exotic ocean destinations. Doubly sad, because the Lycomings would have made it much more maneuverable on the water. Just thinking about the smuggling possibilities used to give Larry a hard-on, he just knew he could have gotten the weight down, but the plane went away in the 50s."

"So, now I don't get where you're going with this."

"Simple. About fifteen years ago, there's a guy who got fascinated with the whole Bird Conversion thing, he found some backers, some guys floating in computer bucks," she smiled that smile again, "guys like you, Harry. Anyway, his idea was to do exotic tours, but also to enable remote exploration, sort of like that guy Paul Allen who goes around finding sunken warships. This guy had a bug about Amelia Earhart, but he was also a good enough businessman to know that the market for exotic tours had opened up once again, much bigger and better than fifty years ago. Anyway, he bought three good Super Cats in Canada. They'd been retired from fighting forest fires not long before. Anyway, he decided that if he was going to have something really fancy, it'd be good to have even more power. You know, if more power is good, a lot more power is better. So, he commissioned an aircraft restoration outfit back over in Europe to use his three Cats as the basis for a new-generation Bird Conversion. Same concept, but better, since the little Lycomings that are available now have a lot more oomph for the same weight than the Fifties originals. And he specified use of a lot of state-of-the art lightweight materials for the structural upgrades and the interior fittings. A stronger and lighter design then, and now certifiable for water landings." Two of them were finished, then it was 2008, the housing bubble burst, and the guy took a financial bath and ran out of money, all of this just as the planes were being finished. The builders took title to the planes and put them up for sale. One of them they sold on to some Russian oligarch, he seems to fly it all over Siberia, but the other one they couldn't move. Eventually they hangered it, but they had the good sense to put it in a full state of preservation, hermetic seals, climate-controlled environment, the works. But they've been trying to unload it for the last few years, and the price keeps coming down. I looked last year, even talked to them, but I couldn't get the loan I needed. My past does work against me. But they were only looking then for $1.35 million. I bet with Covid killing the airplane market, I could get it for that, and make them do what it takes to ensure it's mission-ready."

This bore some thinking.

"We're still talking a very old plane, and a lot of trickery."

"Harry, trust me. You're hiring my expertise, now listen to it. I know the reputation of the people who did the conversion. It's bank solid. Look at the B-52s that the Air Force still flies, they're not much more than twenty years newer than a late-model Cat, and they're still great aircraft. The specs on the plane I'm talking about are like that. Some of the pieces are even formed out of the graphite-reinforced plastic composites, some bits from carbon fiber. The interior is suitable for passengers and cargo, and when I looked at it I decided it would work for parachuting. Sky diving clubs are always good for a little business between bigger charters. I won't claim it's a new aircraft, but it's new enough where it counts."

"All right, you're the expert. If this plane is the one, then we'd better make sure it doesn't get away from us. I'll make arrangements for a line of credit that you can draw on for it."

"Then it's really a go?" She turned around, looked me squarely in the eye. "Harry, you've always been straight with me. I've always trusted you. Tell me one more time. This thing's for real, isn't it?"

"Yes, it really is for real."

She gave me the warmest hug. I held her close for a moment, remembering the one wonderful night so many years ago when she'd taken me into her bed. But then, as on all occasions since, I felt her hold soften, and I let her draw away. I suddenly realized that I was awfully tired. I said as much.

"Oh, Harry, I am sorry. God, it's five a.m. You must be totally wiped out. Here, let's call it a night, we can sleep in, right? Your flight's not until late tomorrow afternoon, I mean this afternoon."

"That's right."

She pulled blankets and extra pillows from the closet, bustling around to help me prepare for bed. As she started to leave the room, she glanced down at the picture of Larry. Then she looked back at me.

"Harry, he really was one of the good guys. He really was."

She said goodnight and left the room. I turned out the light and crawled under the covers. But tired as I was, sleep would not come. As I lay there in the dark, I found myself thinking of Larry Beale. Larry had been just a few years older than me, but already a veteran of Air America flying in Laos, flying impossible missions under improbable conditions, and doing it with a *savoir vivre* that soon made Larry a legend himself. I first got to know him through Lem, my godfather, and in the Eighties we crossed paths in Angola and Mozambique, and then briefly in Central America. But by then he had already crossed the line with the cartels, and, try as he might, he could never seem to completely come back over from the dark side. Moira always insisted that Larry had worked for the DEA, that he had been undercover right from the beginning. Maybe so, but I didn't doubt that he would have invented a comforting lie just to maintain Moira's good opinion. I'm enough of an old fraud myself to know what an old fraud will do to preserve the love of a young woman.

It all ended badly, a 21st Century remake of a 'Miami Vice' nightmare. Larry and Moira were in Miami, and doing the town in style.

They had dinner, then moved on to a place called Neon Leon's in South Miami for desert and after-dinner drinks. About ten o'clock they left and walked out to Larry's Maserati. Larry's taste in cars matched his taste in women. Larry helped Moira into the car on the passenger side and was walking around to the driver's side when they blew him away. I remember seeing the wire service photograph that went around the country, depicting a stunned young woman, kneeling in the gutter at curbside, screaming as she cradled her lover's head, his brains spread over the front of her evening gown. When I realized it was Moira, I immediately tried to contact her, only to find that she had disappeared, hiding where even my Agency contacts couldn't find her. It would be almost five years before I received a letter postmarked "Dublin" and found that Larry's lady had become Moira Finnegan, citizen of the Republic of Ireland, proprietor of a small company offering "Flying Tours of the West Country."

Having found her once again, I kept up with her, and when I took on a security-testing project in Finland, I hired her for the relative handful of jobs that involved a parachute insertion and required a pilot. Not long after that project folded, Moira Finnegan returned to the United States. She made a modest living as a free-lance, part-time corporate pilot, a sort of "Kelly Girl of the skies". She supplemented this income by writing articles for aviation magazines. For fun she flew an inexpensive aerobatic airplane. She kept her private life private, and upheld an image of Larry Beale that probably no one else in the world completely shared. And I still asked myself, "why him, and not me?" For a long time afterwards, I wondered at the obscure test I'd somehow failed. But that, too, was the past, and nowadays, except for the momentary twinges, I don't torment myself about it anymore.

I rolled over and went to sleep.

CHAPTER 8

WE COULD HEAR the sound of gunfire as I turned down the driveway
leading to the long brick building. A faded sign marked the entrance,
the name "Quinlan Mill" still readable, but barely. I found a place to
park between Grady's old Jeep Cherokee and a tan Ford Econoline
van with the words "Public Safety Assistance Project" stenciled in dark
brown on each door. Retrieving my black gym bag from the trunk, I
led Moira down a gravel path, toward the sound of the firing.

"This place is something else," said Moira. "How did your friend
Grady come up with it?"

"Long and involved story. You'll have to get him to tell it, if you
want all the ins and outs. It's an old textile mill, closed, reopened,
closed, reopened, one of the early casualties of off-shoring. They tried
making it over for other uses, but it never really took. It could have
been a good warehouse, Grady tells me, but this part of West Virginia's
too off the beaten path to make that viable. What are you going to
store here? Anyway, maybe fifteen years ago, the county chased a bunch
of meth cookers out of the far end—you still shouldn't go in there,
it's nasty—and, since the owners still couldn't find any takers for the

building, the sheriff took it over in lieu of property taxes. For a while, the county just let it sit, didn't really know what to do with it. Then one of the fire departments in the area discovered it, decided it would be a good training site. Apparently, they're always on the lookout for abandoned buildings. Then Grady tied into it a few years back for his law enforcement training thing, one of his old Marine buddies was a local deputy and they had already been using it for tactical training. That was only part time, but it gave the county a little revenue anyway."

"I'm glad they didn't burn down the mill," said Moira. "I hate to see old things disappear. It's really a very nice building. The brickwork is superb. You just don't see that kind of thing anymore." The trail curved, taking us behind the mill. Moira was right. Caught against the backdrop of the surrounding hills and the bright blue sky, the mill was magnificent, with a rustic splendor like an industrial-grade version of a Wyeth barn.

"And now we have it?"

"Exactly. We made a nice contribution to the county and promised to donate our gear to them when we're finished here. So, we get use of the facility. It's private; if anyone wants to know, we're involved in an innocuous training project that Grady put together. We hired a little motel up the road, about twelve rooms, and we made a deal with a little diner to do meals. Grady's got it set up like the colleges are planning to do for their sports teams, everyone's been Covid tested, and then they stay sequestered as a group. We're supporting local business in a small way, and, believe me, right now they're desperate for it."

As we talked, we continued along the gravel path, descending into a small glade that became a carpet of old leaves, several seasons' worth, squishy from the spring rains. The sounds of gunfire were louder and more distinct, volleys interspersed with single shots. I also heard voices in the intervals between firing.

The path climbed again, and we stepped out of the glade into an open area about half the size of a football field. At the far end the hillside rose almost vertically, forming a perfect backstop for the firing range. The customary B-27 silhouette targets were mounted on wooden frames at the base of the hill—eight of them—one for each shooter on the firing line, which was some fifteen yards from the targets. About ten yards further back stood a shed, with three rows of bleacher seats and a couple of tables for cleaning weapons. A tall, vaguely familiar figure wearing gray battle dress utilities strolled behind the firing line, stopping to converse with each shooter in turn. It took me a moment to realize that this man was Grady, but a Grady shorn of his big beard and bushy hair, a Grady who looked remarkably like the young Marine I had first met nearly thirty years ago. He saw us walking over to the bleachers and joined us there. I introduced him to Moira, noticed the brief appraising glances they exchanged.

"Jesus, Harry, what took you guys so long?" He turned to Moira. "Now the old guy's a big-time wheeler-dealer, he starts sleeping late all the time. Harry, if you hadn't brought this beautiful lady here with you, I'd be really pissed with you."

"What's the program?" I said to Grady.

"Well, now that you're here, I'll introduce you around. All I've got 'em doing now is farting around a little, getting to know each other, sizing each other up. Everybody's trying to figure out who can outshoot who with a handgun. We'll do introductions, then go up to the mill, run our tactical drills, get a good look at them."

"What do they know?"

"Not much. It's a job, it's overseas, it will pay well. I let them kinda think it's in Iraq or Afghanistan, maybe guarding some MREs or Ay-rab politicos," he gave me a big grin, "and I told them the pay would be real good. Okay? I've started to refer to the bad guys as 'gomers.' Remember that one? Much cleaner than, 'the Chinese,' or, God help us, 'Wiangaran fucking militia.' Gomers."

'Gomers' was a generic term for 'hostiles,' much used by the fly-boys, but also sometimes by ground-pounders. Good enough for now, since a proper brief would have to wait until we'd made our selections and gotten their acceptance.

"Yeah, that sound's good. What'd you tell them about this session?"

"Told 'em it was a beauty pageant. They look good enough, Bert

Parks sings 'em a song. Some of them are too young to know who Bert Parks is."

"So, they know it's an audition?"

"Yeah, and they know that the Big Kahuna just drove up."

"All right."

"Final cut's mine, right?" said Grady.

"Of course. In the end it's your team."

Grady had come up with eight potential recruits using his various contacts. He and I were here to look them over before taking the next step. Moira was here because I wanted to start her working with Grady. I would've brought Kip as well, but he was flying around three continents chasing gear.

Grady waited for a pause on the firing line, then shouted "Over here," accompanied by the universal hand signals for "Circle up" and "On me." The shooters wore BDUs, but in a variety of colors, some in gray, some in desert tans, some in woodland camo patterns, but they looked more alike than different. All wore baseball caps and boots and pistol belts and holsters confected of ballistic nylon and Velcro. There wasn't a leather belt in the crowd. They were all young, by my definition, the oldest in his late thirties but most in their twenties. All but one had very short hair, and the one who didn't was a young woman.

I had read the individual background summaries that Grady had put together. Now I would have faces to go with the write-ups. But I liked their looks already. They appeared fit; more important, they appeared comfortable with each other and with what they were doing. Still, only time and a little testing would tell.

"Okay, everybody listen up," said Grady. "You've all had a chance to get to know one another, or start to, anyway. I've got two other people here that I want you to meet. Neither one will be directly part of the team, but we'll still be working real close together. First, this lady standing next to me, her name is Moira Finnegan. And the old guy with the white beard next to her, you can call him the "Herr Doktor." He had rolled the words out with a sardonic lilt, but in a precise, accurate German accent. Grady was always capable of surprising me.

"But all of you can call me Harry," I quickly added.

"Okay, then," said Grady. "Everybody take about fifteen minutes, introduce yourselves individually, get some coffee, take a leak, then come on up to where the van's parked. I'm going to go on up to the mill and get the equipment ready for a little exercise."

Thermos bottles were produced, coffee was poured, in some cases cigarettes lit—I noticed far fewer smokers than one would have found among soldiers a generation ago. Changing times. I walked over to the table where the coffee was being dispensed. The master of this ceremony was a tall, slender black man, with the physique of an Olympic hurdler or an NFL wide receiver. I proffered my Styrofoam cup.

"You're James Smith, right?"

"At your service. Call me Smitty."

Smitty was, I recalled, the most experienced of the group. He had spent twelve years in the army, mainly with the 75th Ranger Regiment, and had jumped into Afghanistan with a small, very select Ranger team barely a month after 9/11. Two years later he'd made the 173rd's big jump into Iraq. He'd also served as a parachuting instructor, one of the famous "Black Hats" at Fort Benning's jump school. Then he'd spent ten years as a policeman, mainly as a SWAT team member. Carrying our coffee, we walked to where a small knot of team members had gathered around Moira.

"So, you're the HMFWIC, huh?" said one of them to me, his southern accent almost incomprehensibly thick, the last letters slurred. He was a compact young man with short dark hair and a thin mustache. As he spoke, he performed the improbable feat of smoking a cigarette and chewing on a toothpick at the same time.

"HMF what?"

"Head Mother Fucker Who's in Charge—HMFWIC."

"I guess you could say that. And you are?"

Another young man spoke up. "Why that's the famous Jerry Wolsey, better known as Jerry 'By-God' Wolsey. He's an ugly little man, ain't he? I keep him around cause he makes me look prettier."

The speaker was a short, powerfully muscled man, with a broad, flat, almost Oriental-looking face beneath his high-and-tight haircut.

"Which must make you Ronnie Banks."

"Guilty as charged, boss."

Two of Grady's younger protégés, both recruited out of a SWAT team from a suburban Atlanta police department. Banks had been Army airborne, and, like Smitty, had made the jump into Iraq with the 173rd. Like so many others, he'd left the army because his wife didn't like the long separations. Now, according to Grady, they were permanently separated. Wolsey was unique in the group in that he had no military experience. He'd been a fireman and an EMT before becoming a policeman. Grady envisioned him as the team medic, but more important, in Grady's view, "He looks great in training—he's got the moves of a Recon Marine." From Grady, there could hardly be a higher accolade.

We strolled back to the parking lot alongside the mill. Grady had opened the back of the van and set up a folding table behind it. On the table was a pile of web gear, each with a series of small reddish-brown plastic nodules about the diameter of a ping-pong ball, but cone-shaped. Looking into the back of the van, I could see a row of M-4s, the short-barreled carbine version of the M-16 rifle. Unlike a standard M-4, however, each of these weapons had a small green metal box attached beneath the barrel, just behind the muzzle.

The little green box meant that these were MILES system weapons. MILES stands for "Multiple Integrated Laser Engagement Simulation," one of the most useful tactical training aids ever devised. The military uses the system on everything from pistols to missiles, from tanks to helicopters. What Grady had managed to secure was the most basic version, the small-arms system, and not the latest model of that, but still a small marvel of modern electronics. Each weapon was adapted to fire blank rounds and each time one was fired, the box-like electronic transmitter below the muzzle emitted a laser pulse. If the weapon was on target, the pulse would be captured by one of the sensors—the plastic nodules—on the harness worn by an "adversary." A clean hit caused a buzzer in the harness to go off; a near miss caused a short beep. If the buzzer went off, it continued to sound until a yellow key was removed from the laser box on the weapon and inserted into the key slot in the harness. This did two things. It deactivated the laser in the adversary's weapon, signifying his "death," and it brought the ear-splitting buzz to an abrupt halt. The newer ones dispensed with the yellow key in favor of an even more extensive electronic bag of tricks, but these had been easy and quick to come by and would more than suffice for present purposes.

MILES is not perfect. It has difficulty registering clean hits at very close ranges, and the laser pulse is stopped by barriers—a piece of plywood, for example—that would never stop real bullets. But it takes tactical simulation far beyond the unsatisfactory old days of umpired exercises, notorious for degenerating into arguments over who shot whom. It permits training that moves right up to the edge of real combat. As high-tech gadgetry goes, it is very low tech, at least when compared with something like the Rickman's fancy missile, but more to the point, it is war-winning technology. Historically, green soldiers almost always lose their first firefight against an experienced adversary, because traditional training lacked the ability to replicate the adversary's actions. These days, we may not win wars—that's usually a matter of political will—but our soldiers come to the battle with the skills they need to survive and prevail.

"All right everybody," said Grady, "here's what we're going to do next. The 'Herr Doktor' and his lovely companion will be the adversaries for this exercise. They'll set up inside the mill, somewhere inside that door over there." Grady pointed to the nearest entrance to the mill. "We'll divide up into four two-man teams. Jerry, you and Ronnie are used to working with each other, and that isn't fair to everybody else, so we'll split you up. Jerry, you work with ol' Mike Burnham over there, okay, and Ronnie, you pair up with Robbie—can you keep that straight, then? —Ronnie and Robbie. Smitty, let's have you and Lorayne together. That leaves Brad and Charley. Okay?"

He paused to make sure that everyone was with him.

"Now I'll observe each team. I'll follow you inside, it'll be dark in there. I'll tape a pair of green chem lights to my back and chest, so nobody will miss seeing me or waste a shot on me. Okay, then. I'll pass out weapons, and check for live ammo. One thirty-round mag only. You won't need more than that to take care of the Herr Doktor and his partner. I only want to see mags with yellow stripes in the weapons, those are the ones we loaded with blanks. And double-check the chambers for live rounds. I've checked, but remember, it's your ass if someone fucked up."

Moira drew me aside. "Uh, Harry, one little thing. I've never fired an M-16 before."

"Not a problem. It's an easy weapon to handle, particularly when you're just firing blanks. Besides, this whole business is a test for them, not you."

We lined up to draw a weapon and harness. I found myself standing behind one of the team members I had yet to meet, the young woman. She was slender, with brown hair styled in the shag-cut popular with young women in the military. I tapped her on the shoulder.

"Oh, hello sir," she said. "I'm Lorayne Trippett." Her accent spoke of the hills of Kentucky.

She extended her hand formally for a handshake. I noticed that she was holding an empty Styrofoam cup in her other hand. Lorayne looked absurdly young, although I knew from her data sheet that she was thirty-four. From Harlan County, Kentucky, she'd spent four years in the Air Force, a security police officer guarding nuclear weapons at a former Air Force Global Strike Command base. After graduating from Eastern Kentucky State University with a degree in criminal justice, she'd become a sheriff's deputy in a rural county in the eastern Kentucky mountains, proved herself as a member of a drug strike force, eventually meeting Grady during a tactical training seminar.

I also knew that she was the recipient of a commendation for single-handedly stopping an armed robbery at a convenience store. She had been off-duty, had dropped by the store for a quart of milk and a dozen eggs, and walked into the middle of a holdup. One perpetrator was covering the clerk with a handgun while he emptied the cash register. The other perpetrator had lined up the customers against the glass-fronted refrigerator containing soft drinks, controlling them at the point of a sawed-off twelve gauge. Lorayne had sized up the situation, drawn her off-duty Smith & Wesson 'Chief's Special' from her purse, and dropped the two perpetrators with two shots apiece—the classic "double tap"—all within ten seconds of walking through the door. In the movies this kind of thing is made to look easy, when in fact it reflects nothing short of consummate skill and coolness. In the movies, it also makes Bruce Willis and Mel Gibson heroes. In real life, Lorayne's commendation had been quickly followed by a lawsuit brought by the store clerk, who claimed that being showered with bits of bad guy had left him "traumatized." The suit had been dismissed, but the experience left the young woman looking for alternatives to a law-enforcement career.

I helped Lorayne into her harness, positioned the headband that also mounts a set of sensors. Then she did the same for me. I noticed an odd small bulge in her right cheek, just behind the corner of her mouth, but before it registered, Moira walked up.

"I'm all set, Harry, assuming you can take a minute to show me how to shoot this thing."

"Just a second."

Grady had just finished passing a weapon and magazine to Lorayne. I stepped up to receive mine, but was arrested by the sight of Lorayne spitting a stream of brown juice into her white coffee cup. She had turned and walked over to join the other members of her team before I recovered my composure.

"Just a pinch between her cheek and gum," said Grady.

"I guess that means she's a spitter, not a swallower," said Moira, which caused Grady to nearly choke on his mouthful of coffee.

He was still shaking his head as he passed me my M-4. I say "my M-4" because Grady had set aside for me the one with the holographic sights. I slung it over my shoulder and walked over to the other side of the parking lot, where the members of the team had gathered. At the far end of the parking lot, about a hundred meters distant, Grady had placed a small yellow sheet of metal fitted with MILES laser sensors. This was a MILES calibration target. Before beginning the exercise, each of us would take a few shots at the target to make sure that our sights were properly zeroed-in. When everyone else had finished Moira and I took our turn. I went first.

"All you have to do is, first, seat the loaded magazine in the magazine well"—I demonstrated with my weapon— "check the safety lever, and pull back on the charging handle." I hooked my index and middle fingers around the handle and drew it back fully; then I released it, chambering a round. "Off safe and you're ready to fire. This weapon has selective fire, so you can choose between semi-auto—one shot per trigger pull—and three shot burst. Set the switch to semi-auto and take a few shots."

The entire M-16 family of weapons is easy to handle, particularly for someone already familiar with firearms. After several shots Moira was thoroughly comfortable, and registered several hits in a row. Now it was my turn. I had insisted on the optical sight for a specific reason. My eyes are old, and I wear bifocals, which makes it very difficult for me to keep open sights aligned. I don't have this problem with a handgun, at typical handgun ranges—I'm quite good at point shooting. But hitting anything beyond seven meters requires using sights, and the holographic sight, a magical gadget that fixes the target in a

tiny screen with minimal need for sight alignment, placed fewer burdens on my aging vision. I'd done well enough on behalf of Kip and Bobby, but even then, I'd been using a scope, which is easier on old eyes than open sights, and I hadn't tried to hit any moving targets. With this trick sight dialed in, I could hit what I wanted. When it came down to the mission, each team member would have an individually assigned personal weapon and a choice of sights, although I'd insisted that everyone's optical sights be backed up with an infrared laser dot system that would work with night vision.

Moira and I went into the mill. Just inside the door, we were below a row of large outside windows that ran the length of the building. Although the windows had been painted over, enough outside light seeped in to make things quite bright in the immediate vicinity of the wall. Further back into the building, however, it was almost totally dark. The room we were in was a large bay, which had once housed huge looms. Now it was empty save for a scattering of boxes and old machinery, a rusted-out lawn tractor, a backhoe, and a collection of less recognizable bits and pieces, which collectively produced an interesting array of odd shapes and shadows. Better was a metal catwalk about three meters up that followed the interior wall of the building, just below the level of the big windows. Best of all, about ten meters down from the door, the paint had flaked off almost completely from one of the windows, allowing a shaft of excruciatingly bright sunlight to shine through. I had my first set-up.

I reached into my bag of tricks and took out two sets of knee and elbow pads, not the fancy ones that the D-boys favor, in fact designed for skateboarders, but adequate to the task.

"Here," I said to Moira, "put these on. You'll enjoy this a whole lot more if you aren't worried about banging yourself up."

"What're we going to do?" she asked.

"The first one will be simple. I want you to get back over in the shadows opposite the door where they'll come in. Back there by that stack of wooden pallets will do nicely." I pointed out the position for her. "When they come in the door, you'll see them clearly. Now the door is in shadow, but when they open it, they'll be backlit. Let them come in almost as far as the tractor, then give them a quick burst. Set it on three shot burst, just blip the trigger. Then roll back behind the crates and run like hell for that door back in the shadows. They'll lose you after that burst."

"What if I miss?"

"Don't worry about it. That's my problem."

She held out the carbine to me. "You said set it on 'three shot burst'—I don't know how."

I showed her how to manipulate the selector switch and then gave the weapon back to her. As she got into position, I started climbing the metal ladder that led to the catwalk. I was about halfway up when

Grady came in the door, shouting the traditional "controller moving" warning.

"Ready?" he called out.

"Just a minute," I shouted back.

He looked up, following the sound of my voice. By then I was in position.

"I can't see you, Harry," he said.

"Of course you can't."

I was looking forward to this one. Old men really shouldn't be allowed this much fun.

"Who's coming in first?" I asked.

"Wolsey and Burnham."

"Send them on in."

Grady stepped to the door, pushed it ajar.

"First team's up," he yelled to the team outside. Then he moved down the wall, well away from the door, but where he could still see. From my perch, prone on the catwalk, in the shadow directly below the shaft of sunlight, I couldn't see the door being opened. But I heard a slight scraping of metal. I hoped Moira was watching carefully.

They came in moving well, not bunched up, using the available cover. But, as I had expected, they were focused narrowly on the area to their front and sides, and weren't scanning upward and behind. After clearing the first five meters from the door, they would have to cross an open space.

One of them, I couldn't tell which, moved into the open, while the other hung back to cover him. But he didn't hang back far enough. He was just far enough from the catwalk to allow me an angle of fire. As the first one popped out into the open, Moira unleashed a quick burst. Even the relatively soft "pop" of the blanks rang sharply in the stillness. I shot the cover man in the back, then shifted my aim to the dead zone behind the tractor. As I'd expected, the lead man had gone to ground there. It was good cover, but only against fire coming from Moira's direction. The shaft of sunlight above my shoulder spotlighted him perfectly, but the same light robbed him of his ability to pick me out from the shadows below. It was almost too easy. I "killed" him before he even had a chance to figure out where the fire was coming from.

Grady went over to them and reset their buzzing harnesses, then asked me to stand up and show myself before sending them back outside. Although not the main purpose of the exercise, we'd given them an unforgettable lesson in checking up high and to their sides, and in not moving too quickly. But this also meant giving up my wonderful ambush position. The first team would surely tell the others about it, and then they'd come in expecting me to be there.

Ronnie and Robbie entered next. My new position lay deep within the shadows, behind some old equipment, while Moira was proned out along the back wall, about twenty meters down from the door. She would have a clean shot at them when they came through, and I was hoping, she'd force them to turn their flank to me as they responded to her fire. It didn't work quite that neatly. Moira was taken out, and I had to exert a real effort to outmaneuver them. But in the end, it was even more satisfying than our first victory.

The third team, Brad and Charley, were either unlucky or clumsy. They walked right into Moira's field of fire; she took them out before I could even get them in my sights. But the last team, Smitty and Lorayne, made me reach deeply into my bag of tricks. They cleared the door quickly, found good cover positions, and quietly scanned the room, watching and listening. The team moved forward carefully, avoiding most of the obvious mistakes, but eventually the rows of old junk channeled them straight into our kill zone. At my signal Moira fired a quick burst and had the satisfaction of hearing a buzzer go off—this later proved to be Smitty. But Lorayne did an almost perfect forward tactical roll, dodged under my carefully set up shot, and came up firing in our direction. This kid was good.

As we'd planned, Moira went left and I went right, which, unfortunately, took Moira right into Lorayne's field of fire. Another quick burst, and Moira was "dead." I responded with a snap shot which, predictably enough, missed Lorayne completely. Then I faded back among a row of boxes, ready to play cat and mouse. But Lorayne didn't respond, at least not at first. Instead she went to ground, waiting, sizing up the situation. The object of the exercise was to make her do the work, to show what she could do. But now I was feeling my oats. One against one. She had skill, youth, and agility on her side. But I'd been doing this sort of thing for real since long before she had been born. I had a trick or two left, and over short distances I could still move pretty well. And I knew how to do so very quietly. I don't think she ever knew I was there, not until I shot her in the back.

Grady went outside to reorganize the teams. We didn't want the same people working together all the time. Moira and I moved to a part of the building that was subdivided into smaller, office-like spaces. The next time around we had a much harder time of it, and the third time harder still. As much as I was getting a kick out of the game, the greater kick lay in watching Grady with his young charges, the way he charmed with a mixture of blunt compliments and gentle abuse, the very opposite of the drill instructor persona that he'd once been trained to display. At one point Moira remarked, "He's really just an old sweetheart, isn't he?" and I allowed that this was true, although I didn't think he'd much appreciate the term 'sweetheart.'

After the third round, we broke for lunch. When Moira and I first stepped outside the building, it was like exiting a bar or movie theater at mid-afternoon. We were half blinded until our eyes adjusted to the bright sunlight. We collected box lunches out of the back of the van and gathered at a pair of picnic tables in a shaded grassy area on the other side of the parking lot. Grady and Moira and I didn't discuss the morning's proceedings, and none of the others raised the subject. There was a tacit understanding that individual performances were under scrutiny and were therefore not a fit subject for lunchtime conversation. Instead, the discussion fragmented as everyone sought to avoid the business at hand. I made the mistake of asking Grady about Daisy, the sick hound. He gave me a bleak look.

"Dead, Harry, just a couple of days after you were there. She never came home from the vet."

There was real pain in his voice, and Moira, who was sitting beside him, reached out and placed her hand upon his. After saying that I was sorry to hear it, I didn't know quite what else to say. But Moira began speaking of other dogs, dogs she had obviously loved, dogs that she had lost. Grady listened, and then did an astonishing thing. He began to speak of his feelings of hurt, of loss. Suddenly they were in a world unto themselves, talking about dogs and the sad emptiness left behind when they are gone.

Feeling somehow excluded, I turned my attention to the rest of the group as it began wandering back toward the building, loosening up for the afternoon's exercises. Finally, Grady and Moira joined us, and we resumed our series of tests. This time, however, Grady decided he wanted to swap roles with me. This struck me as a good idea, since it would give us a different perspective from which to judge the prospective team members. Besides, it would further his interaction with Moira.

By the end of the first afternoon cycle I'd pretty much made up my mind. Jerry Wolsey would've been a keeper, even if we hadn't needed his EMT skills. Smitty and Ronnie Banks looked equally good; moreover, I was mindful of the fact that both had actually seen combat and performed well. All other things being equal, I'd take the men who'd earned a Combat Infantry Badge. Lorayne continued to be a pleasant surprise, and she, too, had shown great coolness in a life-or-death situation. She was clearly a keeper. None of the others measured up, and, while we were desperate for numbers, the proverb about 'weak links surely applied here. My first special ops tactical mentor had put it bluntly: "Two good men get the job done—ten assholes get you killed." Waiting to start the second cycle, I watched Grady start to flirt with Moira in a gruff Marine gunnery sergeant kind of way. I'd wanted them to bond, and it looked like it had worked.

We did one more cycle before wrapping up for the afternoon. I took Grady aside, shared my observations, and asked Moira if she was ready to leave.

"We'd better be on the road," I said. "I need to go soak these old bones in a hot bath." This was the simple truth. What had been at most a light day for these kids had been hard on me. I was going to be pretty sore the next day.

"We hate to see you leave," said Ronnie, "but leastways Grady managed to talk this pretty lady into staying."

"Oh?" I said, looking at Moira.

"Yeah, Harry. I mean, Grady says I can be of help here tomorrow and the next day. I've already lined up the plane, but I can't take delivery for another couple of days, and since it's sitting out on Long Island, staying east avoids wasting time with a trip back home. That's the first of next week, so I've got time to help out here."

"What about your second pilot?" Somehow, I didn't want her to stay. I'd vaguely entertained the notion of her coming back with me to Virginia Beach.

"Same thing. I know who I want, and I know he'll do it, but I want you to talk to him. I've got it set up in Vegas four days from now, that's where he lives. You can make it back from Europe in time, can't you?"

"I'll make it. Are you set for a room here?"

"Yeah, Grady doesn't think it'll be a problem at the motel where everyone's staying, but if it is, then Lorayne says I can share her room."

"You sure you can't stay, too?" Jerry asked me. "Give me another day and I'll take you every time."

"Yeah, Herr Doktor," said Lorayne, trying to imitate Grady's pronunciation, "I've gotta say you move pretty good for an old guy."

Before I could say 'thanks,' Ronnie jumped all over her Kentucky country drawl.

"Hair Doctor—that's it. I kept wondering what Grady meant when he introduced you. But now that Lorayne here has translated it for me, I understand. Hair Doctor? You just do the Rogaine thing, or can you maybe do surgery on this bald spot I'm getting?"

With that I gained my team nickname—the Hair Doctor.

CHAPTER 9

Two hours after landing at London's Farnborough business airport I was struggling with driving on the wrong side of the road, passing through the London suburbs and into the Surrey countryside. Usually, when I visit England I rely on public transportation, but Covid restrictions had made that problematic. At least I'd managed to finesse the restrictions on travel from the U.S., taking advantage of the Estonian passport I'd acquired after claiming dual citizenship a few years ago. U.S. visitors still had to endure a 14-day quarantine, but I'd flown first to Tallinn to do a little coordination with my sister and to check out the ship. I'd also picked up a crate of Covid test kits, a product of one of my sister's companies, and a further means of easing my entry into the UK.

The day was one of those wondrous English summer days, all shades of green and watery gray, a background that somehow made the reds and yellows and blues, the phone booths and delivery vans and painted cottage doors seem unusually bright, almost luminous. As I drive into the village of Godalming I glanced down at my watch, which read 11:30 a.m., In spite of my hesitant driving, I'd hit almost precisely the ETA I'd given when I called the day before.

He was waiting on the steps of an older, white stucco building, waving and smiling, wiry and tall, his long pale face, bright blue eyes, and gray-tinged reddish blond hair bearing testimony to the Viking contribution to the English gene pool. My good friend, Peter Rudd, late of the Royal Marines' Special Boat Squadron.

"And a good day to you, Harry," Peter said. "Did you have a good flight?"

"Good enough. I'm spending too much time on airplanes these days."

"Ah, yes, lots of travel, big doings, things you want to talk about face-to-face. Nothing we could do with a Zoom meeting?"

"That sums it up. I'm hoping you and I can sort things out this afternoon."

"And then it's off for the Continent tonight? That's what I understood when you telephoned. You've not had lunch, I'm sure. Let me just pop in here for a quick word with the wife, and then we can head up to the street for some takeaway curry. Sorry, but we can't manage any kind of indoor sit-down meal just now."

"No, that sounds good."

"There's a churchyard and a park nearby. We can find a bench, eat our lunch, then, a nice walk in the park, feed the ducks, have our talk. If it starts to rain there's a nice shelter in the middle of the park, last year it would have been full of secretaries and little clark girls, but these days not so much." He'd lost me for a moment with "clark girls," before I recalled the English pronunciation of "clerk."

Peter's wife worked inside the building where we stood. It looked just like a country inn and, in fact, had once been exactly that, a place for travelers on the rail line from Portsmouth to London to stop for the night, get a warm meal and a soft bed. As train speeds improved, however, the inn became irrelevant—no journey on the London to Portsmouth line required an overnight stay. For many years, it had housed offices for a firm that, pre-Covid, had restored and sold rare and vintage automobiles. Since the pandemic, the firm had taken advantage of its precision metalworking and fabricating capabilities to make some bits and pieces essential to the manufacture of ventilators. The firm had also had a sideline brokering pre-World War II art and artifacts related to the automobile, such as Art Nouveau advertising posters, shipping them throughout the UK and around the world. This was the province of Peter's wife, Gillian, who had now lent her expertise to managing distribution of their ventilator parts.

Entering through the back door, we came to a small room with a dining table and a couple of vending machines. Two young women were sitting at the table, their brown-bag lunches spread before them. Two men, one fortyish and balding, with long side whiskers and tattoos on both forearms; the other younger, taller, bearded and blond, played darts while standing at the far end of the dining table, sailing their missiles over the heads of the women towards a dart board on the far wall next to the drink machine. The women—they seemed scarcely more than girls—were apparently totally unconcerned about the sharp metal objects flying above. Nor, evidently, did they care much about Covid inside their little break room. Not a soul wore a mask.

"How are you, Major," the bald man said. "Here to see the missus?"

"That's it, Will," said Peter.

"She's tied up right now," said one of the girls. "On the phone, again, with NHS, trying to sort out a delivery. They'll be at it for a while, I should say."

"We'll be off again, then. Would you tell her I was by? Oh, I'm sorry, this is my good friend Harry York from America. Harry, this is Fiona," he said, gesturing to the young woman who had spoken, who looked, deliciously, like a Fiona, "and Maida," who called to mind a 6x6 truck. "The ugly old rascal with no hair is Will, and the handsome young devil with the darts in his hand is Vince. Say 'hello' to Harry, children."

"Hello, Harry," they said, almost in unison.

"Right, then, now say 'good bye' to Harry."

We continued up the street, past the post office and a bank, stopping at the curry house on the corner of the High Street.

"They're just barely making it these days, but at least they're still open." Unlike the place next door, it seemed, a restaurant now shuttered. "Sad story, that place," said Peter with a gesture, "they spent a lot of money last year taking the place up market, made it a fancy grill room, which seemed very smart now that we've become a posh bedroom community. But the pandemic hanged them deader than Dick Turpin."

We took our curries to the park, found a bench, and, despite the circumstances, dined enjoyably and, toward the end, hilariously. Peter was like that. The sun had come out and the breeze had picked up, the warmth of one compensating for the chill of the other.

"Colin's going to be able to make it, isn't he?" I asked.

"Should be along any time now. He's living down in Brighton, part-time student, of all things, at Sussex University. He has one of those fierce great motorbikes, Japanese, with the fairing and all, comes tooling down the road looking like he ought to be doing the Tourist Trophy race on the Isle of Man. Same old Colin. Has a new girlfriend."

"Will that bar him from taking on an overseas job, three weeks, maybe a little more?"

"I shouldn't think so," replied Peter. "He still has the old girlfriend as well."

"Same old Colin indeed."

"Right you are. And, Harry, would you be wanting me too, then, for three weeks and maybe a little more?"

"Yes, of course. I want you both."

"Sounds like a big project."

"Very."

"But you want to wait for Colin so that you only have to go through the details once?"

"That's right."

"It truly should be any time now. That's why I keep looking up toward the church."

A modest stone church with a sharp pointed steeple, pleasingly proportioned, stood at the far end of the park, a couple of hundred meters away. We were on slightly higher ground, looking over the stream that ran through the middle of the park, and we could see clearly the gravel parking lot alongside the church. It was empty.

"I told him we'd meet him there."

"Why don't we just walk on in that direction?"

We ambled along. The path was lower than the hill where we'd been standing, and we could no longer observe the churchyard, but Peter assured me that we'd hear Colin's arrival even if we failed to see him.

"His motorbike makes a monstrous noise, just awful," said Peter. "Filthy loud things, those machines. You'd think the boy'd had his fill of loud noises by now."

I enjoyed his reference to Colin as a "boy." Colin Graham was at least a couple of years past forty, had enlisted at sixteen as a Marine. The Brits encourage these juvenile enlistments as a kind of apprentice-ship program. He had completed 17 years of active duty, mainly with the SBS, around Basra in Iraq, Helmand province in Afghanistan, and, along the way in a lot of other "dodgy neighborhoods," as Peter tended to call them. Of course, Peter was nearly fifty-eight, enough older to think of Colin still as a boy. But they both seemed like boys to me.

Still, my wars and Peter's had overlapped a bit more. He had been born in 1962, the son of a schoolteacher in one of those sad little factory towns in the Pennines. He'd been bright enough to overcome this, first by acing his GCSE school-leaving exams, then by success-fully passing the commissioning course for the Royal Marines, just in time to serve with some distinction with 42 Commando during the Falklands War. He'd done tours in Northern Ireland when it was still a hot zone, and, after becoming a member of the Special Boat Service, in his own long list of dodgy neighborhoods, several of which we had shared. He'd been around for both Iraq Wars, the latter just, having become a Major before, in the time-honored phrase, saying

"I'm getting too old for this shit." He'd earned a degree in War Studies at Kings College, London while still on active duty, and, retired, after several false starts, earned an honors degree in analytic philosophy at Oxford. Teaching satisfied him for a short period, but then came disappointment (in his words, "the Inklings were all dead, I was never going to be A.J. Ayer, and besides, the undergraduates were more dull-witted and less interesting than a whole battalion of Marines.")

Now he was retired, doing a bit of security consulting and entertaining himself by writing, pseudonymously, a nice little series of detective novels, staying fit by swimming ludicrous distances and running the occasional marathon. He was, in short, a perfect example of that admirable breed of Englishmen, the T.E. Lawrence's, the Fitzroy Maclean's, the David Stirling's—gentlemen, scholars, thugs. I'd tapped him for a few African projects since setting up the Foundation with Kip, and I suspected he'd be very much up for the mission. He'd implied as much when we'd spoken on the phone, without knowing the slightest about what I had in mind.

We had stopped some distance short of the church, waylaid by a flock of ducks. Peter produced some bread from his pocket that I hadn't even noticed he'd taken at lunch.

"The poor ducks get neglected in this park, especially now when everyone's staying at home," he said. "There's four or five big swans at the other end, nasty great buggers, they get all the attention from the mommies and the kiddies. I can't imagine why, they're such mean-tempered brutes. I save my goodies for the ducks."

I've never much cared for ducks, or chickens, or any of the rest. I only like any of them when they are roasted or fried. I was on the verge of saying so when the distant roar of a motorcycle engine announced Colin's arrival. We dispensed the rest of the bread in large handfuls, and headed toward the church. As we reached the parking lot, Colin was taking off his motorcycle helmet and lashing it to a strap on the seat of a lime-green and white Kawasaki. We all shook hands.

"Long time no see, boss," Colin said to me. I cannot begin to capture the flavor of Colin Graham's accent. He was a product of the border region, bred to the warrior's way by a millennium of strife between the English and the Scots. It was always a treat to see him with Peter. The physical contrasts were stark; Peter was tall and fair, while Colin was short and dark. Peter was languid, Colin intense. Moreover, they were separated by age, by background, by every sort of interest, and by the gulf that all services create between officers and enlisted men. Yet the bond between them was stronger than steel.

While strolling with them, I gathered my thoughts, then began. "I would like both of you to participate in an operational mission. Not an exercise, not a performance test, but an actual strike on a facility. I've already developed a preliminary plan, and have the approval and the financing to go forward. I believe that the operation has an excellent chance of success, as long as the right people are involved. I believe that it is worth doing."

It was as if I had thrown a rope around them. They both stopped dead in their tracks.

"An American job?" asked Peter. "U.S. government sanctioned?"

I wished I could simply say "yes."

"Not exactly," I said, and then began to explain about the Letter of Reprisal. The very idea of this delighted Peter.

"Right, Harry, I'll be Captain Kidd and you can be Blackbeard, or maybe 'Whitebeard' would be better." The tone was lighthearted but his expression was guarded. I wasn't overly concerned about getting Colin's agreement. Colin would do something like this, as Grady would put it, "just for the cornbread hell of it." But Peter would be more thoughtful, consider the larger implications. Colin, as I expected, allowed Peter to speak first.

"Terrorism," he began, "state-sponsored terrorism, and on the grandest scale. I haven't much cared for what they've done to Hong Kong or how they treat the Uighurs, but this just beggars belief. I like the Chinese people I've known, but the CCP? Bloody hell."

"Right bloody bastards," Colin chimed in.

"That's almost an understatement," I replied, following his lead. "I don't know much about how this weapon will work, but we don't need to know much. We're seeing it illustrated every day, all around us, only much, much worse. Your NHS will be flattened, people will be dying on the sidewalks, and, when the Chinese announce their vaccine, people will be selling their souls to get it. At the epicenter, it will make the Rwanda genocide look like a Saturday night pub brawl. But the spread beyond Africa will be really quick."

"How many casualties did you say?" This was Colin.

I waited while a young woman pushing a stroller passed by. "What's the latest count of Covid deaths worldwide? The last I looked it was over a million. Just in terms of sheer virulence and sheer deadliness, maybe ten or fifteen times over in the same period of time. The only real limit will be when Xi decides we've all had enough, and offers the vaccine to every government prepared to kiss his ring."

"Or his ass," injected Colin.

"And you're quite confident this really exists?" asked Peter. "This isn't going to end up being poor old Tony Blair, hounded by the BBC to prove that the WMD really existed?"

"The intel on this is rock solid." Instead of belaboring the details for Peter's benefit, I simply said, with all the conviction I could muster, "I truly believe that this will lead to something big, and very bad, and that if we don't stop it, it's going to happen soon."

"It should be a job for the government, or the governments, in this case," said Peter. "But the politicians and the bureaucrats just don't want to know, do they? They're all set to funk it."

"That's the way it seems," I said.

"I've spent most of my life doing counter-terrorism," Peter continued. "It's what soldiering has become. The Falklands was a glorious anachronism, and so, too, the Gulf Wars, all those tanks and bombers and battleships. Now it's all "grey zone" and "hybrid" and all the other buzz words, but it's about decency versus monstrosity. It's about good people trying to work, have children, raise families in places like Belfast or Beirut, without having to worry about being blown up at the bus stop. It's about finding a way for people to go to church in France without having their heads cut off. It's about not having to worry about Xi or Putin and all the wannabe masters of the world. I don't care much for great causes anymore, but what we do these days, it's about protecting the poor little sods who stick Fords or Toyotas together all day and then go home to the missus and the wee ones at night, isn't it? Tell me, Harry, have you read much Orwell?"

"Some. *1984*, *Homage to Catalonia*, a few essays."

"Wonderful man. Kept wanting to be a Communist or suchlike, but was much too decent a man to give in to it. He's very sound on these things. He once wrote: 'People sleep peaceably in their beds at night only because rough men stand ready to do violence on their behalf.' That's what it's about, isn't it? The chance to act, the chance to save lives, be it one or a thousand."

"If I didn't think so, I wouldn't be part of it. I wouldn't ask you, I wouldn't ask Colin or anyone else to be part of it."

This was becoming difficult. It was easier to approach in terms of professional challenge, even in terms of monetary reward. But Peter was one of those special men who soldiered from the heart outward. Speaking what was in his heart was part of making the decision. So, I spoke from my heart.

"You'll take the lives of, perhaps, forty people, but they're all people who've lent themselves to this monstrous undertaking. There are no innocent bystanders at that facility, no children, the women there are contributors to the terror," I said. "On the other hand, in real terms, there's no measuring how many lives we might save. Maybe none at all. There's no assurance that these people would ever enact the threat they present. But as you say, maybe millions. And by the time we know for sure, the opportunity will be gone."

"I like your 'Letter of Marque and Reprisal' agreement, by the way."

"I can't claim that it really offers much protection to us."

"Not my point, Harry. I'm far too old a dog to believe much in protection like that. We'll find our protection in doing the job right and doing it quietly. That way, no one will want to know, will they?"

"That's how I read it."

"No, I like the thing about punishing piracies. I read something the other day in the on-line edition of your *Washington Post*—I have to keep up with you dangerous Yanks now, don't I—and the author made the point that your 9/11 Commission had gotten one bit horrendously wrong."

"Go on," I didn't really want an intellectual discussion at this point, but I knew Peter was still working the whole thing out for himself.

"He said they shouldn't have focused on 'Islamist' terrorism only, says instead they should have focused on the whole business of terrorism itself, whoever does it. That we need to go after anyone who practices it, like we once went after slavery and piracy. We have to make it unacceptable behavior."

"Sure." I was suddenly afraid that he was talking himself away from the mission, and he must have read the fear in my expression.

"No, Harry, no fear. It's not just about wagging your finger and saying "bad person" to a pirate. It took that, but it also took a few good hard men to go out and kill the odd pirate as well, and some of those men sailed under Letters of Marque and Reprisal. I think your *Post* man was right. None of this bloody nonsense about 'one man's terrorist is another man's freedom fighter.' I've seen enough, and I hate the lot of them, and mostly their precious causes are just bollocks. It's just like that bloody business in the Sudan. You've got *Doctors without Borders* who want to go and help people, but when you've got bad men with guns in the way, you can't get the doctors in. It's like what you've been doing with your foundation."

Colin piped up. "So sometimes you need some 'Killers without Borders' to help out the doctors. Dead fucking brilliant that would be."

Peter smiled. "Yes, exactly right."

"So, does that mean you're in?" I asked.

"I can't say no."

"But, Peter, it has to be a strong affirmative, a "yes" you can live with all the way."

"Yes, Harry. Definitely, yes."

I looked at Colin.

"Sign me up, guv'nor."

We had crossed the big hurdle, but in this case, there was one more hurdle ahead. I wanted to hold back for a minute, catch my breath so to speak, before tackling it; but Colin, without realizing it, forced the issue.

"Will you be the head boy, Harry?" he asked.

"No, not exactly. I'm in charge of putting things together, and I pay the bills, but I won't be part of the team."

"So, you're running the head shed, our one-man rear echelon. Well, I wondered a bit. I figured if an old crock like you was doing the job, it would be a piece of cake."

The smile on his face told me that, however serious the question itself, I was being ribbed. I responded in kind. "Why I've forgotten more about soldiering than you'll ever learn, young Colin."

"Aye, and a rare shame it is what old age can do to a good man's memory," he countered. I couldn't win, and I couldn't avoid the real question any longer. This was delicate. By virtue of experience and military rank, Peter deserved to be team lead. My only reason for favoring Grady was the feeling that he was a bit better at pulling disparate personalities together into a team, that and the fact that Grady and I had more history together.

"Remember Grady Dawkins? The Gulf, back in 90? I've asked him to be the team leader, and he's agreed to do it. I'd like you to be second-in-command."

Peter came through, thank God, as I had hoped he would. "The estimable Mr. Dawkins, yes, very good, Harry. Are you putting together an all-bootneck show?"

It took me a second to recall that "bootneck" in British parlance was the same as our "leatherneck," both terms referring to the leather pieces worn around the neck by eighteenth century marines to protect against the slash of a cutlass. We talked for another hour or so about details. Peter would be a good second-in-command, precisely because he had a knack for detail but never got lost in it. And while I felt that Grady was the better man to weave a team together on short notice and then to lead and motivate such a scratch-built crew, if things turned to shit, if, for example, something happened to Grady, then there'd be no one better than Peter at extracting a team in trouble, and that was the role I was casting him for.

Peter also brought some special skills to the table, skills in orchestrating and operating electronic countermeasures, in this case jamming facility communications once the attack started. We discussed equipment, and he recommended a Racal unit that had worked well in Iraq.

I also had technical matters to discuss with Colin. I wanted Colin on the team partly for his experience and tactical ability, but mainly because he was an expert at deceiving or bypassing electronic intrusion-detection systems. The British government, down through the years, had spent a considerable fortune to cultivate his natural propensities to be a kind of military cat burglar. I needed to start him thinking about a couple of special technical problems.

Finally, I brought up the subject of recruiting. Disappointingly, no potential candidates garnered their immediate agreement. As various names were mentioned and then dismissed, I found myself regretting that I'd told Grady to be selective. We might simply not have enough people to get the job done. We desperately needed more time.

The sun was beginning to set by the time we concluded these preliminaries. We'd walked back around the park, taking a second path away from the stream, and were standing alongside Colin's motorcycle. A Vauxhall sedan drove up, parked. Two middle-aged ladies got out and went inside the church. I gave Peter and Colin a telephone number where Kip could be reached, explained that he coordinating personnel movement and logistics and would provide them with information concerning where and when to report. I told Peter that I'd need him in the States almost immediately, and I invited him to link up with Moira, Grady, and me in Las Vegas, where we were going to meet Moira's choice of a co-pilot. Colin picked up his helmet and straddled the seat of his motorcycle.

"Must be off," he said, "lots of home-front politicking to be done if I'm going to leave for the States in a couple of days."

"I would guess so," I said.

"Don't want to come home after three months and find an empty flat. See you soon, Harry. And, boss," he said, turning to Peter, "I'll ring you up tomorrow, we can do a bit of coordinating."

He settled the helmet over his head, hit the starter, and was shifting up to third gear by the time he hit the blacktop. Peter and I turned back toward town.

"What about you?" I asked. "Much home-front politicking to do?"

"Not too much. The prodigious sum of money you've promised will stifle any questions she might ask about what I'll be up to, and it will certainly ease the pain of my absence. Besides, my second son has just moved back in with us from university, and there's no telling when he'll be moving out again. The house will not be lonely."

"The boy having problems?"

"Just the pandemic. He's up one day wanting to be a painter, the next an actor. Talented little bugger, too, much more so than the older one. He could be whatever he chooses. Perhaps I shall use my forthcoming vast wealth to subsidize him, sponsor his first showing, bribe gallery owners."

"More effective to bribe Colin and have him threaten to kill them."

"No doubt. Probably cheaper, too."

"What about the other one, the oldest?"

"Prospering mightily, that one. A sociologist, thinks he's the Ralf Dahrendorf of his generation, had some sort of obscure but important job on the staff of the British delegation to the European Parliament. Brexit killed that, but he found his feet in Brussels anyway. Only twenty-eight and already going great guns. Of course, the demand for bureaucrats never diminishes, and now we've a great silly European establishment laid on top of all the national ones. I wonder—is he a 'Euro-bureaucrat,' or have they already coined something like 'Eurocrat?' If I read *The Economist*, I would know, I'm sure. But it all fits. He's just married an Italian girl, lovely, looks just like Luciana Paluzzi, the little red-headed villainess who tried to kill James Bond in *Thunderball*, wonderful tits even if she is my daughter-in-law, she works as a translator in Strasbourg at the Euro-bureau there. So, my

Euro-son has a Euro-wife and I, in the fullness of time, will have Euro-grandchildren." He paused. "Assuming of course, we all live to see the day. My beautiful daughter-in-law's parents are having a very bad time of it in Milan."

We had reached my rental car.

"I take it, Peter, that you're not pleased with the new Europe."

"Perhaps, and least of all when the voice of the new Europe seems to be a bunch of superannuated '60s' radicals, who're now all set to lecture the poor benighted Anglo-Saxons about what fools we are to be leaving them. Mind you now, I'm not at all keen to go back to the old days, when the Germans and the French and all the other tribes were always set to have a go at one another. No, really, I'm not talking politics. I'm just not much pleased with my eldest son. One can love them, you know, and still find them unbearably tedious. Still, his mother thinks he's wonderful, and when I deliver this dirty great pile of cash you're paying me, she may decide that I'm wonderful too. Oh, and Harry. Someday maybe you'll tell me how you came by all of your loot. I know it didn't come from soldiering."

"The tooth fairy left it under my pillow."

And then I was off and running once again.

CHAPTER 10

I DON'T MUCH care for Las Vegas, even in the best of times, but now it seemed quite haunted, the bright lights illuminating an almost spectral emptiness along the streets below. Although some of the Covid restrictions had been lifted as summer progressed, business, clearly, hadn't recovered. Still, our hotel boasted of a first-rate restaurant on the 16th floor, which promised good food and allowed us a wonderful view all the way to the Stratosphere Tower at the opposite end of the Strip.

We—Grady, Moira, Peter, and myself—had declared a truce when our meals arrived, and I, for one, had enjoyed my steak. The restaurant owner had been patrolling the room and reached our table just as we ordered after dinner drinks. He lingered with us, most likely because of Moira and her spectacularly décolleté burgundy velvet cocktail dress. Grady glowered at him, which I attributed at the time to the general bad temper around the table. But I was still grateful for the distraction, since it delayed our return to the delicate issue that had exploded in our faces earlier that day. I wanted to proceed carefully.

Our nominal reason for assembling in Las Vegas was to meet the man Moira had selected as her co-pilot. He would, after all, become a key member of the team, and it was only fitting that he get off to a good start with the senior members of the team. I would've had Kip present, but he and his friend Jean-Paul were still chasing equipment. We were supposed to be celebrating an important milestone, for, with the addition of Moira's co-pilot, the team was finally complete. But instead we were arguing about his suitability in terms that threatened the operation itself.

It had nothing to do with his credentials as a pilot, which were unquestionable, and which, in any event, were Moira's to judge. But there were other concerns regarding Eduardo "Dito" Saumarez, concerns that, to his credit, he'd insisted on airing. A squat bear of a man in his mid-forties, stout, with a curly dark fringe of hair over the ears of his mostly bald head, a bushy moustache, heavy eyebrows, and a thick cigar. He dressed like a janitor. His English was perfectly understandable, but his Cuban accent was thick and unpleasantly nasal. From the outset he came across as down to earth, straightforward.

His resume was impressive. He'd entered the Cuban Air Force in 1984, at the age of nineteen. After qualifying as a fighter pilot, he'd undergone several advanced training tours in the Soviet Union, flown combat missions with the Cuban forces in Angola, become a senior flight instructor, and acquired multi-engine and rotary-wing ratings. He'd even done a brief turn as Castro's personal pilot. A naturally gifted flyer, he could make a fighter plane 'sit up and do tricks.' His familiarity with Africa, albeit somewhat dated, was an obvious bonus. But the real advantage was that he had recent experience flying amphibians as Moira's co-pilot and that they knew each other well and trusted each other's skills. We had no reason to question his ability as a pilot.

Nor did we have any problem with his trustworthiness. I'd run him by a friendly Agency contact just to make sure. The background was interesting. In 2007 he'd turned up in Port of Spain, on the island of Trinidad, offering himself to a representative of the British Secret Intelligence Service, who soon shared their prize with the CIA. He was screened and vetted repeatedly over many months before being pronounced solidly reliable. He then spent a year being wrung out by debriefers on a broad range of technical and political topics. Then he was loaned to the CIA's operational side, where he floated in the background on a variety of Central- American operations, chiefly as a source of information on certain senior Cuban military personnel who appeared to be working with the drug cartels. It was from this period that his friendship with Moira dated. Eventually, when his usefulness in this role was nearly exhausted, he was offered to the U.S. Air Force. The Air Force brought him to Nellis Air Force Base in Las Vegas and made him a "coach" for the Red-Flag aggressor squadrons, whose role was to provide fighter pilots with realistic practice against opponents who flew in accordance with Warsaw-Pact training and doctrine. Finally, after several more years, he was given a modest pension and put out to pasture. A few years later Moira'd run into him at an air show, and they'd shared old times, a new friendship, and an occasional flying partnership in the years since.

His "little problem" first surfaced in 2006, while on assignment in Venezuela after the U.S. arms embargo had opened the door to Russian and Cuban involvement. Having spoken a shade too frankly of his growing skepticism of the Castro regime, he eventually drew the attention of the security policeman assigned to the project. The policeman's first attempt to have Dito returned to Cuba had been dismissed out of hand, which only made the policeman more determined. He scrutinized Dito's actions more closely than ever, seeking his opportunity. Unfortunately, Dito was vulnerable, and in the tight community that was the Cuban military mission, the policeman discovered his weakness.

Being a patient man, the policeman carefully arranged a trap and then waited patiently to spring it. Came the day, and he burst into Dito's quarters while Dito was energetically sodomizing a handsome young construction worker. Fortunately for Dito, the policeman was less diligent about following up his advantage than he'd been when contriving his plan. Instead of arranging to have Dito packed off on the next flight to Cuba, he allowed himself to relax and enjoy his triumph, giving Dito the opportunity to slip away. The policeman, one surmises, was not rewarded for his efforts when he returned to Havana.

My preference was to ignore the issue. We needed a second pilot, Dito was supremely qualified and wanted to do it, and Moira wanted him. We weren't, after all, blessed with a large pool of applicants with the necessary amphibian skills. But Dito had chosen to view his situation as an issue, and insisted that we confront it head-on. So, we'd spent the afternoon at Dito's condominium in North Las Vegas, engaged in what the diplomats call "a full and frank exchange of views." Dito had responded to every question directly, and with considerable dignity. Peter and I had both been deeply impressed. But Grady had been less receptive. Since leaving Dito's, he and Moira hadn't exchanged a word. I wished that I could simply impose a decision on them, but I had tried, successfully thus far, to build a consensus behind all the key decisions. They were the ones who would be risking their lives. I would be sitting back on a freighter off the African coast, waiting and praying for their safe return.

Now the time had come to decide. Moira broke the silence.

"I can make this very simple," she said. "I want Dito as my copilot. Period."

"He has very good credentials—" I began, but Grady cut me off.

"This isn't about his fucking credentials, it's about having a faggot on the team."

There it was. The lines were clearly drawn. Moira eyed him balefully. "So?"

"So—I don't like it."

I tried to redirect the discussion.

"Peter?"

He took a deep breath, apparently wanting to choose his words carefully. "I liked the man. Very dignified, he was, even though the whole business had to have been unpleasant. We hit him with some quite nasty questions now, didn't we?"

"Has he got the guts?" said Grady, which provoked a mumble of disgust from Moira. She started to say something, but Peter gently overrode her.

"Can't answer that now, can we Grady? But not just about friend Saumarez. We have others on the team that we're taking a chance on. Take your man Jerry Wolsey, for example, he's never heard a shot fired in anger, or how about some of the others, who've seen far less action than Saumarez. And what about the rest of us? I've held it together under fire before, but we all know people who went to the well once too often. Could this time be when I lose it? Could it be your time?"

"That's not the fucking point."

"Ah, well, is the point then that fairies lack guts? Some do, I suspect, but that says nothing about this man. Besides, I don't know that fairies lack guts. I mean, I've known a few Guardsmen with bags of guts who were still rather light in the heels."

"So, are you for having him on the team?" I asked.

"Yes," said Peter.

I could have counted that as a second vote in favor, and my vote would make it three to one, but we weren't voting. I wanted to put this to rest, and turned to Grady.

"We need a good copilot," I said. "Do you have another one in mind?"

"I just don't want a cocksucker on the team."

Moira broke in tersely. "I've sucked a cock or two in my lifetime. I'm told I'm very good at it." She gave him a look that I couldn't quite interpret. "Does that mean you don't want me on the team?"

"That's not what I meant, and you know it."

"You don't know what you mean."

They glowered at each other.

"Now wait a minute—" I began.

Just at that moment the waiter came to refill our coffee. The enforced break allowed them both to back down a step.

"Aw, fuck it," said Grady. "Bring him on. All he has to do is help fly the fucking airplane."

It would have been fine if he'd left it at that. But he didn't.

"Besides," he added, "all the damned air-wing pukes were candy-asses anyway."

For a split-second I thought that Moira was going to throw coffee in Grady's face. But after a very tense moment, she released her grip on the cup, took her napkin from her lap and dabbed at her lips, and then very deliberately stood up. I knew that Grady's first wife had cuckolded him with an 'air wing puke,' but that hardly seemed the point.

Moira looked from me to Peter, then back to me, before finally shifting her gaze toward Grady. When she finally spoke her tone was level, deliberate, plainly straining to maintain control. "Grady Dawkins, you're the most infuriating man I've ever known. This is my decision, and I've made it, and if you cannot support it, then to hell with you. Turning to me she said, "Harry, if you can't get this sorted out, then you can find another pilot."

She picked up her purse and began walking away. Then she turned, eyes blazing, her finger a dagger pointed straight at Grady's face. "You are totally full of shit," she said, spitting out each word and stabbing at him with her finger, "just totally full of pompous mud-Marine shit. Well let me tell you something, Mr. high-and-mighty infantry martyr. Just let me tell you something. In World War II the U.S. Eighth Air Force, in two years of running bombing missions over Germany, lost more men than the entire U.S. Marine Corps lost in the entire Pacific War. More than Tarawa, more than Iwo Jima, more than Okinawa all rolled into one. You think about how much guts it took to fly those missions. Then you better get down on your knees and pray forgiveness from all those poor men you just insulted. And if you can't do that, you can just stay down on your knees and kiss my ass."

With that she stalked away, the eyes of every man in the place following her, Grady half-rising out of his seat as if to go after her. So much for my idea that having the discussion in a public place would enforce civility. We'd made quite a spectacle of ourselves.

"This is stupid," I said to Grady. "Get your act together and go apologize. We don't have time for this."

With raised eyebrows he thought about this several seconds. Then he rose and went after her.

"I didn't manage that very well, did I?" I said to Peter.

"Well, now that you mention it."

"I should have just told Moira not to even let Dito bring it up, and I should have told Grady that 'Team Leader' only means the ground team."

"With the wisdom of hindsight, of course."

"I wanted all the possible kinks worked out. I wanted some consensus."

"Harry, I think you might just shut up. Consensus? I thought you were the lord proprietor of this little fiefdom. Maybe Moira thought Grady wouldn't really mind. Who knows, and, frankly, who cares? You shouldn't. What you should do is go outside and, if they're still arguing, tell them both to shut up, tell them Dito's on the team, and, above all, remind them that you're the boss."

Peter and I got the waiter's attention and paid the bill. Stepping out the front door, we looked around. Peter spotted them first.

"Over there," he said.

I followed his gesture and saw the two of them standing in the parking lot next to our rental car. They didn't appear to be angry any longer. To the contrary.

"Had I been given the opportunity," said Peter, "I would have said something like 'kiss and make up.' Do you think, then, maybe they read my mind?"

There was a kind of bemused appreciation in his voice as he watched their embrace. I started in the direction of the car, but he took me gently by the shoulder and restrained me.

"It does no good to interrupt them now, does it? Let's just give it a minute or two."

A few moments later, Moira brushed past, her eyes wet, mumbling something about needing to go to the ladies' room. No sooner had she disappeared inside than Grady walked up.

"I was out of line back there, Harry," he said. "I think it's all straight again now."

"I hope so. We don't have the luxury of fighting each other if we're going to pull this thing off."

"This man Saumarez wants to do the job," said Peter, "wants to risk his life with us, why should we cavil about what he does in private?"

"What's this 'cavil?' You college types talk some strange shit some times. You know what, Harry?"

"What?"

"She's a great woman, and she knows what she's doing. I guess I kinda had my head up my ass. I really didn't mean to piss her off." Almost as an afterthought he added, "and I didn't mean to piss you off either. Anyway, we'll make this team work, we'll get everybody together. I guess I really don't give a shit, you're right, we do need a good copilot, and the airplane is Moira's business. Point is, Harry, I honestly don't give a good goddamn, as long as he just wants to do the job, as long as he's just a trooper, not one of them that wants me to cut 'em some kind of fucking break because they're different, because they're so bad off, so disadfuckingvantaged. People like that should've grown up shoveling cow shit like I did. But now take Lorayne. Take her out of her BDUs, put her into a dress, and she probably looks like somebody's prom date. But that little lady will kick ass and take names, big time, and she'll always carry her own weight. And Kip and Smitty—they're black, but they don't ask for no favors, and they definitely have all their shit in one basket. So that's it, then. I mean, take this Cuban faggot. It sounds like he knows his shit. If he was the kind of guy who wants you to hold his hand and say 'Gee, it must be tough being a pansy,' then he could just go piss up a rope. But Moira says he's good troops, says he knows how to carry his own weight. He does that, he gets my respect. Far as I'm concerned, as long as he can fly the goddamned airplane I don't care if he sings ba-ba-loo every time he gets cornholed."

As a statement of principle this left something to be desired, but it sufficed; the crisis was past. Moira returned, saying that she'd call

Dito as soon as we got back to the hotel and give him the good word. We weren't going to discuss it further, not among ourselves, not with anyone else on the team, our own version, I guess, of "Don't ask, don't tell." We walked together to the car and drove back to the hotel.

The next morning, I was up early, standing outside the front entrance of the hotel, watching the cars as they approached along the circular drive. The cars either stopped before reaching me or drove on past. Finally, one pulled up where I stood, the window lowered, and I saw Toby Parks beckoning from the driver's seat. Incongruously for Las Vegas, he was dressed in a dark business suit and white shirt. I opened the near-side door and sat alongside him. As I buckled myself in he pulled away from the curb and threaded his way through traffic toward U.S. 95, the road leading northward through the desert toward Reno. But Reno was a long way away. We drove in silence along 95 until we were clear of the suburbs and on a desolate stretch lined on both sides by pink mountains. There was little traffic in either direction, and the only sign of life along the road was an Indian reservation's cut-rate cigarette stand. Parks waited a long time before speaking.

"Time's about to run out on us," he finally said.

I considered this for a few moments. "Two days ago, you when I called you, you said we were good for another two weeks."

"That's changed. We've got a problem."

I didn't like the sound of this.

"What's changed? What problem?"

I saw the sign indicating that we were approaching the tiny town of Indian Springs—two service stations, a restaurant, the inevitable roadside casino, and a small Air Force base, which served as a support facility for the immense bombing range that stretched deep into the desert mountains. For the next hundred miles there was nothing, I knew, but a couple of little towns south of 95, notable only for their brothels, and north of 95, the Nevada Test Site, where nuclear weapons had once been tested.

"How far do you plan on driving?" I asked Parks.

He answered by pulling into the Shell station across the road from the entrance to the air base.

"We can turn around here. I just wanted to be well away from everything while we talked. Damn, Harry, this whole thing is really working on my head."

He waited for a couple of cars to pass, then pulled onto 95 heading back in the direction of Las Vegas. The silence expanded, filling the car.

Finally, he said, "I think you've been blown."

"Blown? Blown how?"

"Somebody, I shouldn't say who, couldn't help bragging about what a clever trick this 'Letter of Reprisal' was, it got back to one of my idiot fellow congressmen, who started nosing around. I don't think it's gone any further, and we've got some people who are trying to sit on him, but a Chinese interest and all bets are off. Plus, his senior aide is none other than your old friend Sandy Sawyer. If she gets wind of this, she may start digging, and, give the devil his due, she's a helluva digger. And if she turned up a connection to you, then Katie bar the fucking door."

"Shit."

"Yeah, deep shit. I'd like to think we've got things plugged, but this is D.C., one leak and the whole boat starts taking on water"

"So, what do we do? It will take at least a week for the ship to be in position, and Grady needs to bring the whole team together and exercise it at least for a day or two. This is really working on a shoestring, already."

"You can't go on using that old mill as a staging and training area. It's too close to the flagpole. You were going to do your final staging out of that place on Reunion Island. Start pulling up stakes as fast as you can, get there, and launch as soon as possible.

I thought about the logistics for a moment.

"I need 72 hours. Can you buy me that much time to move the team?"

"Yeah, sure, I think so."

"And another seven days to launch?"

"That's still good, but barely."

"Maybe another couple to buy the best weather window."

Now it was Parks's turn to hesitate.

"I'll do the best I can, but you need to be ready to move as soon as the ship is in place, and if you can hurry that up, then all to the good."

On the way back to the city I went over the plan with him. On the one hand, there were all sorts of good reasons why he didn't need to know the details. On the other hand, he had a proper special ops background and was, besides, a very smart man. I guess I just wanted a second opinion and he was there and couldn't very well refuse to listen. As I hoped, he gave me just the kind of feedback I needed, zeroing in on several of the sticky points, not bothering to raise the obvious point, namely the fact that the team was, essentially, thrown together, with very little time to build any real unit cohesion. Then he raised yet another good point.

"I need some kind of cover story, just in case I get backed into a corner on this."

"Cover story?"

"A fake version of your plan, something that people can pick at without any clue what you're really doing. Even some of our friends want to know more than I've given them."

I thought about this for a moment.

"Okay, use this. Before I came up with the idea of Moira, and before we settled on her trick airplane, I first thought of using some French contacts I've got in Chad to provide a staging base, probably down around the city of Sarh in the southeast. What I mapped out used three Chinooks, cover story supporting an oil exploration team, one to transport the team, the other two carrying fuel bladders to refuel the team chopper for the necessary range. Sort of like the Iranian hostage rescue mission, and a bad plan for the same reason—too many moving parts, particularly as a shoestring private venture."

"I like it," he said. "The similarity to the Iran mission will help it play in people's minds."

"Even so, don't give it to anyone unless you absolutely can't avoid it. And, assuming we actually go in within ten days, push our notional launch date out another week." I figured I could leave it at that, but then another question formed. "Do you have any more nasty surprises for me?"

"Well, shit, Harry, there's one more thing," he said, glancing over at me before focusing on the increasing traffic as we edged into the built-up area north of the city.

"One more thing? After what you've already hit me with?"

"Your insider at the bio lab, Dr. Shih Yang. She's got to come out with the team."

"You mean she's still there?"

"Exactly."

"Grady will have a shit fit. The job on the ground's already complicated enough. Can't she get out in advance?"

"Not if you want to keep getting intel from inside."

I stopped short on that one.

"We owe her, Harry. Think about it. She's the one who sent up a red flag on this in the first place, she's the one who got us the hard evidence. She was going to bug out after feeding us the original intel, but we persuaded her to stay put, so we could still have some good on-the-ground intel for you guys. She finally agreed, on the condition that you guys get her out. She knows she won't survive the aftermath of a raid. Like I said, we owe her. She's your best guarantee that the team won't walk into a shit storm, and besides, there wouldn't be any fucking mission without her. Anyway, if there's no plan for getting her out, how do you keep from killing her along with the others? She doesn't deserve that. And we need her when all this is over, if and when we decide to go public with what the Chinese were up to."

He was absolutely right, and it shamed me to realize that I'd not thought it through. There was nothing else to say, so for the rest of the drive I said nothing. But when we pulled up into the circular drive at the front of the hotel, Parks waved off the doorman and took me by the arm. "It's a good plan, Harry, and you've got good people on the team. I think they can pull it off, even with this other little wrinkle, and get out in one piece. Oh, one other thing. If this starts to unravel, maybe I can lay a false trail for the hounds, put them off by giving them a fake plan, let them chase the wrong lead for a day or two."

"It's worth a try. We may need all the time you can buy." I thought about it for a moment, then told him to use a variant of the original plan we'd talked about, one involving three Chinooks, two carrying fuel bladders, one for the team, and with a much bigger team. I figured it would be convincing, since it represented the way a SOCOM-type with real assets to play with might go about things.

He said he would use it only if he had to, and then, as I got out of the car, he wished me 'good luck and good hunting.' I took this as a benediction, probably the best one I was going to get. I went up to my room feeling somewhat better about the fact that I was sending 14 people, some of them my very good friends, on a mission with almost no preparation worthy of the name, with a plan that seemed increasingly like something drawn in the sand with a stick.

I had a sandwich sent up to my room, and then started the process of getting the team onto a charter flight to Reunion. I hated putting all our eggs in one basket, but my original plan, having them arrive in ones and twos, had just gone out the window. Once this was in motion, I called my sister, encouraging her to push our ship along if at all possible. Peter had already departed for England, but I left a message for him to call me as soon as possible. I caught up with Kip, and, after a cryptic explanation, had him start directing our gear for the base camp he'd organized through his French friends on Reunion. All of this done, I went looking for Grady and Moira. Better to tell them both face-to-face. I couldn't find them in either room, so I decided to look for them in the just-reopened coffee shop. Then another possibility occurred to me, and I went looking for them at the indoor pool, which the hotel manager had proudly told us had also just been allowed to reopen, "with proper social distancing."

As soon as I stepped past the glass door I felt a rush of humidity. I sensed their presence before I actually saw them, then heard their playful voices. Grady and Moira. I saw them splashing and playing at the shallow end of the pool, the childlike play suddenly giving way to a lengthy intimate embrace. And then Moira pulled away, and climbed out of the pool and up to the diving board, her bright orange two-piece suit wet and clingy, emphasizing her breasts, hips, and pubis. Grady swam toward her, positioning himself to watch her dive.

I heard the splash and the peal of laughter that followed, hesitating, not wanting to intrude. But I needed to talk to them both, right away. I walked straight over to them, waved as I drew close.

"Harry, hey there," said Moira, waving back. "How was your meeting with Mr. Power Pants?"

Mr. Power Pants? But Moira was, of course, Moira.

"Let's talk about it," I answered. We pulled three of the deck chairs close together and I explained the new timetable to them, as well as the reason why. I held back on the matter of bringing out the scientist, since I wanted to have a plan I could offer to Grady before springing it on him. Moira was perfectly at ease with the challenges posed by the shorter deadline. The plane was ready at an airfield adjacent to the conversion facility on Long Island. Kip and Jean-Paul had already seen to the loading of our tactical gear and would accompany it on the charter flight from Europe to Reunion. Moira and Dito would fly to Long Island tomorrow, then leave with our PBY the following afternoon, taking it by stages to the Azores, Malta, Chad, Tanzania, and the Seychelles, before joining us in Reunion. Moira had hired two other pilots to help them fly as far as Tanzania, telling them they were delivering the plane to the set of an 'Indiana Jones' knockoff African adventure film. As cover stories went, it was thin as tissue paper, but Moira had assured me that her friends were not the kind to ask too many questions, particularly as they were being very well paid. Besides, the story didn't have to hold for very long.

I explained to Grady that I'd already booked him on the same flights to as my own, leaving the next morning. We went over a few more details, but then a couple of other swimmers showed up, making whispered conversation awkward. In any case, there was really little else that needed discussing, except for the thing that I didn't want to discuss. We changed the subject to lighter things and talked some more for the next half-hour. Moira seemed perfectly at ease between me and Grady, her fingers casually seeking out his arm, or shoulder, or back, touching him needfully in the way lovers do. Grady, however, didn't appear as comfortable. Finally, Moira announced that she was hungry, and was going up to shower and change, and that she'd meet us both in the coffee shop in forty-five minutes. Grady trailed behind.

"We need to talk a little, I think." He was glancing away from me as he spoke.

"Okay, Grady. Go ahead. I'm listening."

"I didn't go looking for this," he said.

For a moment I considered making it hard for him by playing dumb and asking what exactly "this" meant. But I didn't. Instead I said, "I guess I would've been surprised if you had."

"Harry, you've known me for a long time. You know how I feel about Mary Anne. I haven't messed around since I met her. It's not like the old days. But this isn't just some TDY romance, I'm not counting down to a PCD."

TDY—Temporary Duty, an official abbreviation for a term that required no explanation. PCD, an abbreviation for an unofficial term, was one that I hadn't heard in a long time. It meant "Pussy Cutoff Date," usually calculated as the date of returning home after a TDY, minus the number of days to identify and successfully treat a sexually transmitted disease. I wondered what impact HIV had made upon the calculation of PCDs.

"I know you've never screwed around on Mary Anne."

I didn't know this—I couldn't know this—but I believed it just the same.

"Things just happened. That Moira, she's something else. Back there at the Mill, the second night, it just happened."

It just happened, like it had once happened to me. But with Grady it had kept on happening. Why him and not me?

"I was gonna tell you about it, but she said no, said I couldn't, said she didn't want to hurt your feelings. I tried to tell her that you were a tough old bastard and you didn't have much of that kind of feelings, and that you'd be more pissed if something was going on in the team that you didn't know about."

"What'd she say?"

"She just said I wouldn't understand, and told me I'd have to leave it at that."

I just looked at him.

"Harry, I don't know what I'm gonna do when this is all over."

"I can't help you there."

He had toweled down as we talked and were now out of the pool area, walking along a corridor toward the elevators.

"I should stop," said Grady. "I mean, I guess I'll be going back to Mary Anne when this is all over."

"Yes."

"But I probably won't, not yet."

"No."

We reached the elevators, pushed the "up" button.

"She's really fantastic."

I didn't want to continue talking about it.

"I'm sure she is." This was close to saying more than I wanted to say.

The bell tone sounded, the "up" arrow glowed, and the elevator door opened. I stepped inside and pushed the button for my floor. Grady pushed the button for his.

"Harry, you remember the old saying, don't you? 'What happens in the team, stays in the team.' Right? We're still together on that?"

"Yes—we're still together on that. But there's another old saying, too."

The elevator stopped at my floor and the door opened.

"Which one's that?"

"Don't shit in your own mess-kit."

CHAPTER 11

"THEY'RE A COCKY bunch," said Grady.

"They'd better be," I replied. "Isn't that part of what we were selecting for? If they didn't believe they were ten feet tall, they'd have never signed up for this one."

"Sure, yeah. Mind you, I'm not complaining. If they can strut on a night like tonight, we know that morale is good."

We were standing just outside the front door of the team house, the centermost and largest in a row of five small cinderblock buildings. Technically, we weren't on Reunion Island, but rather a smaller island just off the coast of Reunion, a location, now abandoned, that had once served the French military as a training area, but now kept up as an occasional destination for birdwatchers. We'd hired it using our cover story as a movie production team, paying generously enough to deflect any close inquiries about our activities. The accommodations were not bad, dormitory-style sleeping quarters with military surplus bunk beds, hot and cold running water, ceiling fans to relieve the heat, and even electric light, all powered by a diesel generator. On our right was a small cove, with a dock where our Catalina was moored. Beyond the cove, across several miles of open water, lay the main island, and a modest shoreside village whose lights provided the only illumination for miles around. In front of us lay a steep bluff, carved at its center by the intriguingly named Infarction Creek.

The team emerged suddenly from the night and fog, coming towards us down a steep and muddy path that ran alongside the creek bed, with Peter and Kip in the lead. As they drew closer their individual shapes became sharply defined, and their faces took on an otherworldly appearance as their night-vision goggles became visible. When the head of the column reached us, Peter pushed his goggles up onto his helmet and gave us a gesture somewhere between a wave and a salute. Then he continued past us to the team house, followed closely by the others.

While Grady had stayed back with me at the team house to settle several logistics questions, Peter had taken the team out on a limited-scale exercise up on the bare slopes of the ridge, little more than a five-mile march combined with a couple of hours of two-on-two MILES engagements out in the forest. The real challenge, I suspected, had been the weather, for the gentle drizzle in which the team had departed at sunset was now, shortly after midnight, a miserable mix of fog and rain. We'd been lucky with the weather for most of the week, which had made us discount the promise of rain for the night, so the sheer ugliness of the downpour had been a nasty surprise. Still, as the team filed past us, their spirits were obviously high.

We fell in behind the team as they entered the main building. Inside they gathered around a large table, peeling out of muddy boots and preparing to give their weapons a quick cleaning. The MILES laser transmitter contains a miniature acoustic sensor that transmits a single laser pulse every time a blank round is fired. Blanks are notoriously 'dirty,' firing a lot of them, as we were doing, quickly gums up a weapon. Besides, cleaning weapons whenever the opportunity presents itself is a habit of good soldiers, and, even though these were not the actual weapons the team would use on the mission, the habit had asserted itself without any prompting on the part of the team leaders.

The odor of powder solvent and gun oil mingled with the still strong odor of fresh sweat. Although the temperature had been mild, the team had exerted itself heavily. The work around the cleaning table went quickly, accompanied by the sounds of easygoing byplay among the team members. The smell of brewing coffee soon joined the other aromas, and soon a line had formed at the coffee pot on a side table.

Grady wandered from table to table, sharing a joke with one group, asking questions of another. He'd accepted the new task of rescuing Dr. Shih Yang with unanticipated grace, largely because I'd worked out a way of doing it that would have minimal impact on the overall plan. With that done, he'd gone back to his primary concentration, getting the team ready. There'd been almost no time for team building, for all the little exercises and activities that endow a group with confidence in each other. But we'd done well with their recruiting, selecting not only for the martial skills essential to the mission, but also for the equally critical personality traits. Part of the group, the Quinlan's Mill element, had been together now for some time, while the rest had seen each other for the first time upon our arrival on Reunion. But as a unit they'd already started to jell.

I circulated some myself, speaking briefly with Kip and Peter, spending more time with the members of the team that I'd only just begun to know. From the original crew at Quinlan's Mill Grady had selected Smitty, Lorayne, Jerry Wolsey, and Ronnie Banks. Kip's had contributed two ex-Legion comrades, Jean-Paul Gautier, and the Dutchman, Cornelius 'Kees' van Veghel. Kees was quiet, not easy to warm up to, but Kip's confidence—and Kees's obvious technical skills—sufficed for me.

Grady had also made offers to two more of the Quinlan's Mill team, but they'd turned him down. Left with no apparent hope of making the necessary twelve, I turned to two young men that I'd not wanted to use. One of them was Tommy Naburje, Bobby Naburje's older brother. Tommy had called me after Bobby's funeral, making it clear that he didn't for a minute buy the 'accidental discharge' explanation for Bobby's death and indicating that Bobby had shared far more of his activities than a good covert operative should. Tommy had made it very clear that, if the occasion should arise, he wanted a chance to get back at whoever it was that had caused Bobby's death. Instead, I'd engaged Tommy usefully—and for him, I knew, rewardingly, in the on-the-ground work of the Foundation, including our protection work and training efforts. He'd acquired some high-level tactical skills—and parachute training—with the Kenyan Army's Ranger Regiment, but his only combat experience had been anti-poaching sweeps. On the other hand, he knew the target area better than anyone; in fact, he'd been who I turned to for conducting the depth soundings for our landing area on the lake. Still, I hated the very notion of involving him. I didn't think that Bobby's parents deserved to lose a second son, and, frankly, hadn't wanted to personally assume that responsibility. But still I'd hesitated until it became clear that we would struggle to make up the numbers for the team.

In much the same manner I'd invited my young cousin, Lem Lauristen, to become the twelfth and final member of the team. I'd only worked with Lem in his capacity as a helicopter pilot, but he'd been a ground-pounder in the 82nd before becoming a pilot, and, along the way, had also picked up a fixed-wing twin-engine certification. The latter won Moira's endorsement: "It can't hurt to have a spare pilot, even one with no seaplane experience." Grady had simply grunted and said, "Well, we really need another shooter—I'll just have to get him up to speed." For me, somehow, it seemed fitting that the name 'Lem Lauristen' was associated with the team, doing something his father would've, as the saying goes, given his right nut to be part of.

Lem had also brought a very special and unexpected tactical gift. For several years he'd been building a second career in the advertising and film industries, flying small camera equipped drones to produce the artsy overhead shots that directors craved, while saving them the expense of hiring a helicopter. He'd arrived with one such device, small enough when disassembled to fit in a large backpack, large enough to carry a compact thermal imaging camera—and virtually invisible, and scarcely audible, particularly at night. I'd already pictured his mission assignment as providing overwatch from the hillside above the facility, but this took things to an entirely different level. I'd read a great deal about drones, and the Foundation had even worked with an organization experimenting with using them to deliver medical supplies to doctors working in remote villages. My failure to include one in my original tactical planning reminded me rather painfully that my old age was showing.

While I'd worried about both Tommy and Lem, now I was glad that I had taken the chance, for both were proving to be real assets. Lem's value was obvious, more so since Moira had taken time to give him a basic familiarization with the idiosyncrasies of the Catalina. But Tommy had provided the totally unexpected surprise. He quickly emerged as a key player, more tactically capable than expected, and gifted with a kind of quiet confidence and resolution that drew others to him. He was a natural leader and, he'd become a magnet for the younger members of the team.

As I looked around the room I realized that they all looked tired. Then again, the entire team had worked virtually non-stop since our arrival five days previously. Much of that had been devoted to ground tactical rehearsals, but, once Moira and Dito had arrived, we'd also conducted four parachute jumps, smoothing out the ability of the entire team to make a quick exit from an aircraft that had never been intended for such a role. They'd organized the weapons and gear, cleaning the mission weapons that were fresh from the manufacturer of their preservative coatings, organizing ammunition into combat loads, arranging harnesses, tactical vests, and web gear for both the parachute jump and the operations on the ground that would follow.

For my own part, I'd divided my time four ways. I spent some time each day observing the training, participating whenever I could contribute something useful. I flew with Moira and Dito on their flight tests and served as jumpmaster for the parachute jumps. On the last jump, without telling Grady of my plans, I made the jump myself after the rest of the team had exited. Jumping wasn't the big adventure it may seem. With the new, highly-steerable rectangular parachutes and some skill in reading the wind, landings were no more jarring than falling out of a hammock, which even an old man like me could manage easily. And I thought it was a good thing that the team could see that I wasn't just their planner and paymaster, that even though they'd not see me on the ground, I would share as many of their challenges as possible. For the same reason I'd shared in the cleaning of weapons and other mundane tasks, including taking the lead in meal preparation, assisted, primarily, by Moira and Dito, whose time was less occupied and whose energy was less in demand. I'd worried that they would somehow find this demeaning, and especially feared that Dito would find this chore a comment on his masculinity, but these fears proved groundless. He undertook every task with a smile, and soon had won over every member of the team, even Grady, albeit somewhat grudgingly. In the meantime, Moira deftly sidestepped the admiration of the male members of the team, making a subtle 'girls against the rest' alliance with Lorayne, with whom she shared the smallest of the quarters. We were far too busy and had too little privacy for Grady and Moira to continue their affair physically, but I could see in their occasional exchange of glances and touches that the feelings remained strong. I wondered if there were others—besides Peter, of course—who were aware of this undertone, but decided probably not. Everyone was much too focused on the task that lay ahead.

While working alongside Moira and Dito in the kitchen I also quietly made alliance with them against Grady in another matter. The Catalina was capable of carrying the sixteen fully-equipped personnel I'd called for in my original plan, plus the two pilots. Even with an increase in the fuel load to provide an extra cushion of range, it looked as if there'd be room for one slender old man to ride along, staying with the plane, to be sure, but sharing at least one more portion of the risks. On the return trip it would matter even less, since we'd be leaving behind a lot of weight in the form of expended explosives, heavy weapons, and special equipment.

The most vital of my four activities consisted of maintaining contact with our 'source' inside the bioweapon facility. For this I had a secure channel satellite link back to a contact designated by Parks, who relayed any fresh information. I had no idea—nor any need to know—regarding how Dr. Shih Yang continued to communicate, but, at this juncture, I expected very little. Obviously, all of this communication was one way. We couldn't risk even attempting to communicate elements of the tactical plan to her, not even the date of the attack. All she needed to know had gone in one simple message, relayed early on via what I presumed was a CIA contact. She would hear a loud explosion and then she would have ninety seconds to rush to the main gate house, wearing a white lab coat for identification. There she would be met and led away. I hoped that in the middle of the night there wouldn't be too many women in lab coats running around the site, since there was very little else I could offer as an alternative.

When the team members finished cleaning their MILES weapons, they stacked them in a rack mounted against the wall of the cleaning room. The laser weapons would not be used again that night, and, if the weather front broke, they might not be used again. Our mother ship had comfortably exceeded the original estimates of its progress and now looked like being on station within the next twenty-four hours. Equally critical, it looked as if the necessary weather window was opening up, and, if it did, we'd spend tomorrow in final preparations and in loading the Catalina, and we'd take off the following morning. Just in time, too, since we were racing both the Chinese and Sandy Sawyer to the finish line. I'd come to dread the buzzing of my satellite phone.

Despite our looming departure, and despite the evident fatigue, the team seemed pretty loose. A large part of that was Grady, who tolerated no grab-ass, but encouraged a lighthearted tone. I went over to talk to Colin about the rubber boats we were using. His SBS background made him, along with Peter, the resident experts on this aspect of the operation. Tommy joined us to share a few thoughts about the river that would carry us down to the lake. Even as we spoke, Ronnie Banks and Jerry Wolsey came over with a question.

"We've been talking," said Jerry. "When the 'Hair Doctor' here briefed the plan the other night, he mentioned something about having to lie up in the woods overnight after we make the jump."

"That's right," I said.

"Ronnie here's been worrying about those gorillas in the woods."

"That's a good worry," said Tommy, with just the hint of a grin. Tommy and I had made this up, just for fun—there wouldn't be any gorillas in the target area. But perhaps some had missed the joke.

"Yeah, well you were explaining about the gorillas, but you didn't say what to do if one tries to crawl into my sleeping bag."

By this time several of the others had gathered around, and I could see Grady lurking over their shoulders, getting ready to call the team to its next task.

"No," said Tommy, "I guess I didn't." He smiled at his audience and continued. "Truth is, we Africans don't worry much about gorillas." I knew that most Africans see themselves as something less generic than "Africans," but Tommy had recognized almost immediately that the distinction was lost on most of his comrades. "What you do is you treat your gorilla just like you would your girlfriend if she crawled into the bag. Stick your tongue up its ass and wiggle it around. Gorillas like that kinky shit."

Grady allowed the laughter to subside and then summoned the team through the door into the next room, which served as the armory for the mission weapons. The live fire weapons and ammunition, of course, were kept carefully segregated from the MILES weapons. It wouldn't have done, for obvious reasons, to load a live round into one of the MILES weapons before going out to play lasers. This has happened in MILES training, with predictably tragic results. The last exercise of the night—the last exercise period, given our departure tasks on the morrow—would take place at the live fire range, which we had established about a half mile down the coast at the aptly-named Murder Point.

I hung back as the team geared up and then disappeared once again into the darkness. I would have enjoyed watching them out on the range, but I was also expecting a message from our support ship, and I didn't want to take a chance on missing it. But before going back to the office to retrieve the satellite phone, I paused for a moment to pick up and examine one of the weapons once again. I checked the chamber and then sighted in on a stack of ammunition cans across the room. I liked the way it felt.

This was the team's primary weapon, the H&K 416 carbine. Grady and I had considered various exotic weapons before deciding that time was too short and that the team would be better served by a weapon familiar to most, and easy to master for those who came to it fresh. The H&K amply fulfilled this requirement. We'd fitted Aimpoint sights, chosen for their ruggedness and their compatibility with night vision devices. Combined with the state-of-the-art night vision goggles we had a night vision and night shooting capability that equaled most military special operations units.

We also had equipped the weapons with sound suppressors. This would not completely eliminate the sound of a round being fired— that only happens in the movies—but it would significantly reduce the muzzle blast, leaving only the crack of the supersonic 5.56mm rounds as a distinct noise signature. Grady had insisted on this as a means of ensuring that the sound of an unsuppressed weapon would not warn an alert adversary. He'd also specified that at least a couple of the 416s be equipped with a 40mm grenade launcher. Instead of being a separate weapon, it attached under the barrel of the 416, and operated a bit like a single-shot, break action shotgun. With this arrangement, the gunner didn't need a backup weapon. He could lob grenades or spit 5.56mm rounds depending on the target requirement.

In addition to these weapons, Grady had also selected a couple of short-barreled Ultimax light machine guns with similar sight and a heavier sniper rifle in .338 Lapua Magnum. These were supplemented by a Swedish-built Carl Gustaf shoulder-fired anti-tank missile launcher, similar to, but better than, the U.S. Army's AT-4. This was a gift from Parks, who'd cadged it from one of his mysterious sources. If the mission went as planned, the team would need the sniper rifle only briefly, and the Carl Gustaf not at all. The guards didn't have any armored personnel carriers, the militia responders drove Toyota HiLux pickup trucks with DShK 12.7mm machine guns mounted in the truck bed—classic "technicals," nasty firepower, but soft-skinned. The helicopter that the lab used for tests was normally hangared twenty miles away at the railhead. If we got in hard and fast, as planned, it wouldn't ever come into play.

I returned the 416 to the rack and went back into the office, made my call to the ship, and then decided to go out to the range. It was still dark outside. From the beginning, we'd turned everyone's body clock around; since the mission would be at night, we trained at night, often continuing until well past dawn. I put on my rain gear, turned out the light, and started along the greasy slick path to the range, wishing that I'd thought to draw one of the spare sets of night vision goggles from the armory, or at least had remembered to bring a flashlight.

Every time I approached the range while the team was shooting I got the strangest feeling. For almost all my life I've been around firing ranges, and they are always loud, but not our range, not with the team's suppressed weapons. Moreover, since all our range work was conducted at night, using only night-vision equipment, there wasn't much to see until one reached the firing line itself. And even then, the entire exercise remained a kind of shadow play.

Finally, Grady was satisfied and decided to call it a night. The team formed column and started up the small hill that separated the range from our base camp. I fell in at the end of the column, my head down, planting my feet gingerly in the sloppy footing. We were about a third of the way up the hill when the column abruptly halted. I heard shouts, curses, from up ahead. A flashlight flared at the middle of the column. I hurried forward as fast as I could climb. When I reached the source of the commotion I saw a figure lying in the mud, but I couldn't see who it was. Grady leaned over, shining the flashlight at the figure's leg, next to which Jerry Wolsey crouched. Lorayne and Smitty appeared to be helping. Two other team members were rushing up the trail to the team house while the others tried to spread their ponchos to form a makeshift shelter.

By the faint illumination of the flashlight's beam I recognized the figure on the ground as Ronnie Banks. I could see that he was in great pain; his lips clenched and his eyes wide and darting. Jerry, our trained EMT, had already reached Ronnie's side. He looked up at Grady.

"It's broke, boss. No fucking way it's not broke. I just don't know how bad."

"Leg?"

"Ankle. He's really fucked it up good."

"Shit."

Ronnie moaned softly. Jerry took his hand. "I'm sorry as all hell, partner. We'll get you up and out of this shit as soon as they get back with the stretcher. Better this way. If we try any other way of getting you up the hill in this goo, we'll probably drop you and fuck you up even worse."

Grady handed the flashlight to Jean-Paul, stripped off his own poncho, and wrapped Ronnie as comfortably as possible under the circumstances. Just then Kip and Lem materialized out of the darkness up above with a stretcher. They must have run all the way to camp and back, and I wondered that neither one of them had slipped and fallen. Under Jerry's supervision, the team gently placed Ronnie on the stretcher and Kip, Tommy, Kees, and Smitty each took one of the corners. Everyone else helped by sharing out the stretcher-bearer's weapons and equipment loads. At the top of the hill we found Dito, and Moira waiting, the lights on in our little mess hall, a table situated directly under one of the overhead lights. Ronnie was placed on the table while Jerry ran to get his medical kit from the team house. This was the back-up kit. The one that would go on the mission was untouchable, but it was identical in every respect, a fully equipped Special Forces field medical kit that would support virtually every procedure short of major surgery. Jerry looked at the crowd that had gathered, told Kees, Colin, and Lem, who each had some field medical training that he wanted them to stay, and then shooed everyone else out. It was already painfully clear that, after this initial treatment, we would have to make arrangements with the locals to take care of Ronnie and see to his safe return to the U.S. I couldn't help but ponder the irony; we'd bent over backwards to ensure that no one on the team was lost to Covid, and now we'd lost a critical player to the most prosaic of stupid accidents.

Grady dispersed the rest of the team to their cabins, and signaled for me and Peter and Kip to follow him into the small office we'd set up in the team house. Inside we silently went about the business of making ourselves dry and warm. Finally, we sat down around the table, coffee in front of us, no longer able to avoid the urgent business at hand.

Grady broke the silence. "We're fucked."

His pronouncement brought a gloomy chorus of assent.

"I'm so fucking stupid. I should have called things earlier."

"No, Grady," responded Kip. "Not stupid. We're trying to get a team ready. We can't call training on account of rain."

"Kip's right," said Peter. "Besides, we have no time for spilt milk."

We all looked at each other.

Finally, I said, "We always figured that twelve was the minimum."

"And we were fucking right," said Grady. "It's always been a stretch, even with twelve."

For the next half-hour we wrestled with the tactical plan, trying to convince ourselves that it would work with a team of eleven. But each time we came back to the simple inescapable truth: the whole concept had been built around dividing the team into six task teams, each with two members. To go with eleven meant assigning one task to a single individual. It *could*, of course, be done, but that would violate a principle we all firmly believed was vital, namely, not leaving anyone without backup. Worse, it also meant that, if the one individual went down, a task might go undone, and that would place the entire team and its mission in jeopardy.

"We simply have to find another team member," said Peter.

"How?" asked Grady. "It was hard enough to come up with twelve good people in the first place."

"Is there anyone we can think of?" Kip asked.

We considered this.

"Never mind that we have no candidates," said Peter. "The important thing is that we have no time."

"Then it's eleven or no fucking mission," said Grady.

And then I said it. "I can do it."

"Aw, shit, Harry."

Kip and Peter both eyed me speculatively.

"No, I mean it. I can do it. I did well enough when we were back at Quinlan's Mill, and, if all goes well, our time at the target won't be much longer than that. I know every piece of the plan. I can still jump. The only thing I might struggle with is the hump from the DZ, but even that's not a really long haul." And even as I said my piece, I knew that it was the only answer, and it was the right answer. But I wanted Grady to know it, in his heart, where it counted. I needed his confidence because, in the end, I knew that he'd need to have confidence in me.

Peter spoke up. "I think Harry's offered us the solution. He's right. If the plan goes right, it will be one of the least physically demanding raids in the history of special operations. There's no long overland hike to the target area, not a lot of ground to cover at the target. And Harry's still a good shot."

And now Kip weighed in. "And the Major knows what it's like to be shot at, and how to hold it together when things turn to shit, and that's more than we're sure of with some of these kids."

Grady looked back and forth from one of us to the other. I knew he was feeling the responsibility of the decision, knew that when I'd made him the team lead I'd also made him an implicit promise not to overrule him about anything related to the operation on the ground. It was his call, and it had come down to taking along a deficient team member, who was old slow, and had not done all the training, or going shorthanded, or pronouncing the mission undoable. Finally, he said, "You all keep saying 'If everything goes right?' What happens if things really turn to shit, and we have to hump out of there hard and fast? What happens if you can't keep up?"

"Then leave me behind, Grady. I'd never ask for anything else."

"Goddamnit, Harry, there's no fucking way. Look, it's not that I don't think you'll hold your end up. That's not it at all. But I couldn't leave you behind."

"We've already talked about it with the whole team. Everybody knows that we'll try to get people out, but that medevac isn't part of the equation. I'm not taking anything on that I haven't asked the rest of you to do."

"Dammit, Harry, that's not what I mean. Listen to me, you old bastard. When the shoe was on the other fucking foot, you didn't leave me. You threw my young ass over your shoulder and hauled me through the fucking desert for two fucking klicks, all the way to the extraction point. And you think that I could leave your sorry old ass behind." He looked straight at me, real pain in his expression. "I can lead this fucking team, I can carry what I need to carry, but I don't think I've got enough extra anymore to carry you out like that. I think I'm just too fucking old myself."

Kip stepped forward, put his hand on Grady's shoulder. "You wouldn't have to do it by yourself."

It had all gotten to be a bit too much for Peter.

"What is it you Yanks call one of these, a Hallmark moment? Might I remind one and all that, as Grady put it a while ago, 'we've got no fucking time for this.' We have to decide, now. All Harry has to do to get out is jog a few hundred yards, ride a rubber boat, and fly out on the bloody airplane. Harry, I know that Grady's your team leader, but this is your party. You need to decide."

"Grady?"

"Well, hell. If something happens to the plane, if we have to go through the escape-and-evasion drill, then we're probably fucked anyway. We're gonna be right in the middle of fucking Wiangara."

"Right—so it really makes no difference, does it?" responded Peter.

"Grady," I said, "I don't like it either. I never pictured myself doing anything like this ever again. It scares me. I mean, going in doesn't scare me, no more than it should, but it scares me that I might take this on, and then something would give out, some brittle old bone would break, something would let go inside me, maybe, and I'd let you all down. But that could happen even to the kids. It happened to Ronnie tonight." After a pause I said, "It's the only way."

He hesitated before speaking.

"All right, Harry—you win. But, hey, if you get your skinny old ass busted, don't count on fucking Medicare to fix it."

CHAPTER 12

I'VE BEEN AROUND small boats for as long as I can remember, and I can honestly say that I've never been seasick. But the motion of the Catalina as Moira held it alongside the *Vaanu* for refueling was like nothing I had ever encountered. The up-and-down chop was sharp enough to produce that light-stomached feeling that comes when the bottom drops out on a roller coaster. There was a gentler side-to-side sway, but this too was interrupted by sudden jerks as Moira used the little Lycoming turboprop on the outward wing to keep the Catalina from drifting too far aft of the midships fueling station. After only a few minutes I felt the first twinges of nausea, a feeling made worse by the stink of aviation fuel that hung in the air. I tried closing my eyes, but that only made things worse. I took no consolation in seeing that Lorayne and Jerry Wolsey also looked a bit green. Then came the sounds of relief: the metallic clatter and shouts from the small boat under our starboard wing as the refueling crew detached the hose coupling and the boom operator swung the hose back aboard ship.

Moira's voice came over the intercom, telling us to prepare for takeoff. Then came the firing of the outboard Cyclone, then the inboard Cyclone and the second Lycoming, and now all four engines were running strong, and we edged away from the side of the *Vaanu*. We picked up speed slowly, the hull pounding against the waves. And precisely at that moment I recognized the theme song from *The Magnificent Seven* blaring over the intercom from Moira's music player in the cockpit. Now we were moving faster as the hull began planing smoothly on top of the water, and then came a sudden smoothness as we became airborne, if only by a few feet. Soon the music died away and my stomach started to settle. I caught Peter's eye and saw him mouth the words "Dam Busters." He'd realized more quickly than I, the feeling behind Moira's musical exuberance. This was her moment, her starring role as Wing Commander Guy Gibson in *The Dambusters*, her turn as Van Johnson in *Thirty Seconds Over Tokyo*, her emancipation from all those who'd dismissed her as merely a charter pilot or worse, a drug flyer.

Unlike the typical airliner takeoff, we experienced virtually no sensation of climbing, largely because we did no climbing to speak of. Moira inched the Catalina up to an altitude of roughly one hundred and fifty feet and then locked it in. Our purpose, of course, was to stay below the detection threshold of surface-based radars, a necessary stratagem, but one that prevented us from seeking a smooth cruising altitude. Still, even though our first few minutes in the air were bumpy, my stomach felt much better. With our water landing and takeoff behind us, I hoped that the most eventful part of the flight was over. Regardless, I could do little more now than enjoy the ride, so I decided to do precisely that. I unbuckled my seatbelt and started forward, as if headed for the flight deck. But I stopped short in what had once been the space shared by the flight engineer and a small galley, where I reached up to open a small hatch. Then I pulled myself up through the opening in the overhead into the flight engineer's observation compartment, nestled in the pylon that supported the huge wing. No one else on the team had evinced the slightest interest in this space on any of our test or training flights. I suspected that some still didn't know that the tiny compartment existed. But I had gravitated to it early on, and now thought of it almost as my own private space. I made myself as comfortable as possible in the bare metal seat of the compartment. Looking outside I could see nothing but dull gray sky over the dark steel blue of the ocean's surface, not exactly the conditions for an enjoyable day at the beach, but perfect for our purposes.

When I'd first discovered the engineer's compartment, I'd been surprised at its roominess. Moira explained to me that in the original Catalinas, the flight engineer had actually played an important role in managing the engines, and the compartment had contained several banks of controls and gauges. The Bird Conversion that we were flying was controlled entirely from the cockpit in the manner of all modern aircraft, making these items superfluous. Removing the equipment had created a generously sized compartment. When we'd finished the load plan for the mission, it became evident that we had no need of this extra space. Since we would be well within our load limits for the operation, even packing the four extra H&K carbines, along with the spare boxes of 5.56mm ammunition that we hadn't used on the range. Little did I suspect then just how important those weapons would become.

I had also decided that we had enough takeoff reserve to allow me to stow a personal item. I reached underneath the engineer's seat and retrieved the tiny iPod I'd placed there before takeoff. Instead of using the foam-tipped headphones that came with the unit, I'd modified a large set of earmuff type phones to use instead—this did a very nice job of shutting out the noise of the big Wright Cyclones a couple of meters from my head. I spun the selector, considered the Edith Piaf collection, but decided that it was a night for looking forward, not back. I selected a Loreena McKennitt album, punched "play," took my paperback book out of my pocket, and started to read. When my eyes grew heavy, I set the book aside, closed my eyes, and drifted for a little while. When I opened my eyes again it was noticeably darker. This was mainly due to the dense cloud cover, which gave us the equivalent of a moonless night. No ships or other aircraft in sight. No running lights of our own, no interior lights save those in the windowless kitchen and bunk compartments. No lights from the cockpit just ahead, below my little cubbyhole. Wrapped in the low cloud, I could just barely make out the engines through the portholes on either side. I changed tracks and floated sightlessly toward the coast of Tanzania with Borodin's "The Steppes of Central Asia" reverberating through my head.

Suddenly I became conscious of a change in the pitch of the engines and of the lengthy shallow turn we were making to port; one couldn't make sharp turns in such a big aircraft at this low altitude without running the risk of digging a wingtip into the sea. As we completed the turn and leveled off, I looked out to starboard. Through a break in the clouds I could see, faintly, what appeared to be the running lights of a ship.

We were, I knew, not using our active radars. Instead we relied on a combination of inertial navigation and GPS, with a little bit of dead reckoning thrown in. There's no point in trying to be stealthy while radiating a big active radar signature. Moira and Dito had probably picked up the ship's radar emanations with our passive radar detectors, large military versions of the devices used by motorists to detect police radar. For a moment I wondered if our mask of invisibility had been somehow penetrated. Still, there was no point in worrying about it. If we'd been detected, I could do nothing about it, and we'd already discounted the risk of being called to account by a random freighter.

I went back to my music. But now I was wide-awake and restless, wondering how the rest of the team was doing. I decided to abandon my solitary perch. The contrast between the darkness above and the brightly lit galley was like the sensation one experiences when stepping out of a dimly lit bar at lunchtime into bright afternoon sunshine. At first glance the two figures at the tiny counter next to the stove appeared scarcely more distinct than silhouettes. But it took no more than a few seconds for my eyes to adjust sufficiently to recognize Grady and Peter industriously brewing coffee and piling up sandwiches on a big aluminum platter to pass out to the team.

I left them at their labors and moved forward to into the old radio and navigation compartment. This space, once filled with electronic equipment, now served as one of the two main personnel areas. Jean-Paul, Tommy, Colin, Smitty, and Jerry occupied five of the six seats. I visited with them briefly, then pushed through the forward door, where Lem had wedged himself between Moira and Dito, just behind the flight deck. They were busily discussing the subtleties of flying a four-engine aircraft. Lem had a fixed-wing single engine certification in addition to his various rotary-wing tickets, and he was trying to learn as much as possible about flying the Catalina. I squeezed up alongside him. Moira and Dito were illuminated only by the light from the monitor of the thermal imaging system and the fainter glow from the instruments. Both appeared to be relaxed; at this point the autopilot was doing most of the work.

"Feet dry in about five minutes, Harry," said Moira. "We're right on schedule, everything's running smoothly, and fuel consumption is right as predicted. Dull as dishwater."

"But it may get a bit more interesting as we close in on the coast." This was Dito. From the smile on his face I could tell that he was looking forward to the 'more interesting' bits to come.

"We're also going to run into some weather about a half-hour inland," said Moira. "There's just enough time for everybody to get a bite to eat, stretch a bit, and take a leak before securing everything and strapping in again."

Kip came forward with the coffee and sandwiches, which required Lem and me to give up our place so that he could serve Moira and Dito. Once this was done, I allowed Lem to resume his multi-engine orientation while I followed Kip back aft. As I passed through the galley, I took a couple of roast beef sandwiches and a big Styrofoam cup of coffee, which was delicious. The superb coffee we owed to Moira, who had had over-ridden Grady's coffee procurement plans with the tart remark that "Starbucks Breakfast Blend weighs no more than some miserable GI coffee." I ate standing as I talked with Grady, while Kip took the remaining coffee and sandwiches aft.

Grady spread his hands expansively and remarked, "Beats the hell out of a C-130, don't it?"

I found it easy to agree. Small as it was by modern day standards, it was still a very large aircraft for carrying twelve passengers, even passengers with much more than two suitcases worth of lethal baggage. Much better than a C-130 full of paratroopers, or even a C-17. This was the Business Class version of going to war.

Well-fed and nicely warmed, I moved aft to the second personnel compartment, what had once been a space for four bunk beds—in its original patrol configuration—the Catalina had been meant to stay aloft the better part of eighteen hours and had been designed with the need for crew naps in mind. Now this compartment housed four seats and a set of equipment stowage racks, as well as the door that would serve as our parachute exit. To my great surprise, the compartment was empty save for Peter, who was sound asleep. I pushed on back to the last major compartment, ducking my head as the fuselage started to taper back toward the tail. This was the former waist gunners' compartment. The huge Plexiglas gun blisters had been faired over, and the .50 caliber mounts removed. Now it served as equipment storage and as a place where, perched on bags of gear, Kip, Lorayne, and Kees were trying to start a game of cards.

"Play Hearts, Major?" asked Kip. "I was just about to start forward looking for a fourth."

"I'm rusty, but I think so." I found myself a place to sit. "Why back here?"

"The seats up there aren't right for card playing," answered Lorayne.

"Well, we've really got no time," I said, explaining what Moira and Dito had reported about the inland weather. We conversed pleasantly enough as we took our proper seats, despite the heavy drone of the engines in the background. Lorayne regaled us, improbably, with stories of babysitting, and Kip and I swapped tales of our various misadventures, stories we'd shared many times before, but new, of course, to Kees and Lorayne. Although he seemed to be enjoying himself, Kees held back, as he had since the moment he'd arrived. At first, I'd taken this as stereotypical Dutch phlegm, but, when I commented on this to Peter, he supplied a more likely reason. Kees had begun his military career as an enlistee in the Dutch regular army, and had been one of the soldiers present in Srebrenica in 1995, ordered by his feckless commanders to stand by as Serb forces massacred thousands of Bosnian Muslims. He'd left the army in disgust at the end of his enlistment and had joined the Royal Dutch Marines for a three-year hitch because, in his own words, they were the only part of the Dutch forces with an ounce of self-respect. But even that hadn't been enough, and he'd moved on to the French Foreign Legion. I'd worried that he'd bottled too much up inside, and was pleased that, however stiffly, he could laugh along with the rest of us and even managed an awkward sally at teasing Lorayne about her tobacco habit. I decided that I had no cause for concern.

We'd just gotten settled when Moira gave us the 'buckle up' warning over the intercom. I promptly fell asleep, continuing soundly until shaken awake by Kip with word that the time had come to harness up and get ready. The others had practiced this evolution several times, but I hadn't had a chance to jump with the team. Still, there wasn't much mystery involved in getting into my gear, and Grady had, over my protests, re-distributed the loads so that I wouldn't have to deploy a leg bag. My relative lack of jumps with the team also caused him to make a further adjustment. Although the Catalina was roomy, it had never been intended as a parachuting platform. The jump sequence that we'd worked out required the first six to form a row in the jump compartment, while the others worked their way single file from the compartments forward. With practice this had proven to be acceptably fast, but, since I'd missed all of this, Grady decided that I'd better not simply take Ronnie's accustomed place. Instead he told me I'd be first out the door, no maneuvering inside the aircraft required. And so, I found myself standing there, hands hooked outside—never inside—the open door, waiting to hear the word—we had no 'red light, green light' routine—through my radio headset. I felt Moira throttle back sharply and knew we were on the verge, and then Grady's 'Go,' and I hurled myself out the door.

The jerk of the chute was abrupt, but not sharp, nothing like the military chutes of old. I looked up and checked the canopy, running through the checklist litany that goes with the new steerable chutes: "Is it big, is it square, is it stable?" By the green-tinted light of the NV goggles it was clearly all three. I reached up and cleared the brake lines from the risers and turned into the wind. If Moira had dropped us correctly, the site would be off to my left. And sure enough, although I was already too low to see the site itself, I could see the glow of lights against the sky, like a small city on a distant horizon. I did a rough count of the other chutes around me, and then decided to relax.

No matter how many times one has made a parachute jump, the innate human resistance to jumping from great heights makes the act both a leap of faith and a tremendous adrenaline rush. And then, in the moment when the chute is right, one feels a pervasive inner peace. I've never meditated in the Eastern manner, but I cannot imagine a greater tranquility than that which comes from floating under a parachute. But this tranquility passes quickly as the ground rushes up at you. Landings at night can be treacherous, even with night vision goggles, and the possibility of a hot DZ also has a way of undermining tranquility. A jumper is horribly vulnerable to ground fire as he floats to earth. But, as I passed over the DZ and turned back against the wind for my final approach—one flies these seven-cell chutes like a glider—I saw no evidence of a hostile reception committee. Then, close to the ground, the illusion of motionlessness was replaced with a sense of sudden acceleration. I tugged hard on the brake lines, stalling the chute at the perfect moment to achieve a soft stand-up. I ran into my chute, pressing out the remaining air before it could tug me off my feet, bundling the fabric against my chest, and then pulling the release to separate it from my parachute harness. Others were now landing, and, looking up at the sky, I saw the rest of the team close behind. I headed toward the tree line. I stripped out of the parachute harness and, taking the small entrenching tool we carried expressly for this purpose, proceeded to quickly bury my parachute and jump gear in the soft turf. I saw several of the others doing the same, and then we went back out onto the DZ to round up the gear that had been dropped in two metal containers which had been slung, one on each side, from the former bomb shackles under each wing.

Peter was already counting noses and directing traffic when I linked up, and the others had evidently been quicker to complete their concealment chores. Perimeter security was being established, Kees and Smitty were stripping gear out of the equipment containers so that they, too, could be hidden, while Kip and Lem busied themselves assembling the nifty lightweight aluminum cart we'd included to help us with the heaviest gear. We waited roughly a half-hour, scanning the wooded hillsides and the clearing to make sure no one was moving around us. In the meantime, Peter supervised the distribution of equipment. The big sniper rifle was loaded on the cart, with Peter's electronic bag of tricks, and the little lightweight inflatable boats. They didn't need to be sturdy as we'd only use them once. Colin and Lem were the 'mules' assigned to the cart. Smitty, the fittest of us all, hefted the Carl Gustaf anti-armor rocket launcher with its several reloads. Kip carried the other sniper rifle. Kees collected the Ultimax machine gun, Jerry the medical kit. Lem took charge of the drone package, while I drew the little Barr and Stroud thermal-imaging camera, probably the lightest burden. Virtually everyone was assigned a load of explosives; Grady and Lorayne each carried duplicate sets of the custom-crafted main demolition packages.

We accomplished all this without a word being spoken, not hard after having practiced the evolution at least a dozen times. Once the equipment had been issued, Grady gave us a hand signal, and we formed up in a patrol column with Tommy on the point. He had established himself from the very beginning as the best trailblazer for this kind of terrain. Kees followed with the Ultimax, ready to lay down heavy covering fire if Tommy ran into trouble. Kip followed, then Grady, then Lorayne. I took my place behind Lorayne, allowed her about a five-pace lead, and then started up the hill. Behind me I heard the muffled creak of the cart wheels.

Although the slope was not very steep, the going was difficult from the beginning. We had to force our way through a dense stand of trees and patches of bamboo that marked the fact that we were up in the central African highlands; even when we reached something that resembled a trail, we found it badly overgrown and littered with deadfalls. The muttered curses from down the trail told me that Colin and Lem were having a terrible time with the cart. I was grateful for the night-vision goggles; without them, we would run a greater risk of broken bones. It still wasn't easy. Unlike earlier generations of night-vision equipment, these goggles were set up to allow the wearer to glance away from the lens, downward and to the side, without the constant head and neck movement otherwise needed to compensate for the lack of peripheral vision through the night lens. But that only worked when there was enough ambient light, a full moon for example, to allow some measure of unassisted visibility. We'd timed the jump to coincide with the last of the moon, and now the ambient light was fading. Walking safely thus meant turning on the infrared "flashlight" as we used the night lens to watch the ground, making exaggerated head movements to clearly see, with the aid of the lens, what was going on at one's feet or to the side.

The major nuisance, however, had nothing to do with the darkness. Mosquitoes and flies and no-see-ums were everywhere. I'd spent enough time on the ground in this part of the world to know this would be a problem. Not expecting the enemy to patrol this far away from the scientific compound, we'd decided to risk the scent of a strong insect repellent, something that we'd otherwise have been loathe to do. Now I was wondering if the repellent we'd chosen was strong enough. Despite the slight chill in the air, I'd already begun to perspire, and the mixture of sweat and insect repellent made my skin feel greasy. I was glad that Tommy and Kees were making frequent stops to look and listen. Not expecting enemy patrols was one thing, but being careless was something else, and besides, the pace was scarcely taxing.

Soon the trees and undergrowth began to thin. This improvement, unfortunately, coincided with the trail becoming steeper. I was grateful to be carrying a lighter load than the others were and fearful that it might not be light enough. Even though my breathing was already somewhat labored, I silently vowed that I'd drop dead before asking for help. With each step I reminded myself that we had only a short distance to cover, that soon all this would be over. I reminded myself, too, that others were wrestling with substantially greater burdens. From time to time I heard scraping sounds when the awkward loads hung up on outcroppings of rock.

I cursed being old, cursed the fact that a once easy pull had now become a major effort. Over and over I repeated to myself the old commando and Ranger saying, "It's all in the mind and the heart." But by the time an hour had passed, I knew it was in the muscles and the joints as well. Fortunately, just when I thought that I could go no further, Grady called a halt. We were approaching the point where we'd cross the crest of the ridge. Grady wanted to scout the other side before the team went across. In days gone by I would've stayed on my feet, relaxing from the exertions of the climb without allowing my muscles to tighten. But now I simply sank to the ground in the first comfortable spot.

"Okay, there, Hair Doctor?" Lorayne whispered the question from her position alongside me.

"Fine, thanks," I replied. But it took virtually the entire fifteen-minute break for me to recover a regular, easy breathing rhythm. So much for old man's vanity, so much for the illusion that being in good shape 'for 70' was the same as actually being in good shape. At that particular moment I was deeply discouraged.

But that, as it turned out, was the low point. Once we resumed our climb, I found that I could maintain pace more easily. Crossing the ridgeline put us first upon a gentle downhill and then upon the relatively level ground of the saddle that connected the ridge we were on with the lower just above the objective. Crossing the ridgeline also gave us a brief adrenaline rush, since it gave us our first view of the facility, during the few minutes before we descended below the military crest of the intervening lower ridge.

The facility was brightly lit, so bright, in fact that I flipped up my night-vision goggles and took my compact binoculars from my cargo pocket for a brief closer look. The view seemed almost surreal, at once totally familiar—for it looked just as I'd expected from hours of studying maps, models, and aerial photographs—and totally alien. I'd never really expected to see it, and now I had only to look to see it spread out below me, only a couple of klicks away.

Now it was all downhill, quite literally so, and my spirits soared. On this side of the ridge we moved even more carefully, even more slowly. Given the thick cover we'd be very hard to see, but sound carries a long way on a crisp, clear night. In any event, I appreciated the slow pace. I concentrated on small things: making sure that I kept contact with Lorayne, placing my feet carefully to avoid snapping a twig or, worse, twisting an ankle. Every ten or fifteen meters we'd stop to allow Tommy to get his bearings, to look and listen. Each brief pause served as a reminder that we were now in 'Indian Country,' but try as I might I found it hard to believe in the possibility of a surprise hostile encounter. For me it had become an article of faith that the lab's protective force wouldn't expect an attack.

Around 0300 hours we took a longer break. At first, I wondered why, then I realized that we'd reached the general vicinity of the location we'd identified as our lying-up point. On the map it had simply been an "X" on a contour line. Even our superb one-meter resolution satellite photos did not penetrate the heavy overhead forest cover. Now we had to wait for Tommy and Grady to decide precisely where we'd go to ground to wait through the coming day. After several minutes Lorayne started forward again, and I fell in behind. But I'd scarcely taken a dozen steps when Grady's form loomed out of the darkness at trailside. He held up a hand, palm outstretched, as I drew alongside.

"How's it going?" he asked.

"Good enough."

"You don't look half bad for an old Army fart."

"Semper Fi, asshole."

He gestured toward the right of the trail.

"There's a space over there, maybe thirty feet off the trail, a couple of downed trees resting on a little rock outcropping. Good overhead screening, room for about eight of us. That works cause I'm gonna have one team tucked in near the crest, watching the camp, and another watching our back trail. We'll rotate just like we planned. You and Lorayne will be third shift, so you've got eight hours. Remember, Tommy and Colin and Lem have to go ahead now while we've still got the darkness and drop off the boats. They won't be pulling a shift. We won't risk putting the drone in the air until just before going in tomorrow night."

"Okay, good."

What he'd just said was nothing more than what we'd planned over the last several days, as we worked out the fine details of the operation. I went over to where the others were already spreading groundsheets. The chance to divest oneself of tactical vest and day pack, of weapons and helmet, to lie back and stretch one's legs represented no small measure of comfort. I took my boots off, massaged my feet, and then put the boots back on, leaving the laces loose. I scanned the faces of the others, decided that no one else looked as tired as I felt, and then decided that it really didn't matter.

I fished around in my pants pocket for a little drawstring velvet bag and took from it an unadorned black beaded rosary, my tactical rosary, as I'd come to think of it. I wasn't raised a Catholic, but a Catholic chaplain had helped me survive a bad time in El Salvador in the 1980s, and a Catholic girlfriend led me all the way to conversion. I'm not a very good Catholic. Whenever the choir sings "O come Emanuel" I can't help but think about Sylvia Kristel orgasming her way through the movie *Emmanuelle*. Appropriate, perhaps, for a man who, in Grady's words, "was led by his dick to the church." I'm not sure what I believe any more, but I find an odd comfort in saying the rosary. By the time I finished saying a decade, I was relaxed and ready for sleep.

As it turned out I slept for nearly four hours, awakening only as the second shift roused itself to relieve the first. I sat up and looked around, trying to take in the sharply different picture that daylight revealed. In our shaded and sheltered location, the sun's rays penetrated unevenly, creating a dappled pattern of light and dark. Next to me Lorayne lay still asleep. Colin and Tommy and Lem, who'd made the trip to the riverbank with the rubber boats, had returned and were now sleeping. Peter and Kees were quietly checking one of the pieces of electronic gear. Smitty was preparing a meal. I decided that I was hungry enough to do likewise.

We'd each only jumped with one MRE, and one of the clever new "First Strike" rations. With plenty to eat before jumping, and the prospect of plenty more once we returned to the plane, it had seemed senseless to carry a lot of food with us. Yet we'd be on the ground for more than a day, too long to go without eating something. After creeping a few meters downslope to relieve myself, I returned to our "camp," sat down with my back resting against a tree, and fished out my MRE from my little daypack. I glanced down at the brown plastic package, noting the "menu no. 17, maple pork sausage patty" stenciled in black on the side. I tore open the package, spilling the contents into the space on the groundsheet defined by the vee of my legs. A sausage patty, maple muffin top, a cracker pack, peanut butter, maple syrup, smoked almonds," plus "Accessory Packet A," with such additional goodies as coffee, creamer, sugar, salt, and toilet paper. MREs represent a real improvement over the old "Lurps" and C-rations, particularly the newer versions. I still missed the canned fruit in the old C-rats, though not the 'ham and motherfuckers.' I set the sausage patty, the muffin, the syrup, and the coffee to one side, along with the heater pack. The other items I stuffed back into the brown package as a snack for later. As I did so, a small gray-green packet caught my attention. The black print on the package said "beverage base powder," and the flavor was listed as "grape." I read the directions to myself: "Dissolve contents of the 34-gram envelope in 12 ounces of cold water. Allow water just chemically purified to stand 30 minutes before adding beverage powder."

I regarded the little packet with immense pleasure, for it brought back special memories. What the army calls "beverage base powder" is a jazzed-up version of what the rest of the world knows as "Kool-Aid." In my experience only two categories of people truly appreciate Kool-Aid, seven-year-old kids and Vietnam vets. I can't claim any special insight into the tastes of seven-year-olds, but I know why vets treasure Kool-Aid. The only safe drink in the field was chemically treated water, which tastes lousy. But Kool-Aid did a wonderful job of masking the chemical taste and thus was a highly valued commodity among line troops in Vietnam. Unfortunately, it was hard to come by. I still have warm memories of a sergeant named Ross, who shared with me the packets sent by his girlfriend, a sweet young woman who kept sending me Kool-Aid, even for months after Ross was killed. Now the army included a generic version of Kool-Aid in every ration packet, testimony that, for once, the quartermaster weenies had gotten something right.

I took out the heating element pouch, slit it open with my pocket-knife, and placed the sausage patty and the muffin pouch inside. After adding a little water from my CamelBak, I propped up the pouch so the water couldn't spill out. In almost no time the chemical interaction with the water made the heating element warm, then hot. In roughly fifteen minutes I'd have a meal almost too hot for the tongue, all done without an open flame. While the main course was heating, I mixed myself a cup of grape-flavored "beverage base powder," and sipped it while I waited for my meal. Using the plastic spoon provided in the ration, I ate straight out of the pouch. A mess kit had seemed a waste of space and weight. I alternated bites of meat with potato sticks, which I'd enlivened by sprinkling them with Tabasco sauce from the miniature bottle supplied with the ration. Next, I used the still hot heating element to heat water for coffee. When I finally finished I tidied up and sat back against the base of a tree. All I lacked was a finger of whiskey and one of those nice little Davidoff cigars.

I looked around at the others, some eating some sleeping, some checking equipment. Oddly enough, no one had uttered a single whisper. Part of this was well-ingrained noise discipline, but the major part, I think, was the general need for introspection. We'd shared the hard work of the week on Reunion, we'd laughed and talked about all manner of things, being by turns supportive and abusive. That was all done. Now only the job itself remained.

I relaxed, napped again until the time came for the next shift change. Lorayne and I drew the back-trail watch. We settled into position, taking turns surveying our area of responsibility, trying to stay alert against a sudden surprise, however unlikely. I hoped that our adversaries across the way were similarly afflicted by the tedium of standing watch where nothing had ever happened, at least until tonight.

My thoughts drifted to Moira and Dito. I assumed, as we all did, that they'd landed successfully and had been waiting for us throughout the day. During planning Grady had suggested a brief exchange of radio messages between the plane and the team. Peter and I had rejected this, with Peter remarking "they'll either be there or they won't—knowing beforehand butters no parsnips." The absence of communications activity was one of the most surreal aspects of this entire mission. Normally an operation such as this would have required repeated coordination with different elements and the all-important regular situation reports to higher headquarters. But the only higher echelon this time was me, and there was no one out there who could have helped if help was called for. So, we had dispensed with everything but the most basic satellite phone communication, enough to connect us to Moira, to the ship, and, through them, to the intel link provided by Parks. We'd dispensed with the burst transmitters and all the other high-tech gadgets that only mattered when they provided a link to reinforcements or air support. One could have, in fact, felt a bit lonely, but the absence of long-distance micro-management more than compensated for the feeling.

Since we were the last shift, we weren't waiting to be relieved. Instead, when our time on station elapsed we simply fell back to the lying up point. Grady circled up the entire team and did a quick "any questions" final review of the plan. This took, perhaps, five minutes. Then we gathered our various burdens and moved out.

Although it was still twilight we moved fairly quickly, taking advantage of a shallow ravine that shielded us from the facility. Our pace slowed as we climbed out of the ravine and crossed the last sky-line on our path to the site. The sun was setting dead ahead, which eliminated the risk of our being backlit, not that we would allow ourselves to be silhouetted against the sky. Beyond the crest we advanced at a patrol pace, roughly three hundred meters per hour, an absolutely glacial pace to anyone save veteran special operators. But this is what you do if you must not be seen or heard—or surprised.

Part of me rued the fact that we were making our final approach in daylight, but another part of me was less unhappy, since the modest light that filtered through the evergreen canopy permitted much more surefooted movement. Relying on night vision is better than coping with darkness, but I'd already grown tired of the grainy, green-tinted view. It begins to feel like you're looking at the world through the side of a dirty aquarium.

We were treated to repeated glimpses of the target facility as we advanced. We were now close enough to watch, with the unaided eye, as the civilian lab workers and brown-uniformed guards scurried among the buildings. The civilian workers drifted in clumps of two and three to the security gate, processed out, and then boarded a couple of dingy blue minivans parked alongside the road leading to town. Only the most critical scientific and technical workers—all of them Chinese—actually lived full time inside the lab compound. Business as usual. I was momentarily surprised by this before reminding myself that they had no reason to feel the same keen urgency that we felt.

These glimpses of the facility, however fascinating, were also the source of increased nervous tension. If we could see them, they could see us. Of course, this was unlikely. So close to the Equator, twilight was brief. Although the remnants of the setting sun still filtered into the open spaces between the various lab buildings, this would give way very quickly to darkness. In contrast, we were amidst trees and heavy brush, our gear and faces carefully darkened, our gray-green uniforms blending in with the greens and browns and grays of the hillside. We were like deer on a wooded roadside, almost invisible until we made sudden movements, and this we tried not to do. Ever so slowly, we crept down the hill.

The sun was very low in the sky when we reached the position we had dubbed 'The Overlook.' By crawling out along a small, shelf-like ledge one reached a position with a panoramic overview of the entire facility, with the gatehouse leading into the Controlled Area scarcely three hundred yards away. Peter and Lem had taken up a position alongside the trail, at the point where it passed nearest to the ledge. Here the cart now rested under a camo net, the sniper rifle, the Ultimax, and the rocket launcher off-loaded. As each one of us passed by, we dropped off the various "tools" we were carrying. I was delighted to rid myself of my own little package. Now all we would carry would be our personal weapons and the various explosive charges. As we lightened our loads, we also took a second for a quick handshake with Peter and Lem before moving on. This was it. As we moved down the trail they would crawl into position, dragging the weapons and other gear they would need to support us from above, and, when we saw them again, the job would be done.

Another thirty minutes and we reached Point X-Ray, the "X" Grady and I had marked on the maps so long ago, the point from which we would split up and deploy to our final assault positions. Now, at last, radios were turned on and Grady performed a quick roll call radio check. Now selector switches were eased from "Safe" to "Fire." Now, in the darkness, we waited and prepared ourselves for the assault. Now there was no going back. If by some horrible mischance we were compromised, we'd have nothing left to do but fight.

We nestled at the edge of the tree line, no longer upslope of the facility, but on the same level. From our prone positions we looked up through the chain link fence at buildings rising high, the nearest one, the admin building, little more than eighty meters directly in front of us. To our immediate left were the twin barracks for the guards and the technicians, and the traffic between the various buildings remained heavy as the last off-shift guards strolled from the mess hall in the admin building to the barracks to settle in for the night. Another hundred meters further to the left was the hut that contained the power generator, and, beside it, the wooden gatehouse for the Controlled Area. A similar distance ran the double fence of the more heavily protected Security Area, and, looming large, the Main Laboratory Building. Behind it, blocked from our view, lay our primary objective, Manufacturing and Storage Block. Our journey had started some 12,000 miles away. Now we had fewer than 200 meters to go.

CHAPTER 13

WE LAY THERE together for a tense but uneventful thirty minutes. The number of wanderers out for a late-evening stroll and a smoke faded steadily to zero. The lights had come on inside the barracks, and the sodium-vapor perimeter lights had warmed up from a dull amber to a bright white-orange. Everything appeared normal. Either the guard force had no clue of the impending attack, or we were about to walk into a well-disciplined and carefully orchestrated ambush.

From their perch high above the facility Peter and Lem had just finished putting the drone into the air. They now weighed in with their first report. "No movement outside the fence line." Peter also had a thermal imaging scope, concentrating on the shadowy areas beyond the glare of the perimeter lighting, while Lem kept the drone high above the approach road, watching for potential reinforcements. Minutes later Peter added, "Foot patrol leaving the Security Area gate house, walking toward the lab." This was expected. We'd known from the earliest planning stages that we would have to contend with a roving patrol inside the Security Area.

After a few minutes came a second report. "No movement outside the fence line. The rover is out of view on the south side of the lab building. Lem is sweeping that way."

I was expecting the word from Grady at any moment, yet, when it came, I was still startled.

"Smitty, Colin—go."

Smitty and Kees lay to my immediate left. They rose into a crouch, moved laterally just inside the tree line, and disappeared into the dark undergrowth. I could not hear or see Colin and Tommy, who were on the far right, but I assumed that they had moved out just as quickly. For the rest of us, the waiting continued.

"No movement outside the fence line," said Peter from his over-watch position. "Rover on the north side of the lab. Be careful, Colin."

The north side of the lab was our side, and Colin and Tommy were moving just opposite where the rover was now positioned. Although the bright perimeter lights would enable him to see anyone crossing the clear zone, they also quite effectively blinded him to any activity in the dark shadows outside the perimeter. And Colin and Tommy both moved like ghosts, rapidly, quietly, with scarcely any evidence of motion.

"I've got slow movement, two crawlers, just north of the Con-trolled Area gatehouse." This was Peter again, the voice of our guardian angel. "Is that you, Smitty?"

"Roger," Smitty whispered. Smitty and Kees had left the pro-tective cover of the tree line, crawling through the shadows toward their objective.

"The rover is still north of the lab."

We continued to wait, watching the area immediately to our front. I glanced over at Lorayne lying next to me, propped up on her elbows to get a better view. Despite the helmet and her blackened face, she looked incredibly young, almost like a little boy dressed up to play soldiers. She also seemed utterly at ease, her face relaxed, only the steady movement of the wad of tobacco between her cheek and gum hinted at nervousness.

"No hostile movement outside the fence line," Peter reported. "The rover entered the lab building by the north door."

"Harry, Kip—let's go," said Grady. "Colin, final approach whenever you're ready."

With only a few meters to go, the three remaining teams broke cover in a low crouching run, which exposed them less than a long, slow crawl. Grady and Jerry reached the fence first, Kip and Jean-Paul just behind. Lorayne and I dropped prone in the shadow, just outside the pool of light cast by the perimeter lights. We didn't want too many people clustered by the hole Jerry was cutting in the Controlled Area fence. This took almost no time, and I could see Grady crawling through the hole even as Jerry was stretching back the fence fabric around the cut. Grady had considered it important to be the first one inside. "It's a matter of fucking principle," he'd said, and I'd chosen not to argue the point. Now Jerry and Kip were wedging two short metal sticks into the fabric mesh to hold the cut open. This done, Jerry crawled through the hole, followed by Jean-Paul and then Kip. Now it was our turn.

I closed the intervening five meters at a rapid crawl, feeling horribly exposed as I entered the pool of light. I paused at the cut in the fence just long enough to glance back to make sure that Lorayne was right behind me. Then I was inside. A few more feet, past the glow of the perimeter lights, and I was once again in relative darkness. Looking around, I saw that Grady and Jerry were already at the corner of the guard barracks laying their first charge. I couldn't see the other team, but I knew that they had to be somewhere in the shadows at the base of the service ladder leading to the roof of the admin building. I dropped my NV goggles into place for a moment and hit the "on" switch. With the ample ambient light magnified literally thousands of times, Kip and Jean-Paul jumped out of the shadows at me. Kip was already ascending the ladder; Jean-Paul had his hands on the lower rungs.

I felt a pat on the rump, just below my daypack. Lorayne, signaling her presence. I killed the NV switch, flipped up the goggles—there was still too much light to use them to best advantage—and off we went, fifteen meters, to the corner of the admin building. I glanced back toward the barracks, but Grady and Jerry were already out of view. Looking now with an unaided eye, I could see Kip at the top of the ladder and Jean-Paul just behind. Keeping to the shadows, we ran along the north side of the admin building. At the corner I stopped, took a quick peek. Nothing. But it was better to wait for Peter's all clear since, once around the corner, we would be very close to the Security Area's double perimeter fence and easily within view of the Security Area rover.

"Team Smitty in position." Smitty and Kees had obviously reached their attack location, the roadside ditch just outside of the Controlled Area gatehouse. Now we really had to move fast, since they were concealed effectively only so long as the two guards stayed inside the gatehouse.

Peter came up on the net once again. "No hostile movement outside the fence line. No sign of the rover."

I peeked quickly around the corner once more, saw nothing, and moved, cutting diagonally from the admin building to the bend in the Security Area outer fence, roughly ten meters away. At the fence I dropped down again, Lorayne right behind me. I checked right, left, and ahead, while Lorayne checked our six o'clock. Another pat on the butt and I was off again, moving fast and hard, discovering, to my vast astonishment, that I wasn't even breathing heavily. And then we were there, at the point where the Security Area outer fence abutted the south wall of the gatehouse. I started to report, but was cut off by the sound of Kip's voice rasping in my earphones.

"Kip and Jean-Paul, in position and set up."

Kip, the consummate professional, had inadvertently reminded me that I'd been about to report too soon. Yes, Lorayne and I were now in position, but unlike Smitty and Kees earlier, our being in position didn't mean the same thing as being set up. I rolled over, saw that Lorayne was struggling with her backpack. I helped her free the lightweight aluminum camera tripod and the Claymore. Creeping up to the corner, I studied the front of the gatehouse and satisfied myself that the base of the window was roughly as we had estimated, about four feet off the ground. I turned to Lorayne, held up four fingers, then continued to cover the gatehouse with my 416 while she extended the tripod to its full length and mounted the Claymore in the special heavy-duty clamp that we'd fabricated to replace the camera mount. When this was done she spread the tripod legs and made sure they were locked in place, but left it lying on its side with the detonator wires trailing to the clacker. Because once we put the tripod in place the Claymore would be visible to the guards through the window of the gatehouse, we would wait until Grady gave the "go" order before swinging the tripod into the upright position. Now we were ready.

"Team Harry ready and in position."

Her hands free again, Lorayne reclaimed her 416 and covered to our rear.

"No hostile movement outside the fence line. No sign of the rover." Peter paused for a second. "Maybe he's taking a nap inside the lab."

Another minute passed, then another. Then, finally: "Team Grady, all set." Grady and Jerry had, of course, taken longer, since they had to lay charges both on the guard barracks and the smaller building that housed the bulk of the technical personnel. I hoped that Dr. Yang was tucked away safely in her office, as instructed.

Colin immediately came up on the net.

"Am I then clear?"

"Is he clear, Peter?" asked Grady.

"Good to go."

"Any traffic on the gomer's net?"

"No hostile radio traffic," answered Peter.

"Then standby to jam," said Grady. "Colin, you're clear to go."

"Moving now," answered Colin.

I pictured Colin and Tommy approaching the fence, anchoring the line on the outer fence and swinging the grappling hook across to the inner fence. Their primary task was to penetrate undetected past the double-fenced and alarmed area that protected, in a separate enclosure, the actual laboratory, production, and storage bunkers. I pictured Colin drawing the first line taut, swinging a second one into place, completing a rope bridge that would not sag into the electronic beam of the microwave alarm. I wished that I could actually see him, but I was facing in the wrong direction and, even if I did an about-face, the bulk of the lab buildings would still be in the way.

"I'm up." This was Colin.

"I see him," said Kip.

Now I could picture Colin on the ropes, inching himself forward from the top of the outer fence to the top of the inner fence, the ropes sagging slightly under his weight. I forced my thoughts away from Colin, focused on my own area of responsibility. Time seemed to creep by. Glancing down at my watch, I was surprised that the brightly-lit tritium markers indicated that less than ten minutes had passed since Grady had given Kip and me the "go."

"Halfway across, just now over the microwave alarms," said Colin.

"Rover outside the lab, south side, heading east." Peter's voice had taken on an urgent tone. "Headed your direction, Harry, toward the gatehouse."

The gatehouse blocked my view in that direction.

"I see him," said Lorayne. Positioned at the back corner of the gatehouse, she could see inside the inner Security Area through the fence fabric. But she would be hard-pressed to take him out, since a shot through both the outer and the inner fences ran a large risk of being deflected, however slightly.

"I've got him," said Kip. "I'm tracking him."

"I've got him, too." This was Peter, high up and with a commanding view from the hillside; he and Lem had the big sniper rifle, but Lem had his hands full flying the drone.". Then, only seconds later. "I've lost him again. He stepped back around the corner."

"Okay, Peter," said Grady. "Kip, you're the man."

"Lining him up," said Kip.

"Everybody easy," said Grady. "Colin, how close are you?"

"Ten feet, maybe."

"Rover's turning north," said Peter.

"Coming your way, Colin," said Kip.

"Fifteen seconds and he's round the corner. He'll have eyeball contact with Colin."

"Jam the gomer's net, Peter," said Grady.

"Jamming."

"He's close to the corner."

"Drop him, Kip," ordered Grady.

"Fuck!"

"Take the shot, Kip, take the shot."

"Can't take the shot, he's not up close to the building, he's out almost along the fence. I've got outriggers and razor ribbon in the way. It'll tumble the bullet. Damn, damn, damn."

"Lorayne, can you take him?"

"Real bad angle, too much clutter in the way, no."

"Don't leave me hangin' in the fuckin' air."

"Listen up, people, the shit's about to get real deep. Peter, can you reacquire?"

"Break," interjected Kip before Peter could answer, "he's stepped away from the fence. He steps out a little more and I've got the shot."

"I'm almost at the inner fence."

"Stay put, Colin, don't try to climb down, the outriggers and the razor wire are between you and him. Stay still."

"I can see the son of a bitch. If he turns around he'll see me."

"Stay still. Two more steps and he gives me a head shot."

"He's turning around."

"One more step."

Dead silence on the radio net. Then I heard the shot. Despite the suppressed muzzle blast, it seemed impossible that the supersonic crack of the bullet could go unremarked. But a long moment passed and then, in a different tone of voice from Kip: "Okay, Colin—you're clear."

"Jesus, Mary, and Joseph—I just about peed me knickers."

A few more seconds passed, then Colin came up on the net again.

"I'm on the ground inside. Give me a minute now."

We waited while Colin moved up to the side of the Central Alarm Station, located in a cinder-block annex attached to the lab building. I couldn't see him, but I could imagine him placing his satchel charge, playing out his line, tucking back behind the corner of the lab.

"I'm all set," said Colin.

"Smitty?"

"On your command, Grady."

"Kip?"

"Good to go."

"Harry?"

Even as Grady had started the roll call I'd motioned Lorayne forward. She set the tripod up outside the gatehouse window, the ugly green convex surface of the Claymore aimed above the ledge. Then we put the corner of the little building between ourselves and the Claymore.

"We're ready, Grady."

"On three—one, two, three. Now!"

On Grady's "three" Lorayne squeezed the clacker twice and the detonation of the Claymore overrode the sound of his "Now!" in my earphone. We jumped to our feet and rounded the corner of the gatehouse. I was dimly aware of several large explosions, one right after the other, somewhere to my left rear: Grady's charges bringing down the barracks. The Claymore had blown away not only the glass window, but the window ledge and much of the window surround. We each delivered a couple of three-shot bursts through the gaping hole. I then turned to the door and aimed a couple of more bursts at the wood around the door lock. The little 62-grain bullets chewed away the wood. I stepped to one side and Lorayne dislodged the entire lock mechanism with a sharp kick. At precisely that moment the light over the door, which by some freak mischance had survived the adjacent Claymore blast, went out. Smitty and Kees had completed their second task, the destruction of the diesel generator. I dropped my NV goggles into place and turned them on. In the midst of all this a voice on the radio was absent-mindedly keying his microphone and transmitting the word "motherfucker," continuing until Grady broke through and sharply told the speaker to shut the fuck up.

I threw open the door and sprayed the interior before entering. Lorayne was on my heels, covering to the right as I covered to the left. But the Claymore had done the work for us, shredding the torso of one of the guards and decapitating the other one. Stepping across the bodies, I went around the desk. As it turned out, there was no need to force the door to the backup control room. The wall of pellets from the Claymore, continuing on their upward angled path, had chewed away the upper third of the lightweight interior door, leaving a remnant that resembled a misproportioned Dutch door with the top part open. I pulled on the door handle and the door, which was missing its upper hinges, flopped away to the side. I stepped through the doorway and stopped dead in my tracks.

A third guard, pressing a handkerchief or some kind of rag to a wound on his forehead, was sitting at the control console. As soon as he saw me he began fumbling at his side for his holstered pistol. I shot him three times in the chest, and he slumped backwards in the chair. Grabbing him by the collar of his uniform jacket, I rolled him onto the floor. I fumbled around at the console, unable to find what I wanted. In this completely enclosed space the NV image intensifier had literally no ambient light to work with. I switched on the infrared illuminator and the lights, so to speak, came back on. I examined the equipment in the room, which now appeared to be bathed in bright green light, and found what I was searching for—the main radio transceiver linking the site with the backup troops in town. Another short burst smashed the radio console to pieces. Now, even if our jamming equipment failed, there was little chance that the gomers could make a radio call for reinforcements. If Smitty and Kees had taken out the telephone lines as planned, the site was now completely isolated. I looked down at my watch. We were right on schedule.

I turned and headed back to the front door. Lorayne was standing just inside it, her 416 trained outward, guarding against any unpleasant surprises. Hearing my movement, she glanced briefly over her shoulder. In the infrared-enhanced brightness I saw her mouth moving beneath the mask of her NV goggles, and could clearly follow the trajectory of stream of tobacco she spat through the open door. As I came up alongside her she flashed an easy smile.

We'd completed our first task successfully. Now it was time to do the job that we'd come to do. I didn't think it worthwhile to fool with opening the vehicle gate outside, so I led Lorayne through the wreckage inside the Security Area gatehouse to the back door. After wedging the door open, I got on the radio to tell Grady and the others what I'd done to save them time as they fell back through the area. Outside the building we paused to look for Colin and Tommy. Not seeing them, I called Colin on the radio and asked his location.

"We've got charges on the outer door of the lab building, and we just backed off around the corner," he answered. "Where are you?"

"At the back of the Gatehouse," I replied.

"Hold there 'til I blow the door."

"Roger that."

No sooner had I acknowledged than we saw a quick, green-tinted flash and—a microsecond later—we heard the sound of the explosion. We immediately set off in a dead run across the compound, linking up with Colin and Tommy just outside the blown weather door. They went inside, set a shaped charge on the main airlock doors, and backed away a safe distance. The charge blew out the mechanism controlling the airlock doors. With Colin in the lead, we forced out way past the two airlock doors. Ironically, in spite of its intended purpose, the Chinese had constructed a fully-compliant biohazard facility. Now we were inside. We were on the target.

Colin and Tommy concentrated on the processing equipment, moving quickly from one key component to the next, planting the small, dedicated charges and linking them with a "ringmain," a double ring of detonating cord. Lorayne and I passed through a small vestibule and entered the storage area, where four rows of filled canisters rested on racks. So little material, I thought—so much death. We hurried down the rows, planting our charges. This went quickly, since our task was much simpler than the one facing Colin and Tommy.

Once the charges were set, we gathered every obviously combustible item we could find—papers, wooden chairs, notebooks and the like—and dragged them into a couple of big piles at opposite ends of the room. Then we moved over to the emergency exit door and waited for Colin and Tommy to join us. As soon as they reached us, Lorayne and I each took one of the special thermite grenades, pulled the pins, and tossed them into the piles we'd made. We'd brought thermite grenades because they will burn anything, even steel. For present purposes they represented overkill, but overkill was what we wanted, white hot flames to consume any of the biological material that survived the explosive charges. The thermite grenades exploded in a shower of white-hot sparks and the piles burst into flames.

Now it was definitely time to go. Colin pushed the crash bar on the inner exit door and out we went, into another air lock. At its end was another crash-out door that we popped through on a dead run. Outside, we were just opposite the point where Grady and Jerry were waiting for us. We dashed over to them and I dropped down beside Grady. I decided to take a break from my green-tinted view of the world and flipped up my goggles. The mix of moonlight and the glow from the burning barracks revealed enough of Grady's expression to instantly kill my elation.

"What's wrong?" I asked.

"You didn't hear?"

"Haven't heard anything."

"Smitty's down."

"How down? Wounded, what?"

"Dead down. Just now, while you guys were inside the factory bunker—it's probably a radio dead spot in there. Kees came up on the net, said our lady scientist had turned up okay, they were getting set to move. Then I hear a burst of shots, loud at first cause Kees's still got his mike keyed, then more shots. Kees comes back up, sounds real shook, says two gomers had come up on them out of nowhere, Smitty shot one and the other one shot him, then Kees shot the one that was left. Kip and J-P responded their way. That's all I know."

It was his smile that came to me as I listened, Smitty's ever-present smile and his ever-ready willingness to take on any task, however disagreeable, and give it his best. But these were thoughts I needed to put aside for later.

"Another ninety seconds, now," I said.

We waited, listening for the muffled thumps that would tell us that our charges had detonated successfully, hoping that we had correctly calculated their destructive power. The charges needed to be strong enough to blow up the lab equipment and vaporize the virus storage bottles inside without blowing out the roof or the emergency exit doors. But before the ninety seconds elapsed, another sound captured our attention.

"Listen," said Jerry.

We all listened carefully, not knowing quite what he'd heard. Then Lorayne picked it up.

"Helicopter," she said. She turned her head and spat a long brown stream of tobacco juice onto the ground.

"No," said Colin, "helicopters—two for sure."

I still hadn't heard anything, but my hearing is somewhat less than perfect.

"How the fuck did they get on to us?" asked Grady.

But the answer had already come to me. "There was a third guard in the SA gatehouse, we didn't get him with the Claymore, we had to shoot him. He had time enough to get off a duress call."

"But we were jamming."

"A hard-wire system, hooked into the telephone land line. I don't know—it doesn't matter right now, does it?"

He shook his head as he got on the horn to Peter and Lem.

"Do you hear them, Peter?" he asked.

"Hear them and see them, Lem's flying the drone toward them. Looks like they're following the road between the ridges. One's big enough to carry troops, something like an old Mi-8, the other's a little scout. Not gunships, anyway, this quick getting here, they must have been on some kind of alert status down in the village."

"They weren't supposed to have two choppers this close."

"Too fucking late to worry about that," said Grady. "Could be a dozen guys or more on the slick. We don't want to fight 'em on the ground if we can help it. Can you hit one with the Carl Gustaf?"

"Negative, Grady," said Peter. "Not until he's on the ground. I'm already tracking him with the Ultimax—that's the best option."

Thank God for a good team, I thought to myself. Just at that moment we heard a series of muffled "thumps" from inside the bunkers. Our charges had gone off.

"Mission accomplished, guys," Grady said on the radio. "Let's take care of these assholes and get the fuck outa Dodge."

At that very moment we heard the sound of Peter's unsuppressed machine gun and saw a line of tracers streak out from the hillside toward the troop carrier helicopter. As the tracers swept the bird, Peter went full cyclic.

From our position on the opposite end of the compound we watched in awe as a sudden bright thunderclap of light and sound signaled the end of the helicopter.

"Got the bastard!" shouted Peter over the radio.

That was the good news. The bad news was that there still was a second bird above us. Even a small scout spelled potential disaster, since, if it had Forward Looking Infrared, it could track our escape all the way down the river to the plane.

"Can you get the second?" asked Grady.

"Changing ammo drums. I'll do my best."

Peter gave it his best shot, but it wasn't quite good enough. We all watched helplessly as the helicopter juked sideways to avoid the stream of tracers, and then started to climb out of range.

"Second helicopter's turning away," reported Peter.

"Bugging out?" asked Grady.

"Negative," this was Lem. "Wait one, I have to concentrate."

We waited what seemed an eternity, listening to the second helicopter hovering above us and out of gun range on the far side of the facility. Then we heard the rotor drone suddenly change to an ungodly screech that grew louder until we saw the flash and then the bang of an explosion on the opposite hillside.

"What the fuck?" said Grady.

Lem came back up on the net, excitement in his voice. "I flew the drone through the pilot side window. I bet those little rotors fucked up the pilot and the co-pilot."

Now, in quick succession, Peter fired our three Carl Gustaf rockets into the crash site of the first helicopter. We weren't carrying the Carl Gustaf out, and, just maybe, there might be a survivor or two around the downed bird. Lem had taken up the sniper rifle and was throwing the big .338 bullets across to where the scout bird lay burning.

"Peter, Lem, good work. Now get the hell out!" ordered Grady.

"Underway," answered Peter. "Ten minutes and we're at the boats."

"Roger, good, keep going, balls to the wall. Break—Kip, got your ears on?"

"I'm here, Grady."

"Throw a couple of 40 mike-mike rounds up the hill, all you got, try to pound the area where the little bird went in. Do it quick, and then *boogie*."

"Got ya, Grady," said Kip.

At that range the 40mm rounds had little real chance of hitting anything, but it was worth a shot.

"Kees, Kees, where the fuck are you, son?"

"Watching the front gate. I've got Miss Yang with me"

"Get your country ass in gear and get out of there now! Grab your lady friend and run, don't walk. Link up with Kip and J-P. They ain't gonna be hard to find just now."

Grady turned to the rest of us. "Down the hill. Now!"

One after another we hooked onto the ropes Jerry had rigged and rappelled quickly down the side of the cliff. By then the first five of us had reached the base of the cliff, on the narrow cleft of land at the river's edge, Lem and Peter were on the rappel line, helping Dr. Yang down the precipice. Predictably, Grady and Kip had waited until last.

"Don't wait for the others," yelled Grady. "Fill a raft and move!"

Colin organized a load for the first raft and we shoved it into the current. I stripped off my body armor. To keep it was to risk drowning if I went into the water. I threw myself into the second raft and away we went.

I'd known that the river originated many miles to the south, in mountains topped by one of central Africa's rapidly disappearing glaciers—yes, there are such still. I had tried to psyche myself up for the fact that it would be cold, but the first shot of icy river water in my face left me, quite literally, breathless. The raft saved me from total immersion, but within minutes I was thoroughly soaked. I tried to wriggle upright, to get my face above the level of repeated splashings, but gave up when I realized I was about to tip over the raft. The current was much faster than the one in the stream we'd trained in—this would make it easier to elude any pursuers—but it made for a pounding hard, wet, out-of-control ride. In the end, I simply closed my eyes and gave myself up to the river. And I didn't open them again until I heard Dito and Moira shouting my name.

CHAPTER 14

WHEN I RAISED my head, I saw Moira and Dito in the dinghy tied alongside the back hatch of the Catalina, waiting to boost us out of the low-lying rafts up into the hatch. I knew that I should reach out to them, but I couldn't make my arms work right. Our raft began drifting aft of the plane and out into the lake. Lorayne reached past me trying to catch hold of Dito's outstretched hands but missed by an arm's length. Colin was sitting in the hatchway, dangling his legs into the dinghy as he pulled off his wet gear and clothes. Seeing our distress, he yanked his wadded BDU pants free of his ankles, dropped into the dinghy, and then dived over the side into the icy water. In a few quick strokes he reached the side of our raft.

"Having a bit o' trouble there, guv'nor?" he asked, his face bobbing a few inches above the surface just opposite mine, his black hair plastered back, a huge grin on his face.

"My arms don't want to work, it seems."

"Not to worry."

He reached up with one hand and took hold of the raft. He then half-rolled into a sidestroke and towed us the few meters back to the dinghy. As we drew alongside, Moira leaned over and hooked her arm around my shoulders, passing her hand beneath the strap of my tactical sling. She helped me over the gunwale while Dito assisted Colin into the boat. Moira unhooked the sling of my 416, and passed the weapon up into the plane. I slumped down into the dinghy, taking a few seconds to catch my breath. I would have gladly taken a few minutes, but Lorayne was waiting and so was Jerry, and they couldn't be pulled in until I got out of the way. So, with a boost from Jerry and a pull from Dito I made it up through the hatch and into the plane. This was even harder than it sounds, since both the dinghy and the aircraft wanted to slide in opposite directions as I stretched between them. Once inside, I flopped on my back, shivering. Looking up I could see Tommy wrapped in a blanket and Colin, stark naked, toweling himself dry, both appearing weirdly spectral in the red cabin lights, an old-fashioned, but still effective means of preserving everyone's night vision capability.

"Better get those wet clothes off," said Tommy, tossing me a towel.

I pulled myself up into a sitting position and pulled off my shirt, then my trousers. Jerry and Lorayne came in through the hatch; from the sound of the voices outside, several more team members had arrived. With my trousers partway down, I hesitated for a moment, suddenly very much aware of Lorayne. But even as I paused, she and Jerry quickly peeled out of their wet clothes and accepted the towels that Tommy was passing out. As I worked my trousers over my ankles I tried not to stare at Lorayne, at her delicate breasts and raisinet nipples, at her round buttocks and her surprisingly luxuriant brown bush. I had grown so accustomed to thinking of her—well, not thinking of her as a woman, as a sexual being. At least being miserably, thoroughly chilled prevented me from embarrassing myself with an erection.

But it wasn't just my penis that was being unresponsive. My legs didn't seem to want to work either, and I wasn't sure why. I took the blanket that Colin more or less dropped on my head, wrapped myself in it, and dragged myself further from the hatch, dodging the weapons that Moira and Dito kept tossing through it, trying to make room for the late arrivals. First Jean-Paul and Kip helped Dr. Yang up into the aircraft. This was my first glimpse of the woman who'd meant so much to the mission, but all I saw was a lab-coated figure whose sodden misery seemed to match my own. Then Jean-Paul and Kip climbed aboard, then Peter and Kees, then Grady and Lem. They dropped their clothes, grabbed towels and blankets, and then, one by one, passed forward into the next compartment until only Peter and Kip and Grady remained with me. That was everybody—everybody except Smitty.

Grady extended a helping hand to Moira and then Dito and then untied the line holding the dinghy to the aircraft. We didn't expect to need the dinghy again. Kip helped Grady pull the hatch door in place. The process of getting everyone into the plane seemed to unroll in slow motion, though it could scarcely have taken more than ten minutes. Despite my personal difficulties, for the others it had been a well-practiced evolution.

Moira took in the bedraggled nudity around her with a bemused expression, then her gaze settled on Dr. Yang, still in her wet clothes, sitting in a daze, hugging her knees to her chest. She mouthed an aside to Dito, who headed forward toward the cockpit and then she extended a hand to the woman on the floor. Gently drawing Dr. Yang upright, she led her aft, helping her over the hatch coaming, and disappearing into the relative privacy of the rearmost compartment.

"Do you think they're close behind?" asked Peter.

"I doubt it," answered Grady. "They'd take a while to clear the site. Besides, Kip and I rigged a few booby-traps to slow them up a little. And we have to assume, at least hope, that they don't have any more choppers on call. At least we broke contact cleanly. But I told Moira anyway that we needed to get the hell on out of here."

"You look very pale, old friend," Peter said to me. "Are you sure you're all right?"

"Yeah, Harry, you look like shit," added Grady. But I wasn't the only one. Even allowing for the dim red light, we were a ghastly looking bunch, not at all the picture of a successful commando team that had just laid waste to a heavily protected facility. Instead we looked more like the survivors of a shipwreck, and I, at least, felt like such. By the dim red cabin light, I could see the other faces around me. We were a pretty grim-looking bunch, not at all the picture of a commando team that had just laid waste to a high-security facility.

As they spoke another chill passed through me, making me shiver and making my teeth chatter uncontrollably.

"I'll be all right," I said, squeezing out the words between clenched teeth. "But I could use some help getting up."

Kip reached down and pulled me up, lending me a shoulder until he was sure that I could stand unaided. I clutched my blanket more tightly around me and shuffled toward the hatchway leading forward.

"Kip, you and Peter secure these weapons, okay?" Grady said. Soldiers being soldiers, not one of us had abandoned his or her personal weapon even though the need for it had passed. "We can't have them loose back here during take-off. Peter, could you grab Tommy over there and start passing out the dry uniforms. Everyone will feel better with dry clothes."

Tommy came through and tossed me a plastic bag with "Harry" magic-markered on a strip of packing tape—my dry set of set of socks, underwear, and BDUs. I knew I needed to get properly dressed, but the effort seemed just too much, so I set the bag aside and clutched the blanket more closely around my shoulders, even as another chill passed through me. I shivered for a moment, then it passed.

Feeling a bit better, I gazed around at the others to try and take stock of our collective condition. Jerry Wolsey, sitting across from me, was having a cigarette. We'd never made much of "no smoking" rules throughout training, relying upon the team to decide such things. Jerry, our only heavy smoker, had gone without a cigarette for the better part of two days. No one would begrudge him a smoke at this moment. To me, the smoke actually smelled good. I thought about asking Jerry if I could have one, but I couldn't get my mouth to form the words. I really was in a bad way. Jerry had supplemented his cigarette with the inevitable toothpick. He was talking to Tommy, who sat next to him, and Lorayne, who was next to me and across from Tommy. I could hear what they were saying, but couldn't actually follow their conversation. Further forward, Lem sat across from Kip. Lem was resting his head against the bulkhead with his eyes closed. Since Kip sat on my side of the plane, I could only see him by leaning forward and looking to my left, past Lorayne. This took more energy than I cared to expend. Then the chill struck me again. My shivering caught Lorayne's attention, and she put her arm around me, unselfconsciously rearranging her blanket on her lap so that it draped over both of us. I was grateful for the gesture, grateful for the extra warmth. At the same time, I felt very weak and pathetic. Leaning my head against her shoulder, I closed my eyes.

I don't know how long I was out—I assumed not long—before Lorayne shook me awake.

"C'mon, Hair Doctor, wake up, wake up. That's it now, sit up, see what we've got here."

I opened my eyes and saw Kip standing in front of me.

"Here, Major, why don't you let Lorayne have her blanket back. I've got something here, not as nice, but pretty warm, and she needs the chance to get up and get something to eat."

He helped Lorayne disentangle herself from me while proffering a dry towel wrapped around something very hot. I pulled back the corner of the towel and saw that Kip had prepped an MRE chemical heating element, tying off the plastic bag to prevent the water from spilling. I tucked the whole thing under the blanket, snug against my chest.

"Thanks, Kip. That'll do very nicely, I think."

"We've got something else here that'll also help."

I realized then that Tommy was standing at his shoulder with a Styrofoam cup full of something hot. He passed it to Kip, who gently placed it into my free hand, not releasing it until absolutely sure that I wouldn't drop it.

"It's tomato soup, Major," he said. "Couldn't find any chicken soup."

"That's okay, Kip. I'm not really a chicken soup kind of guy anyway."

"Well, hey, it's warm."

"Yes, very much so." I took a sip. "Thanks, Kip."

"Hey, Major—it went well, didn't it? We did good?"

"Yes, Kip. We did good." And, I thought, we lost Smitty. But now wasn't the moment to voice that thought.

He reached out, put a hand on my shoulder, then turned and resumed his seat. I downed my soup quickly, soaking in the warmth and the nourishment. After finishing I leaned my head back and closed my eyes, feeling better. When I was sure that I could stand without embarrassing myself, I set the empty cup aside; still clutching the heating element to my chest, I stood up, dropped the blanket, and carefully dressed myself. Heading for the galley, I stepped carefully over the coaming and through the hatchway. The galley consisted of a microwave, a coffeepot, a small refrigerator, and a small worktable, all arranged along a narrow passageway constricted by the wheel wells for the retractable landing gear. My favorite hideaway, the flight engineer's loft, was just above. Colin, Tommy, Kees, Jerry, and Lorayne had all squeezed into the small space around the little microwave and the adjacent counter.

"Looking better, there," Jerry said to me as I wiggled past to the next compartment. This space had originally accommodated the radioman and the navigator. Now it served mainly as additional passenger space, but we'd installed only four seats instead of the six in the after compartment. Grady, Moira, and Peter occupied three of the seats. I sat down in the fourth.

"Just in time, Harry," said Peter, "we've been having a bit of a chin wag and we need your thoughts." He paused, then added, "Do you think they were somehow warned about us? Grady doesn't think so, but…."

"Yeah, but," said Grady, "On the one hand, if they truly had a warning, they sure weren't ready for us on the ground. On the other hand."

"Yes," said Peter, "on the other hand, two helicopters that responded very quickly."

"Even that," responded Grady. "If they knew we were coming, they could've been a whole lot better prepared. I just don't know, but it's bugging me."

"So," started Peter, "the question becomes one of what do we do now?"

Moira spoke up. "Grady wants us to go ahead and take off right now, just to be on the safe side, but I think that would be a big mistake, for all the reasons we built into the plan." I understood instantly. From the beginning, Moira had insisted that, despite the obvious advantages of flying out under cover of darkness, we needed to hold off until first light. She repeated her concern. "I trust our radar once we're airborne, but not as we bounce along the surface of the lake during takeoff, and I'm not real comfortable about it picking up something small and wooden like a fishing boat. If we hit something like that during our takeoff run, we're in for it, big time."

"I hate just sitting here for another hour," countered Grady, "gives them time to collect themselves and come after us."

"Maybe, so," said Peter, "Look, Grady, I feel the same way about giving up a time advantage, but it's only an hour. You said yourself that we'd left them clueless, and the only quick way to get to where we are is rappelling and then rafting, the same way that we did. Surely, they're not prepared for that."

I thought for a moment, trying to weigh things, but knowing the answer I would give. "It has to be the pilot's decision, so Moira, I say we do it your way. But, please, get us up as soon as it's light enough, and no later." The words would come back to haunt me, but I'd left my crystal ball at home.

I could hear them behind us, continuing to talk, their voices loud enough to hear but not clear enough to understand. But now that we were on the verge of being homeward bound, perhaps they simply had a few personal words to exchange.

With that, Peter and I decided to go aft and see how the others were doing. I was waiting for Peter to step through the hatch when the plane reminded us that we were afloat by giving a small sideways lurch.

I reached out to brace myself, grabbing hold of a bracket protruding from the overhead and twirling on it like a straphanging subway rider. As I performed my inadvertent pirouette, I saw that Moira, in the process of climbing back up into the pilot's compartment, had been thrown off balance and that Grady had staggered out of his seat to catch her. I watched them hold each other for a moment as I gathered my blanket around me and followed Peter through the hatch.

The lurch had evidently reminded the others that, having survived the hazards of the raid, they would be foolish to allow themselves to be injured while bouncing around in the aircraft. When we reached the old bunk compartment all six seats were occupied, and no one was standing around. The initial chatter had subsided, and everyone seemed subdued. Perhaps it had started to sink in that we'd lost a member of the team tonight. A good man, a man who, but for my intervention would be going home to a wife and two young sons, something I would soon have to face. But almost as soon as the thought came, I put it aside. Down through the years I've had lots of practice putting such thoughts aside.

My quick scan of the faces left Colin and Jerry unaccounted for.

"They're sitting back in the waist-gunner's compartment with Dr. Yang," said Kip, when I asked where they were. "Jerry's doing his medical thing, making sure she's okay."

"Dr. Yang?" and as I said it I realized that I'd gone for the better part of a half hour nearly oblivious to the fact that we'd not only destroyed the facility, but also rescued the young woman who'd handed the place to us in the first place. I'd not been tracking well.

"How is she?"

"Physically okay, I think. Seems pretty disoriented though. You might want to go see."

I nodded weakly, and started further aft. Walking past an open hatch, I noticed for the first time the odor wafting in through the open door, brackish musty smells compounded of old logs too long in shallow water, of bark and pulp stewed into sponge-like softness, of mud and weeds and moss and scum. It provided an oddly repellent and yet refreshing outdoor contrast to the mingled smells of kitchen, locker room and gunsmith's shop, smells that had come to dominate the interior of the plane. All this, combined with the food and coffee smells drifting back from the galley, contributed to the strange feeling of being disconnected from reality feeling that had grown since our landing.

When I reached what had been the waist gunner's compartment, I saw Jerry and Colin sharing a cigarette, but no sign of Dr. Yang. "Where is she?" I asked, "Is she all right?"

"She's back there," answered Jerry, glancing aft to indicate the hatch leading into the tunnel gunner's compartment. We hadn't used it for much of anything because it was too small to allow someone to sit comfortably upright, much less stand, and filling it with equipment would have adversely affected the trim of the aircraft. "Physically, she's okay, but she seems pretty shook up. Maybe you can talk to her."

"I'll give it a try."

I opened the hatch and stuck my head inside, and there she was lying on her side in the darkness, still wrapped in a blanket, curled up with her knees tucked beneath her chin. At first, I thought she was asleep, but as I crawled into the compartment to check on her, she spoke to me.

"Who is there?" She spoke in an English so thickly accented that I could scarcely make out the words. I couldn't determine much else about her, except that her hair was a mess and that her eyes were dark hollows in a thin, pale face. In the faint light she looked impossibly young.

"Are you ill?" I asked, and, when I got no initial response, I repeated the question, wishing that my language skills extended to Mandarin.

"No," she replied. "I'm not ill."

"What then? The others have prepared something to eat. Maybe hungry?"

"No." So, she wasn't hungry.

"We're happy that you are with us now, and safe."

"I am thankful to you all, and it is good that you have blown up that place." Her words, however, were more positive than her tone.

"So," I tried again, "is something wrong?"

"Nothing."

But I knew something was wrong.

"Dr. Yang, Shih," trying her name for the first time, "something is wrong. You shouldn't be lying here like this—what is it?"

"I got your black man killed."

Of course. "Why do you say that?"

"I was between him and the two guards when they first appeared. He moved me out of the way, but then it was too late for him."

"You don't know that. Too many things were happening for you to know that." I stopped abruptly. No matter what I said, no matter how I might emphasize the role chance plays in a firefight, I knew that I was stretching a point. Maybe having to deal with her had got Smitty killed. If so, it was my fault for putting him in such a situation. For the next few minutes I tried to find words to make her feel better, thanking her for the information that had made the mission possible, telling her that she'd undoubtedly saved many lives. But all those lives were abstractions. A real human being had been carved up within inches of her face by automatic weapons fire. I tried another approach, asking her to tell me about what had happened at the facility, what had led her to turn against Colonel Ma and his crew. She told me a story both fascinating and frightening, culminating in the moment when Ma had ordered a full-scale test on several dozen poor African farmers, killed horribly by the virus, their bodies then destroyed by fire. Her story made me all the more proud of our accomplishment in destroying the facility.

Still, none of this seemed to lift her from her melancholy. So, in the end I just kept talking, talking because I didn't know what else to do, knowing that the young woman deserved comfort, struggling to find the right things to say—tender words that I somehow lacked. But I must have had some effect, for after a short while she sat up and fumbled in her pockets, drawing out two small shrink-wrapped bags, each holding an identical thumb drive.

"I made these for your government, documents and pictures, the whole story of the virus and the lab, with proof. Take them, make sure you keep them safe."

I could only marvel at this further evidence of her courage. I pocketed the drives, thinking that I'd give one to Peter, just in case. I couldn't think of anything quite right to say, so I leaned over and gave her a very light kiss on the forehead, much as one would do in comforting a child.

I sensed movement behind me, looked up, and saw Moira crouching in the hatchway.

"How is she?"

"Physically, okay," I answered, whispering. "But she's struggling some, about Smitty's death, but part of her has to be thinking of all the people she worked with. She can't have really wished the whole lot of them dead."

"I suspect not," said Moira. She sat down on the young woman's other side and drew her away from me, holding her close, whispering gently to her in a voice almost motherly. In a moment she began to gently sob against Moira's chest. I seemed to no longer be needed, but I couldn't readily disengage my arm and I didn't want to disturb the moment. After a time, the sobbing stopped, and then rhythmic breathing told me that she'd fallen asleep. Moira looked over to me, mouthed the words, "help me," and we gently rearranged this brave and now wounded young woman so that she was sleeping on the cabin floor, a spare blanket rolled up beneath her head, another stretched over her recumbent form. We exited the compartment, closing the hatch behind us. If we had no other comfort to offer, then a moment's quiet would have to do. We took Jerry aside, cautioned him to retrieve Dr. Yang and get her properly buckled in before we took off.

I heard a splash from just outside the nearby exit door, then another.

"Who're the swimmers?" I asked.

"Colin, of course," answered Tommy, who was standing next to me. "And Kees."

I couldn't get any closer to the open door, so I stepped back and looked out the cabin window on that side. At first, I saw nothing among the shadows along the shoreline, but I knew roughly where they must be because I'd realized what they were doing. After landing the night before, Moira and Dito had anchored the plane as close inshore as possible, and then had draped some camouflage netting over the aircraft, not much, just enough to break up the highly recognizable aircraft profile. This now had to be cut and pulled away before the engines could be started. Pushing to get this done in the dark meant Grady was getting more antsy, and he was right to be—glancing out the window I could see the first glimmerings of what astronomers, mariners, and special operators refer to as "mean nautical twilight." In higher latitudes this could last quite a while, but, here, near the equator, we could expect full sunrise to come upon us very quickly.

I went forward into the old bunk compartment and took a seat, just as Moira pushed past heading for the cockpit. Even as she passed forward, the engines began to turn over. Dito wasn't wasting any time. First came the whine of the turboprops and the plane began to swing around slowly into take-off position. Moira's voice came over the speaker warning everyone to make sure all gear had been secured and to buckle up. Then the big Cyclones coughed a couple of times, then caught, then settled into an idle as Moira gave them time to warm up. Already, as more light seeped through the window, the higher pitched note of the Lycomings and the deep bass of the Cyclones blended into a single rhythm, rising in pitch until the Catalina began inching forward, then faster, bouncing across the surface of the lake as the hull came up on plane. It seemed as if we were taking an unconscionable amount of time to get airborne, although I hadn't a clue how long it actually took. But when the fuselage finally came unstuck from the water and the seat stopped pounding against my backside, I allowed myself, for a moment, to think that the hard part was over.

CHAPTER 15

THE TROUBLE BEGAN almost as soon as we became airborne. I heard Moira calling me over the intercom, asking if I would come forward immediately to the cockpit. When I got there, Grady was wedged in between Moira and Dito.

"Shut the door, Harry," said Moira. I squeezed in alongside Grady. After a couple of tries, we managed to get the cockpit door to close. While Dito continued to focus ahead, Moira twisted around sideways in her seat to look directly at us.

"I didn't want to put this out to everyone on the plane, but we've got a problem. We're being tracked by radar, some kind of aircraft radar, Dito says he's pretty sure some kind of fighter aircraft targeting radar. He knows more about that than I do"

"Well, fuck me to tears," said Grady. "They must have been in the air waiting for us."

"We can lose them?" I asked.

"I don't know—we're down among the clutter, lots of odd returns and echoes from the ground that they have to deal with, they would have struggled to find us down on the lake, but still, now that we're up, well, it's designed to find and lock on to other aircraft. Besides, the old Cat here doesn't have much in the way of stealth characteristics."

"How long've they been tracking us?" asked Grady.

"I don't know. We picked up the signal as soon as we got airborne. It may have been coming in before. We didn't have the power up, and we didn't test our radar detection receiver before taking off."

Dito chimed in. "For all we know, they had us on the lake and during take-off, but I don't think so. These radars usually have some kind of minimum speed threshold, you know, some minimum speed that a target must be going before it shows up on the screen, something to make sure that what they're tracking is another aircraft."

"I'll try a few things," said Moira, "see if I can shake them while holding course for Ugandan airspace."

"We'd better tell the others," said Grady. "They deserve to know."

He looked at me questioningly. I nodded to confirm my agreement. "Moira?" I asked.

"Yes. Everybody needs to strap in extra tight. This may get a little hairy."

Grady and I found seats in the navigator's compartment where, as luck would have it, Peter and Kip were already seated. Perfect for a council of war between the old heads of the team. But as I listened to Moira make the announcement on the intercom, the full force of our predicament struck me, as did the realization that, from this moment on, we were entirely in Moira's and Dito's hands. There wasn't a damn thing anyone else could do to help.

As if to underscore this thought, as soon as the intercom message concluded the plane made a sudden sharp climbing turn to the right, almost a full ninety degrees, then, equally suddenly, we decelerated sharply—very sharply—and began a gradual descent. I had no window to look through, and even if I had, I'm not sure I wanted to see. But I knew we'd returned to a course that paralleled our original, only now we were much lower, and much slower. We continued in this manner for perhaps fifteen minutes. Then we slowed down even more. I had no idea just exactly where we were in relation to our stall

199

speed, but we had to be close to it, and then Moira was turning slowly, ultimately a full one hundred eighty degrees. Now we were headed back where we came from, still nearly at stall speed. After a couple of minutes of this, Moira turned the Cat ninety degrees to the right. Suddenly we heard and felt the sound of the engines being wound up for more power as we began climbing quite steeply, and then we turned sharply once more.

"Sorry about that, guys," said Moira over the intercom.

After a few more minutes we leveled out. As near as I could tell, after all the twists and turns we'd taken, we were back on something that resembled our original course. I heard a noise from the direction of the cockpit, and looked up to see Moira stepping down into our compartment.

"It's no use, guys," she said. "We can't shake them. Whoever it is that's tracking us has got us locked in but good."

"May I ask a question?" This was Peter.

"Of course," replied Moira.

"We're receiving a signal, which we identify as an airborne of some sort. Correct? Now, do we have any other indication that we are being pursued?"

"No—nothing at all."

"Then, if I might make a quick suggestion, why don't we just ignore them for now. Continue to fly toward the coast as rapidly as possible. Maybe we're getting a clear read of their signal, but are so far away that they're not getting a good return. Maybe they don't even know we are down here. It happened with the *Bismarck*, back during the big war. Our cruisers had lost her, but she didn't know it, she still was receiving their radar signal even though it was too weak to bounce all the way back to them."

I pondered this briefly and commented, "Wishful thinking."

"But so what?" interjected Kip. "If they don't really know we're here, then there's no harm in doing what Peter says. If they do know, but don't intercept us, maybe can't intercept us, then there's also no harm. Thirty minutes or so and we're, what, almost over Lake Albert and into Uganda. The closer we get, the more options we've got. We're just wasting time and energy and fuel trying to break contact. Let's just fly and see if they re-shuffle the cards."

"Moira?" I said. "It's your call."

"No, this affects everyone."

"Yeah, but we're not going to take a vote," said Grady, his voice surprisingly soft, his tone thoughtful. "It's not up to the whole team, not even to those of us here, to decide. I think Peter and Kip are right, but you need to call it."

She gave him a grateful look and turned to me. "Harry?"

"Grady's right. We don't have time for an extended debate, or a poll, and you know the ins and outs of what we're up against better than the rest of us. For what it's worth, I'm with Peter and Kip and Grady. Let's just keep going and see what happens."

"Good enough. That's what Dito had already suggested anyway."

She turned and climbed back up into the cockpit, and as I watched her I wished that I had been able to offer more help, a useful suggestion. But nothing useful had come to mind. I felt helpless, as no doubt did the others.

"I wish I'd been able to suggest something more constructive," said Peter.

"I wish I knew who those guys were," said Kip.

"Well, you guys know the old saying about wishes," said Grady. "You can put wishes in one hand and shit in the other, and see which hand gets full first."

I'd heard Grady use that phrase many times, and thought I'd gotten the point, but I'd never really understood exactly what it means. I'd always suspected it's one of those mountaineer things. But his next comment was absolutely clear and to the point.

"There's another old saying, the one about coming in on a wing and a prayer. I guess we have to leave the 'wing' part to Moira and Dito, but maybe it's time the rest of us concentrated really hard on the 'prayer' part." He paused, then added, "You know, Harry, I was really wrong about Dito—the man absolutely has his shit together."

There wasn't much to say after that. For the better part of fifteen minutes we flew on, each of us absorbed in his or her thoughts. The silence, at least in the compartment where I was sitting, was only interrupted once when Moira came up on the intercom with a progress report—halfway there, but still being tracked. In some obscure way, I found this comforting, as I alternated between imagining the worst and hoping for the best.

I even followed Grady's suggestion prayer suggestion, although it came hard. As a small boy I had been taught that it was wrong to pray selfishly for something. One could pray for the benefit of others, but not for oneself. The object lesson had involved my praying for a pony that I desperately wanted, and eventually got, but not until my parents had delayed things enough to make their point about that kind of praying. The idea that I could pray for a way out for everyone else on the plane seemed a trifle too cute, at least so long as I had no intention of putting on a parachute and jumping out. So, I followed my grandfather's austere Protestant lesson and simply said, "God's will be done." And then I just closed my eyes and listened to the droning engines, carrying us closer and closer to safety.

And then I heard Dito's voice on the intercom, and knew that something was up. He'd always left the intercom to Moira. "We've got company, two small fighters, sitting above us, one to each side, looks like those JL-8s you briefed us on."

It suddenly looked as if "God's will" and my own fervent wishes were very far apart.

"Look, guys," said Grady. "We can't have all four of us sitting up here together. This team's shit's about to get real watery awful damn quick, and some of those kids back in the back are going to want to look into our beat-up old faces for reassurance."

"I'll go back," said Peter.

Kip stood up as well, remarking, "Yeah, Grady, that's me—the spiritual equivalent of Imodium."

"Send Tommy and Kees up," said Grady. "Don't say why."

I thought about it for a few seconds, and then started to get up as well.

"No, Harry, stick around," said Grady. "Listen. If things get real bad, if these assholes shoot us down or something, we may all wind up dead. But maybe not. I've seen some no-shit odd stuff happen when planes and choppers go down."

"So?"

"So. If we crash, and some part of us survives, it's likely to be either some in back or some in front, but not both. If you and me get dead, the survivors have a better chance if Kip or Peter are alive, and vice-versa."

His reasoning didn't particularly convince me, but it didn't seem to matter much. Tommy and Kees joined us, belted themselves in tightly, and waited with us for whatever came next. It wasn't long in coming. From above and behind us, at very close range, I heard a couple of bursts of deep-throated automatic weapons fire, something heavy—I knew the JL-8 could carry a pod-mounted 23mm aircraft cannon. The plane lurched to the right. I felt no impact and guessed that whoever currently had the controls in the cockpit had reacted involuntarily to the shots. Then came another burst.

"Motherfucker! Big fucking green tracers just went by!" Grady was looking out of the port side navigator's window."

The plane straightened out and leveled off. Seconds later we heard the intercom crackle and then Moira spoke. "Warning shots. We just got some warning shots."

This was followed by Dito's voice. "We've got voice contact. Instructions in English on the international safety frequency, want us to climb to three thousand meters and come around 120 degrees right. Maintain 150 knots. He wants us to land at their base. He threatens to shoot us down if we don't. But I don't think he wants that—if he did, we'd be down already. They clearly want to steer us back, make us land, take us prisoner. I've been on their end of things before, I'm pretty sure of that. You guys just sit tight back there. We'll figure something out. But right now, we'd better give them what they want."

In the short time I'd worked with Dito, this was the longest speech that I'd ever heard him make. For all the excitement in his voice, he might as well have been an airline pilot informing his passengers that the Grand Canyon could be seen by looking out the left side of the aircraft.

The plane began to bank and climb, turning away from Ugandan airspace, turning back into Wiangara.

Kees asked the obvious question. "Why do they want us alive?"

"Who knows?" said Grady. "Could be a lot of reasons."

"Maybe they suspect where we come from," said Tommy. "Maybe they want to put us on display, embarrass our government, throw some shit into the election back home."

"Maybe," I said. "But Grady's right. We don't know, and we could spend a lot of time speculating on the reasons. The important thing is that they haven't simply shot us down. This offers possibilities."

My mind raced as I tried to think them all through. How badly did they want us alive? Could we have just kept going, daring them to shoot us down, until we reached Lake Albert? Probably not—if we were, for whatever reasons, more useful to them as prisoners than dead, we were of no use at all to them if we got away. But what then?

Now that we were settled on course again, albeit the wrong course, Grady unbuckled his seat belt and climbed up into the cockpit to talk with Moira and Dito. Standing on the cockpit step, he was only visible from the waist down. After a couple of minutes, he ducked back and motioned for me to join him.

"Dito here," said Grady, "has plotted out the course and distance to this airfield he thinks they want us to go to. It's about twenty-five minutes away, which means we've got about twenty-five minutes to figure out what the hell it is that we are going to do."

"Dito," I said, "does this course take us back where we came from, back over the lake where we were?"

"Let me see," he said, looking down at the chart on his knee. "Not quite, but very close. We'd only be about four, maybe five miles off, less if we can get away with cheating over just a little as we go along. Why?"

I'd already half-formed a plan in my mind, but I needed more information.

"If we land on their airfield, they own us from the moment we stop taxiing."

"So?"

"So, Wiangara may be controlled by the General-President's militia, but they don't have everything locked down. And their air assets are pretty limited, even though it doesn't feel like it right now. If we put ourselves down somewhere other than where they want us, even if only by a few miles, we buy some time and room to maneuver. Maybe get back up in the air while they go home to refuel, worst case, try hoofing it out."

"What, exactly, are you suggesting Harry?" asked Moira.

"This is a seaplane, isn't it? We will be flying back over our lake, won't we? Let's follow their instructions up to the last minute and then put her down on the water instead of on their airfield."

"Then what?" said Grady.

"Then I don't know what," I replied. "Even if we have to walk out, we're only looking at a hundred miles or so of E&E to get free. Tommy knows the area pretty well, and he has the language of the local villagers. Anyway, at least we won't be in the bag, and yet we won't have given them a reason to just shoot us down. Nothing else makes any sense."

"I like it," said Dito. "Dare them to try and stop us from landing where we want to. They can't stay with us forever, and like you say, we're not talking about a real air force. They won't have many friends conveniently on call. Let's put this puppy down and make 'em circle. Better than getting shot down. Dare them to try and stop us from landing. They won't, they'll ask for guidance."

"Yes," said Moira. "It's not much of a chance, but it's better than simply giving up. And we can make this work. They've got us up high because it's easy for them to stay on top of us. And because as we get close to this place, we have a range of coastal mountains to clear. But then we'll have to descend pretty abruptly in order to land. They'll have to let us get right down on the deck, and they'll have to let us slow down. And when we're low and slow, we'll be able to outmaneuver them, at least for a few minutes. They can't go as slow as we can. They'll fall out of the sky."

"What if they decide to strafe us once we're on the water?" said Grady."

"If they wanted to kill us outright, they'd have done it already. If we land in Wiangara, they'll ask for instructions, and before long, they'll have to return to refuel. That's our advantage. The jets can't stay on top of us indefinitely, and it will take them a while to organize to come after us with boats, or helicopters, or on the ground."

Funny how the mind and the spirit work. What we were discussing was nothing less than a long shot: landing right back where we started from, surrendering every advantage we thought our plan had given us. But having confronted total hopelessness, even a long shot now infused us with new life and energy.

"We do need to try and get a message to Parks," I said.

"What the fuck for?" said Grady. "So he can send in the marines?"

I ignored this.

"Try to get a message to the ship," I said. "We're not much more than an hour away from our rendezvous time. They can't do anything for us, like as not, nor can Parks, but they need to know, and who knows, Parks is very resourceful. Come to that, so's my sister. Better they know we're in trouble than not."

"Won't that compromise them?" asked Moira.

"Not if they just listen without acknowledging our transmission. Maybe you should tag the message with a 'do not acknowledge.'"

"It can't hurt, I guess."

Moira took a brief moment to organize her thoughts, keyed her mike, and began to transmit on the cockpit satphone, the only one with the power and the external antenna necessary for getting our message out.

"So, decision time. Are we going to land where they tell us and try to talk our way out?" I asked. "Or are we going to try to break away and put down on the lake?"

"We're going to take our shot at getting away from them," said Moira, "at least as long as I'm the left-seater in this aircraft."

I got the idea that the last part of her response had been intended for Grady's benefit. I wondered, not for the first time, at the apparent complexity of the relationship that had developed between them, at the unlikely mix of rivalry, respect, and love that seemed to be at work there.

"We're coming up on a range of hills now," said Dito.

"Do we need to climb?" asked Moira.

"No, we've got plenty of clearance."

"So now you guys are gonna have to do more of that complicated flying shit," said Grady.

"Looks like," answered Moira.

"We had best let the rest of the team know what is about to happen," I said. "How much time have we got?"

"Maybe ten minutes," said Dito.

"Okay. Grady, let's you and me go back and talk to everybody. This is something that needs being said face-to-face rather than an announcement over the intercom."

"Oh, one more thing," said Dito. "I suspect these two are running low on fuel. They've been up a long time if they were waiting for us when we took off. That may give us something else to work with."

Grady stopped to explain to Kees and Tommy, while I went further aft to discuss the next step with the rest of the team members. As I expected, no one raised any objections to trying to get away. Indeed, the only sign of agitation that I noticed was that Jerry Wolsey started chewing his toothpick a little faster.

"So, what happens next?" asked Colin.

"We land on the water, just as I said. Assuming that we're right about them wanting us alive, the planes will circle and call for help. They'll need something that can get close to us on the water or along the beach, a helicopter or a boat. Regardless, it takes them at least a little time to respond, and this buys us more time to figure a way out of this mess."

"And if you've figured wrong?" asked Kip.

"You already know the answer to that one. Anyway, we've run out of time."

As if on cue, the propellers suddenly changed pitch and the nose of the aircraft dropped. I noticed the look on Lorayne's face and dropped my hand to her shoulder, giving it a squeeze before returning to my seat in the navigator's compartment. Tommy was next to me, Grady and Kees sat opposite.

"We just got the word a few seconds ago," said Grady. "I was back up front with the headphones on when they told us to land. Looks like Dito was right on target."

"Perhaps that gives us an edge," I said.

"Perhaps we should get ready to swim," said Kees. We all three looked at him in surprise. I couldn't remember a similar comment from Kees since meeting him.

"We're edging over toward the lake right now," said Moira. "They haven't yet tried to correct our course. When the lake comes up, I'll make the hard break to line up north/south on the long axis of the lake. And I'll dive hard to get right down on the deck and just bang us down. Stand by."

We continued to descend gradually in the same direction. Then Moira came up on the intercom once again. "We're getting ready to turn and dive. Everybody hold tight on my count of three. Ready, now. One, two, three."

Moira put the plane on its wing in a sharp right bank, shedding altitude quickly. When she squared out of the turn, I knew that we had to be at least five hundred feet lower. With the nose still down, we gained speed as we lost more altitude.

"We've pissed 'em off by the sound of it," said Moira. "They overshot really badly when we dropped out from under them."

Now we leveled off. We had to be right above the water. Moira throttled back hard.

"Lots of pissed off sounding Chinese chatter," said Dito over the intercom. "I see 'em circling, and I think they're trying to raise a ground station for instructions."

How much longer? Time seemed to be standing still.

Cannon shots passed over us, not so loud as before.

"They just swept us from our nine o'clock," said Moira. "They're still way up high and out of position. Real messy traffic," she added. "They're stepping all over themselves, cutting off each other's transmissions, real fired up."

Another burst of cannon fire.

"The ranger didn't like that one, Yogi," said Grady into the intercom.

"I've got the lake lined up," said Moira. "Brace up, guys, I'm gonna put her down."

She leveled the wings, brought the nose up just slightly, and killed the engines. The plane bounced, hard, once, twice, then settled into what felt like a normal water landing. We continued to slow down, with everything apparently under control. I was doing my sums, figuring that we had to be well up the lake from where we'd been the first time. I glanced out the porthole, guessed that we might still be doing roughly maybe twenty knots, but losing speed rapidly.

And then I heard a God-awful metallic screech. We were all thrown hard against our seatbelts as the Cat slewed violently to the left. The whole aircraft twisted crazily on its longitudinal axis, so that now I was looking up at Grady, who was hanging from his seat belt above where I sat, and then, he was past my head as the plane bounced and twisted even further to the left and sideways. And then—bang— it dropped back and righted itself, throwing Grady and Kees back into their seats and floating Tommy and me up, momentarily weightless, straining against our seatbelts. Somehow, we were still travelling in our original direction, but tail first, moving perfectly backwards, aimed directly for the beach. When the lights inside the cabin died, I realized that I could no longer hear the sound of the engines, or was their sound being drowned out by the cacophony of screeches and pops and rips. And then I was thrown against my seatbelt once again as we came to an abrupt halt, accompanied by random metallic noises. Then sudden silence. All I could hear was the waves lapping against the hull. That and the gurgle of water sloshing around my feet.

CHAPTER 16

GRADY REACTED BEFORE anyone else. While Kees and Tommy and I still fumbled with our seatbelts, he produced a flashlight from somewhere, checked each of us quickly for injuries, and then climbed into the cockpit. Almost immediately he reappeared with Moira and Dito. Moira seemed to be all right, but Dito had a very nasty gash on his left forearm, and a smaller cut on his forehead.

Grady was pressing a cloth against the larger wound, trying to staunch the flow of blood. "Everybody else okay?" he asked. "Then, good. It feels like we're hard aground. That's good, I think. We have work to do. Moira?"

"Yeah?"

"I'm figuring this poor old airplane ain't never gonna fly again, right?"

"Not a prayer, Grady. We were fine, and then we hit something out there—I think the float on the port wing hit a rock or something and that spun us out of control. I looked out after we stopped, it's hard to tell for sure, but I think that wing is pretty much messed up."

"No matter—we weren't really likely to fly out of here anyway.

Now we're really committed to Plan B, whatever the hell that winds up being. Okay, look. Harry, take Dito here and see if you can keep him from bleeding to death 'til I can get Jerry up here to take care of him. Moira, take this flashlight and go back into the cockpit. Start stripping it of anything you think might be useful. Rest of us, head aft. Tommy, let Kees here boost you up in the engineer's compartment, feel around, see if you can find anything—there's spare weapons and ammo up there, make sure you get it. Kees, after you help Tommy, start in on the galley. As soon as I come up with another flashlight I'll get to you. We need food, weapons and ammo, stuff to carry things in. Oh, round up some empty cans in case we need to collect rainwater. Most of our stuff wound up back in the waist gunners' compartment."

I took Dito by the arm, sat him down. As Grady disappeared aft, I knelt in front of Dito, trying to hold him where a shaft of light streamed in from the porthole, my knees getting soaked, trying to maintain pressure with one hand to keep the wound from pulsing blood, while fumbling to free Dito's belt to use as a tourniquet. I had just gotten the belt unbuckled when Jerry appeared.

"Here now, Harry, let me take over," drawled Jerry as he sat down next to Dito, resting the first aid kit over his knees. "Forget the belt, I've got something better. Keep up the pressure where you've got it on the wound, and take this flashlight with your other hand. I need more light than what's coming through the window."

This was not as easy as it sounded, but I managed.

"What's it like in the back?" I asked.

"Pretty much okay, except poor ol' Peter somehow managed to break his leg. I was going to try and fix that when Grady told me that you was up here trying to keep Dito from bleeding to death. Hold the light on the wound—there—then move your hand and that bloody rag away so I can see."

I steadied the light, and lifted the rag, getting my first real look at Dito's wound. A big gash, bleeding heavily, but not real deep. At least I couldn't see bone.

"Okay, good, keep the light right there. Take your other hand and brace this first-aid kit so it don't pitch off into the water."

Despite the incredibly awkward posture he was forced to assume, he took out the suture set and began to work. He was still working on the gash when Moira joined us. In one hand she had a short aluminum case, rather like a long camera case, and in the other hand she clutched the strap of a big leather purse, almost like what the army used to call a musette bag. She put down the case and the bag and took the flashlight from me. She pressed the forefinger of her free hand into the wound, taking over from Jerry the task of blocking the blood flow, allowing him to use both hands for his suturing. I shifted my weight to mitigate the increasing discomfort where my kneecaps pressed against the floor of the cabin, concentrating on keeping the first-aid kit from toppling over. From time to time I looked up past the light, to the dimly-lit grimace on Dito's face. I don't know how long it took. As I continued kneeling the water steadily rose along my thighs; by the time Jerry had dressing Dito's wound, the water was above my crotch.

"...now, I know that it's hurtin' like a motherfucker," Jerry was saying to Dito as he finished up, "and it's gonna hurt a whole helluva lot worse before long, but I can't give you any morphine for it yet, we've got to keep you up and running. But we just happen to have a little bottle of Percocet in here, I'll give you one of those, it'll take some of the pain away, but it shouldn't knock you flat on your ass. It may make you a little drowsy, but you won't fall asleep as long as you keep movin' and you gotta keep movin', Grady says, 'cause we gotta get the fuck outa here."

He shook a little white tablet out of a standard prescription bottle and pressed it into Dito's good hand. Dito put the tablet into his mouth and gulped it down dry.

"Did Grady tell you how exactly he intended to do that?" asked Moira.

The almost light-hearted tone in her voice caught my attention. I looked up and saw that she was smiling.

"No, ma'am, actually what he said was to make sure that Dito here could walk 'cause we were going to have to carry Peter, and having one guy to carry was enough. But I think his plan right now is to get everybody ashore ASAP with as much stuff as we can save, and get away from here. That's what it sounded like when he came back to the back just now."

He closed the lid on the first-aid kit, carefully snapped the latches into, and set it aside so that he could stand up. I stood up at the same time, awkwardly, since my legs were a bit stiff. Together we helped Dito to his feet. Moira handed me the flashlight so that she could gather up her bag and case. I shined the light in the direction of the hatch leading aft, and Jerry led Dito and Moira out. After they cleared the hatch, I flashed the light around the compartment one more time, satisfied myself that there was nothing worth taking, and followed them.

By the time I stepped into the galley, the others had already passed through to the next compartment. Here the sunlight from outside was brighter, partly because there were more windows, partly due to a gaping crack in the fuselage. I looked around, first at the now empty rack above the microwave, then at the open doors of the small cabinet on the other wall, above the port-side landing-gear wheel well. Although I was now standing upright, the water was once again at crotch level, and I could feel a current playing around my legs from somewhere below the surface. Clearly the tear in the fuselage extended below the waterline. On the surface of the water odd bits of debris floated through the shaft of light, some cardboard, a bottle. Bobbing on the surface in one corner was the unmistakable brown plastic package of an MRE that the others had apparently missed. I grabbed it and continued into the next compartment, also empty and rapidly flooding. The water was now just below my waist.

The door of the hatch leading to the waist gunners' compartment had swung shut. I tucked the MRE under my arm, freeing a hand to open the hatch. Here, finally, was major damage; the right side of the compartment was ripped wide open, the entire aft section of the plane twisted downward. The dull gray pre-dawn light filtered into the compartment from outside, washing out the stark contrasts between light and shadow that my flashlight had carved in the intact compartments. I didn't bother to check the tunnel gunner's compartment, which was now completely submerged. Instead I turned to the great hole—ironically, the hatch just alongside it remained securely in place—and I looked out. The wing on that side projected skyward at a crazy angle. Below it I could see Moira, Dito, and Jerry wading through chest-deep water toward the shore. I took hold of a protruding piece of metal framing, using it to stabilize myself against the water bubbling up over the opening. I unbuttoned my shirt enough to stuff the MRE inside and then buttoned up again to hold it in place. With my hands thus freed, I was on the verge of diving into the water and swimming to catch up with the others when a thought struck me.

"Hey, Jerry," I called out.

"Yeah, what, Harry?" he responded, turning toward me.

"Find out from Grady if we salvaged a thermite grenade, if we did, see if he can get Colin to swim it out to me."

"Can do, Harry."

He pressed on through the water, holding the first-aid kit above his head. Looking into the gloom beyond him, beyond where Dito and Moira were struggling along, I could make out a narrow strip of beach, maybe eighty meters long, and what looked like bluffs rising beyond. The rest of the team seemed to be huddled there. I couldn't make out individual identities, or even assure myself that everyone was accounted for.

The two fast movers came out of nowhere, maybe two hundred feet off the deck, low enough for the jet blast to assault even my insensitive ears, low enough to actually rock the hulk of the Catalina and nearly cost me my balance. I could hear the thump of cannon fire, see tracers streaking toward the beach, and then they were turning right and climbing. I could see the white-orange circles of the jet exhausts long after the gray shapes had faded in the morning mist. They were moving north, and I wondered if they would come back, and I wondered what they would do if they did.

I was getting colder. The part of me that was out of the water and exposed to the breeze was even more chilled than my immersed lower half. Waiting out here had begun to seem like a thoroughly bad idea. I stepped back from the opening, taking shelter from the wind behind the intact portion of the fuselage. Then I heard Colin shouting from outside.

"Harry, still there, are you?"

I looked outside, saw him bobbing up and down in the water. He held a familiar green cylinder above his head. "You wanted one of these, did you now?"

"Yes. It seems better that we give them a burned hulk to puzzle over."

"Right—Viking funeral for the old girl then. Here you go."

He started to toss the grenade to me, thought better of it, and struggled over to where he could hand it up to me.

"Wouldn't do now for you to drop this, would it? We'd never find it, and isn't it the only one we could find?"

I leaned down to take it from him.

"Be careful in there, Harry."

"I will be."

"Hey, now, I'll stick around out here 'til you're done. Don't be too long now."

I struggled back to the front of the aircraft, all the way to the old bombardier's compartment at the very front, beneath the cockpit. Here is where we had installed the fancy avionics, the modern radar, and all the other electronic gadgetry. These were worth destroying because they were the most traceable components. Moreover, a fire started here had a greater chance of catching hold and spreading because the plane had spun in backward leaving this compartment projecting upwards, mostly above the water level. Thinking solely of my own survival, this compartment also had the advantage of being upwind of any leaking fuel tanks. Starting a fire here offered me a better chance of not incinerating myself in a fireball of burning aviation fuel.

I wedged the grenade between the various 'black boxes,' pulled the pin, and slogged aft as rapidly as possible. But I'd barely gone halfway when I heard a soft 'whoosh' behind me. I pressed on to where Colin was waiting and jumped into the water. With my hands free I decided that swimming would be more efficient than wading, and struck off behind him for the shore. But after only fifteen or twenty meters, things shelved very rapidly, and it was no longer possible to swim. I waded forward, my legs feeling more leaden with each step.

Hearing the explosion behind me, I turned just as the ball of flame completely engulfed the old Catalina, burning so hot and fiercely that, even at a distance of some fifty or sixty meters I could feel the warmth. I paused for a few seconds, watching her burn, and then turned toward shore again. Trudging past the dirty rime that marked the tide line, I soon reached the shelter of the rocks at the base of the bluff, where the rest of the team huddled out of the wind, clustered around two figures lying on the sand.

"Nice fireworks," said Kip. His words were light, but the voice was grim.

"It's about fucking time, you old arsonist," Grady said—again, the words were more jocular than the tone.

Moira, who was sitting next to Grady, had tears in her eyes. As I watched the flames climbing higher, and the huge cloud of black smoke that billowed hundreds of feet higher still, I also felt sad. Not sad because we were clearly in very deep trouble, although there was no mistaking the dangers of our predicament, but sad in the way that a family is saddened by watching their home go up in flames. For the old Cat had been our home, our support, our haven, and our means and hope for escape. It had been, in a very real sense, a part of us. And now it was gone. No wonder Moira looked so utterly forlorn.

And there were other reasons for misery. Peter and Dr. Yang lay there before us. Kees and Colin were busy splinting Peter's obviously broken leg, while Jerry was bent over Dr. Yang, working furiously at her abdomen while Jean-Paul and Lem struggled to hold her still. I stepped around and saw that her belly was laid open and that Jerry's hands were immersed between coils of intestine, trying desperately to find and close off a bleeder. I'd scarcely registered this when she suddenly stiffened and then went limp.

"She's fucking gone," said Jerry, withdrawing his hands, looking down at the mess that reached well past his wrists. "She was cut up all to hell inside. Why the fuck did they strafe us before pulling out? Bastards," he added, gesturing skyward. He started to wipe his hands on his pants, then thought better of it and used the sleeve of the poor woman's shirt. He looked up at me and said, "She won't mind now, will she?"

"How's Peter?" My words were directed to Colin, but Peter himself answered.

"Well, Harry, I've been much better. Bit embarrassed, though—all these years, all the missions, never a burden to anyone, and now look at me."

Jerry edged over to him, checked that the splint was properly applied. I followed him standing at Peter's shoulder as Jerry drew a cigarette out of a damp pack and lit up. The smoke curled up into my nostrils and suddenly, despite the years since I'd last smoked, I again wanted one very badly. He must have read my mind, for he offered me the lit cigarette, shaking another one out of the pack for himself. I took it and greedily sucked the smoke deep into my lungs. I sat down next to him, squatting Indian style, looking into Peter's eyes and trying to get a feel for his condition. Behind me I could hear the others lifting Dr. Yang's body and carrying it up into the rocks. Somehow, instinctively, no one wanted to simply commit her to the lake, and a place in the rocks was the closest we could come to a burial. I thought I should get up and say something, and then I heard Grady's voice carrying from where they'd placed her body.

"Lord, I didn't know this lady, none of us did, but she helped a lot of people, and now she's dead. It's not fucking fair, but I guess you've got your reasons. Anyway, now that you've got her, you oughta be nice to her. She had more guts than most, and she showed us the best of her people, not like the assholes running her country."

Then I heard Kip begin to speak, but the wind had picked up, and I couldn't make out the words, although they were probably something a bit more conventional than Grady's eulogy. Gradually—it seemed like hours, but could only have been a few minutes—the others came down from the rocks and we gathered in a semi-circle around Peter. Lem and Jean-Paul had improvised a litter and placed him upon it, which didn't seem to make him more comfortable, but spoke to the fact that soon we would have to make a move. I scanned the faces of the others as I smoked another one of Jerry's cigarettes.

Relatively speaking, we didn't look too bad. Saddened, soaked through and utterly bedraggled, but not hopeless. Somewhere in the background Kip was bustling about, but I couldn't see what he was doing. Even in just a few minutes Peter was looking better and Dito, although terribly pale, at least seemed no worse than when I had last seen him on the plane. He managed to smile through his pain when I asked him how he was doing.

"There've been better days than this one," he said, "but there haven't been any worse. At least none that come to mind. So, I've achieved a kind of personal best in the category of bad days." He punctuated this comment with another wan smile.

"Okay, people, listen up," said Grady. "Moira and Dito here did their damnedest to buy us a little space before the gomers come after us, but we sit around here like a bunch of old whores on holiday, and we piss it all away. Let's saddle up and get going."

This elicited some mild groans, but no real protest, because the necessity of putting maximum distance between ourselves and the crash site was perfectly obvious.

"Hey guys, over here first," said Kip. "Grady asked me to go through the stuff we saved and organize it into individual loads. We got tac vests for almost everybody, we recovered eight of the 416s, one with a M203 and a handful of 40mm grenades, the two MP-5s," these were the submachine guns that were on the plane as personal defense weapons for Moira and Dito, "and some of you saved the handguns you brought with you. We wound up with a fair amount of ammo for each weapon. We've got exactly five of the First Strike compact rations and nine MREs——"

"Ten," I spoke up, fishing out the one I'd saved from my shirt and tossing the plastic-wrapped ration over to him.

"And one more useful weapon," said Moira, holding up the aluminum case she had salvaged. "My Drilling."

" Your what?" asked Grady.

"An old German hunting weapon," I said. "Sort of a double-barreled shotgun with a single-shot rifle barrel between and just below the two shotgun barrels. The Luftwaffe used to issue them to aircrews as survival weapons."

Inwardly I blessed her for her forethought. If we had to hunt game in order to keep eating, as seemed likely, then the Drilling would be far more efficient than any of our other weapons.

"Okay," said Kip, "we've got more stuff than I thought. We've also got some bread and cheese, a big salami, and sandwich meat out of the little fridge, a sack of Milky Way bars, an unopened carton of cigarettes. Anyway, here's how it goes. Everybody takes a weapon and a share of ammunition. There's also some grenades, smoke and frag. Everybody grab a couple. Moira, you keep your shotgun thing, share out the pistols so that Peter and Dito have one. Tac vests to everybody save Peter and Dito and Moira. Kees, you and Lem will carry Peter to start with, Jerry you've got your medic's bag. Grady and Lorayne have the knapsacks we found, they'll carry the food and the cigarettes. Five Camel Baks and they are full. That's Grady, Lorayne, Moira, Harry, and Tommy. Oh, and Harry, we found two pint bottles of whiskey. You take charge of them. Okay, everybody, get your stuff."

We formed a loose circle around the pile of gear and began to load up.

"After you've got your shit, then form up," ordered Grady. "Colin's got the point. Colin, I want you well out in front. Tommy, you're number two, you try to space it so you can keep both Colin and the main body in view. I know you know the country ahead, but right now I want Colin on point. Kip and J-P will walk rear security until we change out carrying Peter, then they'll be the bearers and Kees and Lem will drop back. Moira, you keep an eye on Dito. Everybody got it? Okay. We saved one satphone, five tactical radios and a dozen spare batteries. Colin, you take one, Kip, and Kees and Harry. I'll take the last one and the sat phone—that's trackable, so only for emergencies." He laughed. "Right now, children, what we have is not an emergency. Kees, don't turn your radio on, save the battery, until you swap out with Kip. Harry, you take the spare batteries. Use the radios sparingly. They're tactical, line of sight, so I don't think they can be tracked, but let's not take any more fucking chances than we have to. Okay, people? Everybody got what you're supposed to have? Okay, Colin—lead 'em out."

"Glad to, boss, but where the fuck am I supposed to be leading us?"

"Inland, away from boats, away from open shoreline where helicopters can land. Take us up that draw over to the right," he pointed to an opening between the bluffs. Let's get about a klick in, and then turn north and work parallel to the lake, we know we've got to get around the lake and then start working our way northeast."

Colin picked up his 416 and headed in the direction Grady had indicated. Tommy allowed him to get almost out of sight, then started after him. After a similar interval Grady led the rest of us out, with Moira and Dito right behind, then Kees and Lem with Peter's litter. Jerry followed them, and Lorayne and I rounded out the main body. As we reached the point where we were beginning to climb above the beach, I turned around and looked back to measure the interval between myself and Kip and Jean-Paul. Looking beyond them, I could see that the fire had burned down and that the sea breeze had spread the pillar of black smoke into a long horizontal layer, less dense now and about a thousand feet up, like a layer of smog over a small city. Distance and the effects of the fire had given the Catalina a shriveled look. It lay black and twisted amidst the flickering remnants of the fire. Conflicting thoughts raced through my head, but there seemed little point in sharing them. After giving Kip a short wave, I turned away from the burning plane and marched up the hill.

Lorayne was already some fifteen meters away. I didn't want to risk falling out of contact if the going became tougher ahead, so I picked up my pace until I closed the gap to five meters. The draw we were following bent gently to the left in a long curve. Although there was no path as such, there was little more than scrub brush to inhibit our passage. We might as well have been hiking along a two-lane road. We could see each other clearly, although the sky was dull and overcast, I could see Colin up ahead, maybe a hundred-and-fifty meters distant. I was glad to have such easy going, but being in the open made me feel uncomfortably exposed. I would also have preferred some shelter from the breeze blowing off the lake. But even this had its benefit, because it helped our damp clothes to dry more quickly.

A half-hour brought us to the head of the draw. Behind the bluffs above the lake rose a more serious set of hills. Grady decided to turn us northward, putting these hills to our left. Maybe they would provide a barrier to truck-borne militia responding from their main camps in Wiangara. For another hour we pushed the pace, taking advantage of our easy "path." But then it steepened abruptly, so much so that, at first, I feared we had hurried our way into a rock-walled cul-de-sac. But, looking up, I could see Colin and Tommy atop the wall about ten meters above and realized that they'd found a way up. Ahead of me the others were disappearing one by one into what appeared to be a broad crack in the rock wall, which proved to be the opening for a kind of rough natural staircase leading to the top. After a very bad start to the day, our luck seemed to have taken a turn for the better.

At the top of the wall Grady called a halt. We rested for a moment and passed the water around. Though we spoke little, everyone seemed to be bearing up reasonably well except Dito, who looked terribly pale. After ten minutes we moved out, with Kip and Jean-Paul now carrying Peter, and Kees and Lem bringing up the rear.

Now we passed through a thick stand of tall trees. Although we were no longer walking in the open, our path had taken us back toward the lake, which lay almost vertically below, a little over a hundred meters down. Occasionally I could look down and see the waves breaking against the rocks, although most of the time our route ran well back from the edge of the cliff. From time to time the sun broke through the overcast; under other circumstances, it would have been very pleasant. Indeed, I was reminded strongly of the nature walks I used to take with Patti. And there was a pretty girl walking just ahead of me, although the overall effect was somewhat spoiled by the carbine slung slantwise across her back. I pictured in my mind's eye a cover of the *National Geographic:* "Exploring Nature's Wonders, with Automatic Weapons."

Another two hours. I wasn't carrying as much as I had on the approach march before the raid, and the terrain thus far hadn't been particularly challenging. But Grady was forcing a rapid pace, and it was beginning to tell on me. Although I appreciated the need for us to push on, I was delighted when he called a lunch break. Lunch consisted of the cold cuts that had been rescued from the little refrigerator, and was offered less because we could afford to consume so much of our meager rations so soon than because waiting would see these items go bad. Still, the meager portion of cheese and sliced turkey seemed to give me a big energy boost.

After we finished eating, Grady cracked the carton of cigarettes, opened a pack, and passed them around to those who wanted a smoke. I took one, thinking that, at the rate I was going on this day, I'd become a heavy smoker again. But dry clothes, a glimmer of warm sunshine, food in my stomach, a few minutes rest, and a shot of nicotine all combined to produce a feeling akin to euphoria. Although our break lasted less than twenty minutes, when we resumed our march I felt capable of leaping tall buildings in a single bound, or at least confident that I could keep up with these children for the rest of the day.

Grady had taken the opportunity of the break to rotate Peter's litter bearers. Now Colin and Tommy had taken on that task, while Kip and Jean-Paul took the point and slack positions and Kees and Lem remained in the rear. At first it seemed that Kip was setting a slower pace, a bit surprising considering his longer legs and superb physical condition. But we were traveling more slowly because we no longer had anything resembling a trail to follow. Instead we threaded our way through the trees, following the contour line, working northward along the shoreline.

Beneath the shade of the tall trees, separated now from the water's edge by another rim of shoreline bluffs, we were completely sheltered from the breeze off the lake. As the afternoon wore on, it became warm enough to make us sweat. When, after another couple of hours, we intersected the course of a pristine mountain stream, Grady called a halt and allowed us to bathe our faces in the cold water and drink our fill. We hadn't any water purification tablets, hadn't thought we'd need any, but the need to stay hydrated outweighed the risk of parasites. Then Tommy took the point, Kees and Lem resumed the task of carrying Peter, Colin dropped to the rear, and off we went.

I think that Colin actually heard the helicopter first. I heard him calling out, I guess to Kip, who was between us, but he was too far behind for me to understand his words. But then, even before Colin could radio the word to Grady, I heard the distinctive sound of rotors and froze as the chopper swept overhead. There was no indication that we'd been seen. For that matter, there was no evidence that the helicopter was even looking for us, but, deep inside, I'm sure we all believed that it was. The flyover had given us all an adrenaline rush. Now there was no question that Kip was obviously pushing the pace, and all of us were more than willing to push right along with him. Any doubts that the search was now well and truly on were dispelled not more than ten minutes later when the same helicopter flew over us again, this time returning southward, but flying at a much slower pace.

Now I understood. Someone had calculated the greatest distance that a group of fit individuals on foot could have covered in the time since our plane went down. The previous overflight had taken the helicopter out to that point, and now the pilot was working his way back, expecting that somewhere along the way we would be observed. Perhaps even now other helicopters were flying similar search patterns along other directions we could have taken. Perhaps whoever was directing the search had assumed, not unreasonably, that we would work away north, but stay close enough to the lake to maintain the closest route to either Uganda or South Sudan. Or, maybe they'd just made a lucky guess. No matter. The helicopter was up there, flying a course that zigzagged very deliberately across our line of march. Had we been seen? I had no idea. But as soon as the helicopter moved out of sight and earshot once again, we pushed forward with a renewed sense of urgency.

About a half-hour later Grady dropped back and fell in beside me. "How you doing there, Harry?"

"Not too bad, considering."

"Considering that you're a decrepit old fart who has no business trying to do this shit?"

"Yeah," I answered, "considering all that."

"Well, I'll tell you what. I'm beginning to seriously feel like a decrepit old fart myself, and my hat's off to you for keeping up the way you have. But I had to sort of see, 'cause we've got a problem building, and I need to know if you're okay, if the problem's bigger than I think even."

"Tell me."

"Kees and Lem, for one. They're not complaining any, but I can see that this second round on the litter is really taking it out of them."

This I could understand, having done my share of stretcher carrying. It's not just the weight, but the way that it pulls at your shoulders and elbows and wrists and fingers, and the way that it makes it hard to maintain a comfortable and natural pace.

"What else?"

"Dito. He lost a fair bit of blood this morning and he's weak. Plus, if he takes something for the pain, it makes him sluggish. If he doesn't, then the pain drags him down. He's doing his best, but he's not in the shape he needs to be in. Neither is Moira. We didn't push physical conditioning for them like we did everybody else. Didn't reckon on anything like this."

"No, we didn't, did we?"

"But I don't want to stop for a while yet, not with that chopper buzzing around. Anyway, Jerry and I are going to swap out our loads with Kees and Lem, give them enough of a break so that we can keep going. But I'm going to put Lorayne on point, and let you take the slack. She's good in the woods, and I suspect you can keep your end up. But it'll be more restful for Kip and Jean-Paul if they're not up front. After Jerry and I've done our stint, I'm going to put the two of them on the stretcher with Colin and Tommy, and see if we can continue better with a four-man carry. Right now, we need Tommy's muscles more than we need his ground knowledge."

"No problem. Lorayne will do fine, and I'm sure I will."

I appreciated not only the reasons Grady had given for these various assignments, but also the unspoken ones. Grady understood that, for all her many capabilities, Lorayne would not be at her best carrying Peter. He knew, too, that though I was keeping up, a stint of litter carrying would likely destroy whatever reserves of energy I could muster. Besides, allowing for the impact of Smitty's death and Peter's injury, he was trying to keep the various two-man teams operating together.

"Okay, then," said Grady.

He dropped off to pass the word to Colin and Tommy—radio silence suddenly seemed a very good idea—while I picked up the pace and caught up with Lorayne. Together we advanced up the column until finally we reached Jean-Paul. I fell in alongside him and explained what Grady had ordered, while Lorayne pressed forward to link up with Kip. A few minutes later I passed Kip standing next to a tree.

"Sounds like our shit's about to get real watery again, huh, Major."

"Kip, our shit's been pretty damned soft since they picked us up on radar this morning. But we'll come up with some way out."

"Got no doubt, none at all. By the way, good news is that I just hit a decent path just before Lorayne caught up with me. It'll make the going a little bit easier for a while."

He walked along beside me and we continued to talk.

"Good paths make me a little nervous," I said.

"But the threat's probably behind. If there is one yet."

"You're right, Kip. And we need a good path."

We walked along together in silence for perhaps ten minutes, enjoying each other's proximity even as we retreated into our separate thoughts. Finally, Kip broke the silence.

"I guess I'd better drop back some. Looks like we've opened up a gap on the rest of the team."

"Okay, sure." But we continued to walk, albeit a bit more slowly.

"Know what I was just thinking, Major?"

"No, what?"

"This could turn into a long-damned walk."

I couldn't think of anything to say, so I just gave him a smile and a pat on the shoulder, which seemed somehow to be the right thing. He pulled up to wait for the others to catch up and I continued ahead, finding the path just as Kip had described it, hurrying around a bend to regain sight of Lorayne, who had charged off at the fastest pace of the day. I agreed with Kip that a good path was a Godsend, now that we were beginning to wear down. But another thought had also occurred to me, one far less comforting. Suppose that the gomers were also aware of this path and that the helicopter that had flown by us earlier had dropped off an ambush team somewhere ahead before returning to conduct its search. I had a lot of confidence in Lorayne, but if she triggered an ambush, I'd have to get her out of it.

Up to now I had given little thought to the possibility of hostile contact. Now I made sure that I had a round in the chamber. I couldn't afford what the SEALs call a "dead man's" weapon. I then gave a sharp tap to the base of the magazine to make sure it was seated properly. With my 416 now resting across my chest, suspended by its tactical sling, I pulled the one smoke grenade I was carrying from my pocket and bent back the crimp that held the pin in place. I was, I thought grimly, as ready as I would ever be.

I glanced over my shoulder, making sure that I could see Jean-Paul who was now the next in line. I looked ahead to Lorayne, who was maybe twenty meters ahead now that we were on a fairly open path. I paid particular attention to the trees and the high ground to either side. Young soldiers have an awful tendency to scan only at eye level and below, and, Lorayne, for all her virtues, was a young soldier. I hoped that I was worrying for nothing.

An hour passed and then another. I was becoming weary from the effort, weary from the mental strain. Around 1700 hours Grady called another brief halt, passing out Milky Way candy bars to everyone. This was dinner. Then we got underway, with Lorayne and me again in the lead. The clouds had been gathering for most of the afternoon, and shortly after we resumed the march, it started to drizzle intermittently. But to our right, over, we could see a line of darker, uglier clouds moving in our direction.

After yet another hour, I wondered whether Grady was going to call any kind of break. Then I heard rapid footsteps behind me and turned to see Jerry hurrying to catch up with me. From the expression on his face, he hadn't come to tell me to take a break. That he motioned me to keep moving rather than holding up for him confirmed this.

"We've got trouble, Hair Doctor."

"How so?"

"We heard the helicopter again, sounded pretty far behind us, but then it was closing on us, and then we couldn't hear it. Grady thinks it may have landed, from the sound of it back where we first picked up this path. If that's the case, we may have gomers pounding up the trail after us."

For an instant I almost gave way to despair. Here we were, shaken by a crash landing, worn by a hard day's march, and now fresh troops on our tail. But I didn't need to take that thought any further.

"I'll get word to Lorayne," I said, and I pushed myself to catch up with her. She took the news without apparent excitement, forging ahead as if being pursued by an armed enemy was the most normal thing in the world. I dropped back into position and followed her along, watching carefully to our front, but with my ears attuned to the first sounds of shots coming from our rear. Tired as I now was, I found a fresh surge of energy. To paraphrase Dr. Johnson, "there's nothing like the imminent prospect of a firefight to focus one's attention."

We came to a small clearing. I could see the storm clouds looming to the east, see ugly bolts of lightning and, for the first time, hear the sound of distant thunder. Thirty minutes or so, and the storm would overtake us. But would the gomers catch us first?

In fact, the storm took the gomers off our backs, at least temporarily. Helicopter pilots tend not to like electrical storms, and this nasty one would be no exception to the rule. I guessed that the gomers didn't really know how close they were to us, or had decided it didn't matter. They could have concluded that, since we really had no place to go, it mattered not whether they caught up with us today, tomorrow, or the day after. In any event, Grady and Jerry, who were now working rear guard, heard and saw the helicopter tracking slowly along the path behind us, then watched as it dropped below the trees. Then, after a brief interval, they saw it rising again, this time not bothering to remain at a search altitude but climbing high as it turned away to the south.

Not many minutes after the helicopter disappeared from view, the big clouds rolled onto shore, and the drizzle gave way to a monstrous driving rainstorm, which bombarded us with bolts of lightning while thunderclaps pounded above our heads. Soon we were as thoroughly soaked as we'd been after escaping from the Catalina. The path turned to mud almost instantly, a slick greasy clay that made each step like ice skating.

I ducked my head, protecting my face against the wind-driven rain, trying to concentrate on where to place each footstep. If anyone wanted to ambush us now, then more power to them. Hunched over in this protective posture, squinting into the wind, I almost ran into Lorayne, who had stopped in the middle of the path.

"It splits here," she said.

"What splits? Oh, the path splits." We'd come to a fork. The left fork led inland, broadening as it dropped down. It looked quite inviting. The right fork was scarcely wide enough for a single column, and it climbed sharply. It was clearly the road less traveled.

"Which way should we go?" she asked.

I looked again at both paths, thought about it.

"Check out the right path," I said. "Quickly now, just see if it plays out in the next hundred yards or so. If it stays good for at least that long, then come back here and report. I'll hold the team up here until you get back."

She had been gone little more than a couple of minutes when the rest of the team caught up. As soon as Grady reached me I explained what I'd done.

"Well, we'll see," was all he said. He looked very tired, they all did. I probably looked beat myself. We stood there in the rain, waiting for Lorayne to return.

"It's not as bad as it looks," she announced upon rejoining us. "It takes a little bend, then it levels out again and widens out. It makes kind of a shelf between a cliff on the landward side and another cliff that drops off straight down to the lake. It's uphill, but except for the first bit, it's not too steep.

Kip was the one who expressed what I'd been thinking when I sent Lorayne to check it out.

"These gomers are probably not much more familiar with the countryside around here than we are. The right path doesn't even look much like a path from here. There's at least a fair chance that they'll assume that we stayed with the obvious path."

Grady looked at Kip, then back at me.

"Don't much matter at this point, does it? We're wasting time here, we need to keep going. Lead us out, Lorayne."

He gestured tiredly to the right-hand path, and we moved out again. It was much as Lorayne had described, with a steep, narrow pitch at the beginning giving way quickly to a wide-open stretch, a broad ledge between the higher inland ridge and the cliff dropping off to the lake. Here the going was easier. It needed to be, for I was now just about done in. Not long after we passed the point to which

Lorayne had reconnoitered, the ledge began to narrow, at first very gradually. After passing a pair of giant boulders, each taller than a man's head, we found that on the other side the path suddenly steepened and narrowed to the width of a marching column of fours, then a column of twos. And then we found the cave.

Grady told Lorayne and me to explore the cave and sent Jerry up the path to see what it looked like. We had just exited the cave, which looked promising, when Jerry returned.

"It's a goddamned dead end," he said. "The path continues to curve around and up, but just past that outcrop up there it narrows down to almost nothing. Maybe it opens out again, but you'd just about have to mountaineer your way around with pitons and ropes and shit to find out."

"Then we need to get our asses back down the trail before we get boxed in," said Grady, picking up his pack.

"No, wait," said Kip. He glanced in my direction before continuing. "We know that the gomers were behind us this afternoon, and some of them could be pretty close. If they start at first light, and the chopper sets them down on the trail where it picked them up this afternoon, and they'll be up to the fork back there in no time. But whichever way we go now, they've got an equal chance of catching us in the morning. It's just about dark, and we won't get much more done tonight."

"Better than being trapped up here."

"No, Grady, you're wrong. Look around you." Kip's sweeping gesture took in the entire group. "Good troopers, every one of them. On a good day we could outmarch a fresh pursuit or fight our way out of an ambush. But this just hasn't exactly been what you'd call a good day. Look around. Look at us. Look good and hard. Soaked to the skin. Tired. Most of all, we've just had the shit kicked out of us. We'd pulled it off, we were almost home free, we were halfway back to the world. Now we've just blown up the freedom bird, we've got no ride out of this god-forsaken country, and they're hunting us like animals. Take this bunch down the mountain right now and somebody else'll break a leg in the dark, and then how do we carry 'em out? Or, for all we know, they've still got a patrol somewhere down there. We blunder back down the hill into a damned patrol and we'll get shot to shit. Major?"

It had been Grady's team from the very beginning—I had always insisted on that. But Kip was right, and I had to say so. "The team needs to lay up, Grady. That cave doesn't look so bad. If it's deep enough we might even chance a fire, get everyone dry and warm. Even if it isn't, it's out of the wind and the rain."

"Give the guys a chance to bounce back," added Kip. "By tomorrow they'll be ready to kick ass again. If they come for us here tonight, we'll fight as well or better than we would back in the bush. What difference does it make? If we have to fight tonight then we're just shit out of luck anyway."

Grady said nothing, seemed to draw into himself. I knew him so well, knew that he just ached to keep moving. When he finally spoke, he addressed the whole group.

"We're staying put for the night. Kees, you and Lem go back down the trail to where it widens out and take up a lookout. Take a radio. If they come after us, call me and then hold the position until we can get some help down to you. Okay? I'll get some food down to you as soon as I can, and we'll get another team down and relieve you in two hours. Everybody else get into the cave. We'll dry out, sort through all this crap we hauled off the plane, get something to eat. Tonight, we get our shit together."

"What about tomorrow?" asked Lorayne.

"Tomorrow?" said Grady, "Tomorrow, children, like Scarlett O'Hara said, tomorrow is another fucking day."

CHAPTER 17

THE CAVE, WE discovered on closer examination, was blessedly deep, maybe fifty feet altogether, and past the low and narrow entrance it widened out, almost as wide as the average suburban tract house, and maybe twenty feet high at the very back. We could possibly get away with a fire, at least briefly, without smoking ourselves out, but even without, I blessed the shelter it gave us from the wind and the rain—and from observation.

By flashlight we emptied our pockets and the miscellany of rucksacks, equipment cases, and plastic bags we'd used to haul the treasures recovered from the plane. This more careful inventory confirmed what Kip had determined on the beach: we were tolerably well supplied with ammunition, less so with food and water. Water didn't worry me, not with the pelting rain outside. As for food, well, we'd figure out something. In the meantime, I volunteered to take Kees and Lem something to eat. I retrieved four Milky Way bars from the sack; although we hadn't yet worked out a food ration, these, at least, we had in abundance. Walking downhill to them, I marveled that my tiredness had eased. Sometimes, knowing that you don't have to keep on pushing is a lift in itself.

I found Kees and Lem at the boulders that marked the narrowing of the trail. I handed them the candy bars, talked with them for a few minutes, and took the chance to look around and size things up. On the way back, I continued past the mouth of the cave, pausing momentarily at the smell of coffee—small miracle, that—before following the uphill path that Jerry had scouted earlier. Returning to the cave, I gratefully accepted a cup of coffee from Tommy and then slumped down alongside Kip with my back resting against the curved cave wall.

This little expedition improved my spirits notably. If our long-term prospects were decidedly bleak, our immediate tactical situation could hardly have been better. Our position was, in effect, a ledge carved into the face of a near vertical cliff, some fifty feet below the top of the cliff and at least two hundred feet above the waves lapping into its base. The ledge was about twenty feet wide at the mouth of our cave, but it narrowed to little more than a toehold only about fifty feet beyond. In the other direction, where Kees and Lem stood watch, the ledge inscribed a gentle right-hand downward curve. There it passed out of sight of the mouth of our cave before gradually expanding to an overall width of about 150 feet. Our position was largely open, dominated by rocks and scrub brush, but as the ledge widened out the dense forest resumed. We were invisible from the air and from the lake, and, as long as we stayed well back in the cave, we were beyond the reach of infrared and thermal sensors. Unless our trackers were led by someone with intimate local knowledge, we weren't likely to attract their attention as they combed the area.

Remaining undiscovered was our best hope. Still, even if we were discovered, we could hold off an attack by a strong patrol, maybe even a platoon. No attacker could come up the cliff from the lake; an assault force that chose to rappel down from above would be terribly vulnerable. Beyond the cave there was no real path. Our trackers had only one tactically viable approach, which was to come up the same path we had followed. Using the good cover afforded by the boulders we had threaded past, we could dominate that approach. Mortar fire from the cliff top would plunge harmlessly past us into the lake below. I didn't think that the resources available to our pursuers were unlimited; if we bloodied them sufficiently, they might well back off, particularly Wiangaran militia who were accustomed to abusing defenseless farmers. Anyway, we had a fair chance of backing them off, at least until we figured out a means of breaking contact again. And maybe they would take the obvious path, the left fork that we had avoided, and maybe they would lose us altogether, long enough for us to double back and work our way out of the box we found ourselves in.

I sipped my coffee slowly, savoring its warmth, and looked around. Someone had placed a flashlight at the back of the cave, aiming it against the wall to diffuse the light. It revealed two rows of spectral figures. Grady, Jerry, and Dito sat along the wall opposite, and the others slumped against the wall next to me, with Peter asleep on his litter in between Moira was sitting next to him, holding his hand, speaking to him in words I couldn't hear. As I watched she got up and went over to sit next to Grady. As near as I could tell, no one else was asleep, but there was no real conversation and no attempt at activity. It was as if after posting a guard, inventorying our supplies, and organizing coffee, the collective energy of the group had simply evaporated. I closed my eyes and tried to marshal my thoughts.

Ideally, it would not come to a fight. We'd lie low for several days, allow the search to move beyond our area, and then move out. Unless, of course, lack of food forced us out. I opened my eyes again, surveyed the huddle of supine bodies around me. I suddenly understood that our most serious shortage was not food or rest. More than anything else, we needed a plan.

I looked across at Grady and Moira, her eyes closed, her head resting on his shoulder. Her plans had been aborted when she put the Catalina on the beach. His eyes were open, but they had the classic "thousand-yard stare." Grady had expended his formidable strength of will and insight in the terrible moments after we put down, when time was of the essence and the team needed someone to pull them together. That done, however, his only plan had been to break away, to march faster than the pursuers. Now he appeared to have folded into himself. I knew that he was strong and resilient; he would bounce back quickly. But Grady, too, now needed what we all needed, which was a reason to believe that there was a way out. I knew that it was up to me to find this for them. I was supposedly the old man, the wise head. I also knew that I couldn't do it alone. I turned to Kip, realized that he was staring at me, noted that his eyes were alert, sharp.

"Major," he said, "it's up to me and you right now."

"Mind-reader."

"It's my Highland great-grandmother, like the hero always says in the adventure stories. You know, second sight."

And he smiled broadly.

"We need to talk," I said. I gestured toward the group and added softly, "Not here."

"Why don't we go relieve the guys down the trail? We can talk while we keep watch. If we're not going to rest, we might as well let them."

We gathered up our weapons and stepped over outstretched legs and piles of gear to the mouth of the cave.

"Wait," said Kip, "there's something we need to do first." He went back, returning a moment later with some pieces of plastic sheet and a couple of the empty cans Grady had thought to save. "If this rain stops, we'll kick ourselves for not collecting more water. We can at least catch some of this rain water."

We arranged the plastic sheets and the cans between some rocks so that they would collect rain water, and then went down the trail. The guard position behind the boulders was a good one, allowing one to observe nearly one hundred meters of the trail below, while providing both cover and reasonable shelter from the pouring rain.

"You're early," said Lem. Even now he was anxious to make sure that he was holding up his end.

"Are you complaining?" responded Kip. "Tommy found some heat tabs and made some coffee. You two look like you could use a cup. You've earned it out here."

"I'm assuming you haven't seen anything," I said.

"Not a thing," said Kees. "Doesn't mean they're not out there. With the rain pounding down one can hear nothing. There could be hundreds just waiting to break cover down there." He pointed to where the trail opened out from the trees and scrub.

"Not likely," I said. "They're on a hot trail. If they'd gotten as far as that tree line, they wouldn't wait to send a patrol up here. Either they've written this one off, or they've not gotten around to it yet."

"No point in sweating it," broke in Kip. "You guys get your asses on up to the cave and rest."

"We'll send somebody down in two hours."

"Damn right you will," said Kip.

I thought of something. "Kees, you two get your rest, but make sure Grady has someone on radio watch." I didn't want to suddenly need the team on alert, only to discover that no one back at the cave was awake.

For the first few minutes after they left we were silent, concentrating on the trail below us and on the tree line beyond, making sure that we were oriented, that nothing would surprise us out of the dense patches of gray mist.

Finally, Kip spoke. "Situation sucks, Major."

"That just about says it all."

"You think if our message got through to Parks that he could organize some way of getting us out?"

"I don't think so. He carries a lot of weight, but I don't think even he could press the government into bargaining us out. That would mean taking responsibility for what we did back at the lab, and the whole idea of the mission was that the government could avoid doing just that. And I don't think he could mount a mission to get us out. If he had that kind of capability at his fingertips, we would've never been drawn into this thing in the first place. Besides—rescuing us would be a bigger and tougher mission than we just pulled off. Who would he get to do it? No, the only hope along those lines is that he might pull some strings and energize some of the friendlies either in Uganda or in South Sudan. I don't know what they could do for us, but it might help somehow."

"Which should we aim for?"

I pondered this. "I'm thinking South Sudan. I know you've got family in Uganda, but right now the U.S. has more pull in South Sudan. From the head of the lake, both are about equidistant on foot. We were flying toward Uganda, so maybe that's where the gomers will think we're heading. Once we get right up on the border, then maybe we come up on the sat phone and see if Parks can arrange a friendly reception when we cross over."

"But we've still got to get there...?"

"For that, all we can do is walk."

"Too long, Major, not carrying Peter, not with Dito. I have what may be a better idea."

"I'm all ears."

"There's a road that touches the northern tip of the lake and then bears north. There's a little town there, if I remember right. Likely there will be a truck or two around. We pick our moment, steal 'em, and haul ass. Instead of an eight-day slog, ducking the gomers at every turn, we maybe do it overnight."

"Still have to get there, and that's a day or two at best from here. But we have to work our way in that direction anyway, so we just need to be ready to seize the chance if it comes."

The rain was slacking off and the clouds were opening out over the lake, allowing just a sliver of moonlight to shine through. For the next few minutes we quietly listened, partly to our own thoughts, partly for the sound of an approaching patrol. It wouldn't do to let anyone sneak up on us.

As the silence lengthened an idea started to form in my head. I played it back and forth, then decided it was at least worth sharing.

"We don't have a truck, but we have Moira and Dito and Lem.

That's two very good fixed wing pilots, plus Lem, who's not bad, and Lem and Dito could manage a helicopter."

"That's true, Major, but the last time I looked our airplane was broken and the gomers have all the helicopters."

"Just means we have to borrow a new one."

"You mean—."

"Moira saved most of her navigation charts, I think. She had copies of them on a smart phone at one point, and I bet she still has it tucked away. If she did, that should give us a pretty good idea of where even the poorest airstrips are around here. This is Africa, after all, one of the most miserable parts of Africa. You and I know better than most that the road net sucks. They use planes and helicopters to link up all the little towns. There must be strips all over the place—I bet Tommy could point us to a couple nearby. We lie low here for a couple of days, let the pursuit ease—I hope—or move past us. Then we try to find a plane that we can take. We find a helo, maybe Lem can take us out"

Kip mulled it over.

"I like it," he said finally. "Even if they have guards out, they can't put a lot of people on every airstrip, and we've still got a shitload of firepower."

"It's not perfect. We may have a lot of cross-country work to even find one, and the first one we find may not have a suitable aircraft. We're going to need some size, some range."

"Beats stealing a truck."

The rain had now stopped completely,

"I've got an idea," said Kip, smiling broadly. "Better than go find one, maybe we just find where the guys on our trail parked theirs and take it away from them. But we'd probably have to fight our way to it. They won't leave it with just the pilots to guard it."

I thought about this. "Maybe, maybe not. They have to be thinking we're all about getting away. Why would they expect us to turn around and attack?"

"When we get back up the hill, let's run it by Grady and Lem, okay?"

The wind had picked up and it had a sharp edge. Apparently, the thunderstorm had been pushed aside by an oncoming cold front, something perhaps off the Ruwenzori mountains to the southeast. The slight shelter from the rock overhang had protected us enough to allow our clothes to continue drying. This, and lack of exertion, and the encouragement of planning a way out, no matter how problematic, lifted my spirits enormously. I could hardly wait to get back to the cave and share the idea with Grady, Moira, and the others. Even with having to carry Peter, I knew we could do it. Despite their condition earlier, the team could handle one more firefight. Except for Peter and Dito they were all in good shape, and even if we went on short rations for a while, everyone had been relatively well-fed up to now. I had known soldiers to march and fight a lot longer on a lot less. I knew, I absolutely knew, I could do it, and, not counting the two casualties, I was physically the most marginal of the entire group. All that had been lacking in the cave a few hours ago had been hope, and now I had a supply of that to offer.

Time passed quickly. I'd felt no urge to check my watch, and when Colin and Tommy arrived to relieve us, it scarcely seemed that two hours had elapsed. My mind was boiling with developments of our escape idea. I was in the midst of sharing my idea with them when Kip jerked my sleeve. I turned and saw that his finger was at his lips.

"Shh—listen!" he whispered.

At first, I heard nothing. Then came the soft but distinct sound of voices.

"They're above us, atop the cliff," said Tommy.

"Did they hear us?" I asked, feeling foolish even as I uttered the words.

"No way," said Kip, and I knew it had to be true. Even our animated conversation about the plan to steal a helicopter had never risen above a soft whisper, one of the wonders produced by instinct and deeply ingrained discipline.

"Two of 'em up there, leastwise," said Colin.

Of course—the voice of one man talking to himself would not

have carried all the way down to us. Besides, it had to be a full patrol searching for us. We were too far off the beaten path for it to be anything else.

Kip reached for the radio, keyed the mike.

"Cave, this is Kip. Respond."

"Kees here, Kip. Go ahead."

"We've got gomers on the roof. Keep everybody inside the cave."

"Okay Kip. Out."

I had a horrible thought. "Can those water sheets we laid out be seen from up there?"

Colin answered, "I doubt it. Even with the moon coming out, it's mainly shadows there now, up by the cave."

There was nothing we could do except listen and wait. We heard the voices again, clearly a group. We heard movement and saw a couple of pebbles as they dislodged from the edge of the cliff top and tumbled to the path just a few feet away. Eventually the sounds faded. Kip whispered a brief radio sitrep to Grady, and we waited. We waited a half-hour, then an hour, then more. The sun came up and we waited. Either they had satisfied themselves with having checked things out from the cliff top, or they'd double back around and come up the path and do the job properly. Still, there was nothing to do except listen and wait—and pray.

CHAPTER 18

OUR WAIT CONTINUED for only a few minutes after sunrise.

"Lookit," said Colin softly.

We had all seen the same thing, the glint of sunlight off binocular glass or bright metal, just inside the treeline below.

"Careless," whispered Kip.

"Long night in the woods for those boys," I added. "They want to go back to their chopper and go home."

"Maybe they'll check things out from down there," said Tommy hopefully.

He had no more than said it, however, when a figure clad in a dust-brown uniform and a black beret emerged from the tree line.

"That uniform says the "General-President's" palace guard, but who knows?" I said, "but I don't think he's just the usual half-assed Wiangaran militiaman." We watched him advance carefully, his weapon, some kind of AK clone, in the low ready position. I could tell that he didn't like being alone in the open. I didn't blame him. "Let him keep coming, let him decide for himself there's nobody up here. Don't anybody light him up."

We were in a good position. Facing down the trail, opposite the direction from which he was coming, we were covered by the solid rock of the cliff rising to our right and dropping off to the sea to our left. Both flanks were solid, at least against a single scout moving up the main trail. The rising sun was now above the cliff top behind us, too high to backlight us badly, but right in the soldier's face as he approached us.

"He's stopping. Maybe he's satisfied."

"No, look!"

The soldier knelt, looked carefully at the ground, looked up toward us, waved back toward the treeline.

"Fuck!"

"Footprint, maybe. Some little piece of shit somebody dropped."

"Two more of them—no, four more!"

Four other soldiers, similarly clad and armed, had stepped into view. They fanned out, forming a loose wedge with the first soldier at its apex. The trail would narrow to our side, funneling them tightly together before they got to us, but by then the point man would have already reached our position.

"Wait 'til he comes round the boulders," I said. "When he does, I'll drop him." I would be shooting at little more than arm's length. I knew my old eyes were good for that, and I knew that I would not hesitate. "Kip, take the two on the left." Kip was the best shot, and the quickest at follow-up. "Colin, the middle right. Tommy, the far right, the one coming up against the base of the cliff. Get them all, quick, as soon as I shoot."

I didn't have to explain that our best remaining hope was that these five were alone and that we could kill them all before one of them got on the radio for help.

The point man drew even with our concealing boulders and slipped out of view. I would see him next when he rounded the corner. I covered the area with my carbine, drew in a breath, and took up the slack on the trigger.

It was like a slow-motion film. He stepped around the corner, started to swing his upper body and the muzzle of his AK to cover the area behind the boulders. I saw his eyes widen, then his cheeks puff as three high-velocity rounds smashed the center of his chest and knocked the air from his lungs. I watched him slump to the ground. I almost added another three-round burst, just to be sure, but thoughts of our limited ammunition supply stayed my finger. I poked his cheek with the suppressor-extended muzzle of my weapon and got no reaction. I poked it a second time, harder—still no reaction. I glanced back over my shoulder.

"Kip?"

"We got 'em all, Major."

"Sure?"

"Sure."

But he decided to double check. Raising his head, he just as suddenly ducked; the supersonic crack of rounds passing overhead mixed with the whine of ricochets bouncing off the rocks.

"Motherfucker!"

Another burst.

"Fucking PKM!"

He was right. Funny how, no matter how long it's been, some sounds you just never forget.

The radio crackled.

"What the fuck? Over." This was Grady.

"Waxed five gomers," Kip reported, "but we got more of 'em with an MG down in the trees."

"Shit." Grady sounded like himself again, not the least bit alarmed, just pissed off. "How many more, Kip?"

"No fucking clue."

"I'm coming down."

"Roger that, bossman. Watch your ass when you close on our position. Kip out."

I crawled past the man I had killed. If we were going to precisely locate the machine gun we needed to take a good long look at the tree line. If we were going to do that without being killed, we didn't dare stick out heads up from the locations where we had raised out heads before—that would be where the machine gunners would expect us. So, I crawled around the boulders and edged out into the open, exposing only my head from the eyes up, staying very close to the ground.

"See anything, Major?" Kip was right behind me, radio in hand.

"Not a thing."

"Grady's coming."

"I heard. Look, we had a good position as long as we were mainly trying to stay hidden and keep watch, maybe ambush a small patrol. But now we've got to widen things out. We need to defend on a broader front to keep from getting pinned back against the cliff face."

"Other side of the trail? In those low rocks?"

"Only other place we've got."

"Crossing the trail means breaking cover"

"Can't just stay here with our heads down."

Just then Grady came up behind us. Kees was with him, carrying our 416 with the under-barrel grenade launcher. I gave them a quick sitrep. Grady listened carefully, lips slightly pursed, his gray eyes hard and cold. He knew what he wanted as soon as I finished speaking.

"Right—here's how we play it. Harry, you and me stay right here. Kip, you and Kees get back up behind the boulder where you were to start with. Keep your asses the fuck down. Tommy, you and Colin are the quickest. I'm gonna pop a smoke grenade, roll it around onto the trail. Let it smoke up good, then straight across the trail you go, low and fast. As soon as you make those rocks, just poke your weapons up and throw a couple of quick bursts down the trail. Harry, you and me the same thing, around the corner of this rock. Mr. Gomer will react toward the firing, away from the top of the boulder. That gives Kip and Kees a chance to pop up, spot him, and put a 203 grenade on him. If the first one misses, everybody keeps moving the threat back and forth so he can't zero in on any of us. Kees keeps at it with his bloop gun until he kills that fuckin' PKM."

"When we get him?" I asked.

"I've got everybody else saddlin' up back in the cave. We take out the PKM, then we clear the woods down there, then we hustle our young asses down the fuckin' yellow brick road."

It went exactly as Grady had outlined it, except for the last part. With the smoke masking their movement, Colin and Tommy made it into position, we got enough automatic fire downrange to get the machine gunner's head down after he fired a quick trailing burst, and Kees dropped a 40mm grenade right in his lap. We ceased firing, scanned the treeline carefully, and got ready to cover Colin and Tommy as they prepared to move down to check things out, and then realized that another distinctive noise had filled the silence left by the lapse in gunfire.

"Rotors!" shouted Colin.

"Inbound, low and fast," Kip added.

"See 'em yet?" asked Grady.

"No, but I can fucking hear 'em," said Colin. "Two, at least."

And then we glimpsed the first helicopter, a big one, some kind of transport model breaking clear above the trees for a split second, flaring suddenly, then dropping out of sight just beyond the trees. Then we saw a second one coming in the same way.

"They're putting down in that clearing we passed on the way up the hill."

Even as Grady spoke, Moira and the rest of the team arrived, Jerry and Jean-Paul carrying Peter, the others laden with gear. It was suddenly very crowded behind our boulder. Hearing Grady's last remark, the new arrivals set Peter down and dropped their gear. Lorayne spoke up first.

"So now what do we do?" she asked.

"We saw the first chopper when it flared out," said Moira. "Coming down the hill we were high enough to get a good look over the trees as it went transitional."

"Mi-8," added Dito. "Troop carrier, like an old Huey, but bigger, maybe twenty troops aboard."

"Well," said Grady, "they didn't bring two big birds in just to evacuate whoever's left down in those trees. That's a platoon's worth, plus whoever's left from the ones who were tracking us. The motherfuckers are coming for a fight."

I looked from one face to the next. It was no great trick to read the tension in each expression.

"Movement at the edge of the treeline!" This was Colin, calling out from his position on the other side of the trail.

"Nobody answered Lorayne's question," said Moira. "What do we do now?" She looked from Grady to me and from me to Grady. But Jerry came up with the first answer.

"I guess this is where we bend over, put our heads between our legs, and kiss our asses goodbye."

"This is no time for a fuckin' smartass," said Grady.

I had been thinking hard about the whole situation. "Look," I said, "they didn't bring up that many troops just to sit back and wait us out. They're going to have a go at us, maybe real soon. We're too bunched up here. We need to extend the line, get more shooters over with Colin and Tommy."

"Right," said Grady. "Okay gang, here it is. We get back into our teams and we work as teams. Jerry, you and me, we spread out beyond Colin and Tommy, tie in our left flank on the edge where the bluff drops away. Kees, you and Lem are a team now, you come with me and Jerry, fill in between us and Colin and Tommy. J-P, you're with Kip on the high side of the boulder, up against the cliff face."

"I'm afraid I can't be much help," said Peter, speaking from his recumbent position.

"Harry, can you and Lorayne get Peter back up to the cave?"

I nodded, although I wasn't completely certain that we could carry the litter up the steep slope. We were, after all, the two members of the team with the least upper body strength.

"Okay, do that and then get back down here quick. Fill in right here, the low side of the boulders, by the trail."

"What about Dito and me?" asked Moira.

Grady paused for a moment. When he spoke up, it became clear that he was already thinking along the same lines that Kip and I had discussed.

"Our best chance for getting out of here now is to hold these guys off until dark and then exfiltrate. Maybe steal one of their helicopters." I'd never had the chance to discuss my plan with him, but, as always, Grady and I were on the same wavelength tactically. "Lem—you can fly one of those?" A nod of assent. "Good. Dito?" Another nod. "Lem, you go back with Moira and Dito. You guys carry as much stuff as you can back up to the cave, stay there, take care of Peter, and take care of yourselves, too. None of us will ever get out of this if one of you three flyers don't stay alive. Besides, someone needs to keep watch up that way, to make sure they don't sneak anyone in by the back door. Jerry, partner, I'm sorry, I wanted to send you back so we'd be sure to have a medic, but we need a shooter more. Lem, swap out your 416 with, let's see, who has one of the MP-5s? J-P? Swap out with J-P, so he has the better weapon."

"More movement at the tree line," Kip said. "Things are getting set to go down."

"Okay, Kees, you and Jerry team up with me, since Lem's going. Let's go."

And he was moving, with Kees right behind him, before Moira could give voice to the disagreement that was plain in her face. As they crossed the trail, a short burst of automatic-weapons fire kicked up dirt behind them. Then I heard the muted thump-thump-thump of one of our suppressed 416s from above and behind and looked over my shoulder just in time to see the brass cartridge cases cascading downward. Either Kip or Jean-Paul, I couldn't tell which, had returned fire.

"Radios?" I asked.

"Good question," said Grady. "Colin and Tommy already have one. Harry, you keep yours. I'll take one, Kip keeps the one he has, and Lem takes one back to the cave. Okay? Good."

Moira and Lem gathered up most of the gear, Dito took as much of what remained as he could carry, and they headed for the cave, hugging the cliff to minimize their exposure. Lorayne and I took Peter and followed them. This was a bit of a struggle, despite Peter's lightheartedly profane encouragement, but we deposited him safely in the cave and then hurried back down to our designated positions. The attack still hadn't begun.

I was kneeling behind the boulder. Lorayne had assumed the prone firing position, with the muzzle of her weapon and the top of her head exposed only enough to enable her to fire down the trail. When the attack came I would stand above her, shooting from the left barricade position. But something was nagging at me, a detail that I couldn't get into focus. I'd liked the tactical setup when we faced nothing more than a probe by a small patrol or even a hasty assault by a larger one. But this was no small patrol. The helicopters had undoubtedly landed a serious attack force. The terrain still favored us, even against superior numbers, as long as they simply came at us head-on, from out of the tree line. But these people couldn't be complete dunces, at least there was no percentage in making that assumption. Even if they saw a frontal assault as their only option, they'd do something to shorten the odds against them. Something—what? Think, old man, thinking is the only thing you can bring to the table.

It was still quiet. Maybe they did intend nothing more than waiting us out. No, they would come after us, at least until we made them pay for trying. They *had* to come after us. Our only chance of slipping out, maybe having a go at one of their helicopters, would come if we chewed them up really badly, and we could only do that if they attacked us. If they just laid back on us, they'd do a better job of maintaining a tight perimeter. We needed them hurt and licking their wounds.

Then it came to me.

"Grady."

No answer.

"Grady, dammit, this is Harry. Get your ears on."

The speaker crackled. Finally, I heard Grady's voice.

"Talk to me, Harry."

"It's the cliff top, Grady. The overhang protects us over here. It probably protects Colin and Tommy." Colin and Tommy were closest in, just on the other side of the trail. "But shooters on the cliff can get enough of an angle to hit you and Kees and Jerry."

"Fuck me to tears. We were all focused downslope. Goddamn tunnel vision. When we get back to the world, I'll buy you the biggest fuckin' steak in the world."

Lorayne was still covering against an attack from the treeline below. I gave her a quick pat on the rump to get her attention, and gestured to let her know I was going back up the trail. If I could get enough height, I could look scan our left flank and try to see some way of helping Grady solve our problem. When I got higher, I realized that Grady had already made a move. He couldn't get any overhead cover, so he did the next best thing. Leaving everyone else oriented toward the threat from the treeline, Grady had taken Kees and moved out as far to the left as possible, to the point where the broad ledge dropped off towards the lake. He positioned himself where he could observe both our front and the cliff top. More to the point, he oriented Kees so that the 203 could be used to fire grenades at gomers looking down on us from above. Hard to hit anything, given the acute upward angle, but he could lob the grenades in a looping trajectory up over the cliff and the fragmentation made it a better bet than our other weapons. Moreover, Grady and Kees were now set up to enfilade a line of attackers coming at us from the trees below. But it still wasn't enough. I went back down and reclaimed the radio from Kip.

"Grady. Harry."

"Go ahead Harry."

"They can still hurt us bad from the cliff top. Why don't I take Lorayne back up the trail and then work our way up there?"

"Good idea Harry, but not you two. I've been thinkin'. Jerry's a better climber and, and he's better in the woods than you are. The top of the trail is a hand-over-hand climb. Lem, you copy? He'll be comin' your way"

"Not a one-man job, Grady," I said.

"Okay, Harry. We'll cut J-P loose. I'll tell Jerry to get Lem's radio, tell Moira they'll have to do without. Harry, get word to J-P. Quick, now."

I returned to the boulders and told Jean-Paul and Kip what we were doing. Jean-Paul linked up with Jerry, and they headed back up the trail. Now the sun was well above the horizon. Were the gomers just going to wait us out after all? Wait out the day? Would darkness help our cause? We had only salvaged four sets of night vision goggles. Maybe they just didn't want to take us on. Maybe they *would* wait. Despite the smart uniforms, these were still Wiangaran militia, accustomed to terrorizing poor farmers rather than fighting real soldiers. How good were they, really?

There was another nagging question: how good were we? The team had trained specifically for a single mission and had performed it almost flawlessly. But the team was not trained, organized, or equipped for the task we now faced. Although many of us had good military backgrounds, the levels of experience were uneven. We had just met one test successfully, but then we'd enjoyed the advantage of surprise. These discomforting thoughts stuck with me as I eased down the trail toward Lorayne. I quick-peeked around the boulder—still nothing from the trees below. I decided to have a cigarette. No need to worry about giving away our position, and certainly no need to worry about lung cancer or heart disease. I took the pack from my shirt pocket, shook one out, and placed it between my lips.

I was fumbling for a match when I heard it, the clear, unmistakable "bloop" of a grenade launcher, followed close by another. I tucked in tight behind the boulder. I registered a third "bloop" and seconds later felt the blast of the first round hitting below and to the left of us, not far from Colin and Tommy. I reached forward and grabbed Lorayne by her belt and tugged her backward. The second round hit alongside us, but well to the left of the trail. The third hit up the trail, close enough to throw up dust and pebbles that rained down on our heads. The fourth round hit even further up, about where I had been standing a few minutes before, and the next exploded against the cliff side and the one after that must have been close to the mouth of the cave. The grenadier was walking his rounds up the hill, and clearly, he didn't have a good angle for dropping rounds behind our big boulders. He'd have to get really lucky to hurt us, but he was making us keep our heads down.

Grady came up on the radio.

"Everybody okay? Team leads check in."

"Team Colin okay."

Another round hit, on the other side of our boulder.

"We're okay over here," said Kip.

"Grady. Jerry. We just made it to the top of the cliff. We're movin' into the woods up here. It sounds like you're in a world of shit down there."

Another hit and a cascade of rocks from above. Trying to drop a grenade round behind our boulder, the gunner had hit the side of the cliff. I felt Lorayne shudder.

"What do ya think, Harry?" This was Grady again.

"I think it's just one guy," I answered. Without really thinking about it, I had measured the firing rhythm and reached that conclusion. "Firing to keep our heads down."

"Right," said Grady. He paused as another round hit. "That was smoke, guys, any minute now."

Someone on the other side was thinking. When the attack came, it would be a frontal assault. Full daylight would have been fine for us, but tactical smoke just might provide the edge the gomers needed to cross the open ground safely. I wished we still had the little thermal imager. Regular night vision goggles can't see through smoke, but thermals can. But it had been lost with the Catalina.

More grenades, more smoke, mainly between us and the treeline. Then a heavy machine gun opened up from the cliff top, a nasty big 12.7mm by the sound of it, the gomers had worked hard to haul that monster into position above us. I couldn't see where the rounds were striking, but they were passing right over our heads, probably seeking our left flank, which now stretched from Colin and Tommy across the trail out to Grady and Kees at the edge of the cliff. I heard the impact of another smoke round, and another.

"Heads up, kid," I said to Lorayne. "They're on the way."

We took up our high-low positions at the edge of the boulder. My hip ached, I didn't know why.

"I can't see shit," said Lorayne.

The wind was blowing landward, driving the smoke clouds against the base of the cliff, billowing them upwards. The big machine gun on the cliff opened up again. From his perch up there our boulder cover wouldn't help much, but he couldn't depress his muzzle enough to do anything but shoot over us toward the lake. A weirdly quiet moment followed—maybe he'd figured out that he was wasting ammunition. Then dozens of small caliber rounds snapped past us from downslope: marching fire, from lots of assault rifles.

"They're in the open, coming fast." Grady, at the cliff's edge above the lake, had the least smoke to contend with.

"Shoot through the smoke," I said to Lorayne. We let off several quick bursts, more to slow them down than in hope of hitting anything. I assumed that the rest of the team was doing likewise, but with our suppressed weapons drowned out by the other firing noises, I couldn't tell. It was the strangest firefight I had ever been in, because it sounded as if only one side was doing the firing.

The machine gunner above us cut loose with another long burst. I glanced up and saw the stream of big green tracers snaking out and down. Just then someone—it must have been Kees down to the left—blooped a 40mm. It exploded somewhere up on the face of the cliff.

"Gomers!" I heard Lorayne shout, and there they were, five or six of them, charging out of the swirling smoke not much more than fifteen meters away. We fired together, and one sagged to his knees. I lined up another and dropped him. I loved the Aimpoint sights, which made snapshooting, well, a snap. A third one dropped as if clotheslined. The others hit the ground and concentrated their fire against us. There were more gomers off to our left, I guessed, but I couldn't see them. A round pinged off the rock just above my head, and I ducked back behind the boulder. I heard another 40mm round hit the cliff. Lorayne continued to fire, short bursts, carefully spaced.

"Shot him in the ass, by God!" she called out. "Silly bastard don't know how to low crawl."

I wasn't holding up my end very well. I wished I had a hand grenade, and I hoped that the gomers on the other side of the boulder didn't have any. I crouched—no use sticking my head out at the same position twice—leaned around the corner and found myself staring right at a gomer's belt buckle. I rolled away from him, creating just enough space to bring up my carbine. From this awkward position I pointed up and snapped off a three-round burst, hitting him beneath the chin. Bone and blood geysered from the top of his head as he toppled backward.

The smoke was almost gone, the sounds of firing dying away, and I could see the gomers falling back into the shadow of the tree line. But the clearing smoke also opened up our own positions, making them more visible to the big gun above us. I could hear the deep thump-thump-thump and see more green tracers as the gunners provided cover fire for their comrades' retreat—he couldn't hit us if we stayed put, but he could if we ventured out in pursuit. I held my position and surveyed the area immediately in front of me. There were four bodies scattered along the trail, grouped roughly ten to twelve meters away. I took careful aim and shot them, one by one, in the head. Cold-blooded, but we couldn't take the risk that one was shamming.

Then, suddenly, it was quiet. I didn't know how long the action had lasted. As always, it seemed like forever and it seemed like no time at all, and it had probably been something like five minutes. I knelt at Lorayne's shoulder.

"Are you all right?" I asked.

She rolled over onto her side, looked up at me, gave me a wide smile.

"Doing real good, Hair Doctor. How about you?"

What could I say? I thought about how long we'd have to hold out, switched the selector switch on my carbine from full auto to semi-auto fire. Time to start thinking about saving ammunition.

Kip called out softly, said Grady was checking the teams, was there something wrong with my radio. Was I okay? Was Lorayne? I gave Kip a high sign, and he reported our status to Grady. I looked down at the radio in its pouch on the front of my tac vest, and realized that the wire connecting the radio to the headset had been neatly clipped. It didn't bear thinking about how that had happened. I yanked off the now useless headset and turned the radio up just loud enough so that I could hear the main speaker built into the body of the radio.

"Say again, Colin," Grady was saying.

Silence.

"Talk to me, Colin,"

"Tommy's binned, Grady," said Colin.

"Say again."

"That big booger on the hill just shot him all to hell."

"Shit—how?

"He climbed up on the rock here, I guess he was trying to get a better shot downhill, put him just too fucking high."

"Fuck. No chance he's alive?"

"Not bloody likely—the poor bastards got half his fuckin' head shot off."

"Shit."

Now I had two Naburje sons on my conscience, but I'd have to put that aside.

"Grady." This was Kip. "Jerry and J-P haven't checked in from up on the cliff top."

Grady called them. No answer. He called again. Then we heard a double click, the sound of a mike being keyed twice: the signal meant "I can't talk, the bad guys will hear me."

To complicate matters further, fog had begun rolling in off the lake, piling up like a blanket in front of us, in places thicker than the chemical smoke that had shielded the gomers' last attack.

Kip came back up on the net.

"We have movement to our front, children."

I looked out, couldn't see anything in the gathering fog. I looked back at Kip, still in his position at the right-hand shoulder of the boulder. I looked again and still couldn't see anything.

Then Jerry checked in, a hoarse whisper on the radio.

"Grady, the woods up here are crawlin' with gomers. We've been trying to get close to that big machine gun, but we hafta' move awful slow."

"Are you okay now? Can you take it out?"

"We're movin' again, movin' toward it."

"Two squads," said Kip, "maybe more, fifty meters out, advancing by bounds."

"I see 'em," I heard Colin reply over the radio.

The big gun above opened up again. I glanced up, caught the muzzle flash briefly and then looked down the trail.

"Light 'em up now," said Grady. "Any closer is too close."

I could hear the faint report as Kip took a shot, then Lorayne kicked in. I looked again, but I still couldn't see anything in the fog. Finally, I picked up a blur of movement and delivered a couple of rounds in its general direction. Except for the occasional eruption of the machine gun above us, it was the strangest of actions: we weren't getting any return fire from the advancing elements. I guessed that they didn't want muzzle flash to give them away. A quiet firefight.

They were getting closer, becoming more distinct when they rushed forward, then disappeared after a few meters as they hit the ground. Others were taking shots. These guys were good. I settled the sight on the nearest man's chest, squeezed the trigger—once, twice. Scratch one gomer. Not too bad for old eyes.

Suddenly the relative quiet was shredded by a burst of automatic fire—loud AK fire—from *behind* us. Then another burst, then the unlikely boom of a shotgun, then another, then an explosion, the sound of pistol shots, a piercing scream that changed pitch as someone took the long dive to the rocks by the water, way down below.

"What the fuck?" asked Grady over the radio.

"Trouble at the cave?'" Kip answered.

"Moira?" said Grady.

No answer.

"Hey, Grady," said Kip. "They've got no radio, remember? You told Jerry and J-P to take it."

"Oh, shit. Harry, take Lorayne and get back there. Everybody else hold position."

Lorayne and I crept back up the trail, moving as rapidly as we dared. As we inched our way close, she tapped me on the shoulder, then pointed upward. Four rappel ropes hung from the cliff top, three trailing limply, one taut and swaying. We reached the bend just before the entrance to the cave. I gestured to Lorayne to widen the angle between us with a tactical roll. She was the agile one, after all. She went prone, positioned her weapon, and rolled out. As she did, I took the corner in a crouch, hoping that if anyone was waiting for us, we'd get the first shot.

At the mouth of the cave lay two gomers. A third hung suspended from the rope around his midsection, his belt held to the rope by a carabiner, his arms and legs dangling as he pendulumed across the cave opening. The air was heavy with burnt powder and the sweet-sour odor of a grenade blast.

I called out to Moira.

"That you, Harry?" she called back.

"Yes—you all right?"

"Yeah, we're okay," I could hear movement in the cave, and then Moira and Dito appeared.

"What happened?"

"We were waiting right here," said Moira, "just inside the cave, listening to you guys, to the shooting, it sounded so loud, from down below. Then here came the ropes, dropping almost on top of us. They couldn't see us, I guess, I don't know, they must not've known about it, about us, I mean, about the cave. Maybe they figured they'd be behind everybody, but they came down right in our laps, right here. I shot the first one with my shotgun, Dito got the second one with his pistol, then—well, God, Harry, I don't know, it all happened so fast. One of them shot at us with his AK. I let go with the second barrel, there was an explosion up there, maybe one of them was holding a grenade or something, and the last one just went flying out over the cliff. I don't know exactly, but it was all over, and I dragged Dito back into the cave, he's shot in the side or the stomach, I don't know, I don't think it's very deep. I tried to bandage it, but it's real long and the bandage won't cover, and we didn't have a radio 'cause Jerry took it, and—well, oh, God, I don't know, I don't know."

She broke off as the sound of heavy firing erupted from somewhere above us, somewhere in the woods atop the cliff, then the explosion of a grenade, and another.

"Got the goddamn machine gun, but the motherfuckers are crawling all over our asses." It was Jerry, on the radio, obviously no longer needing to conceal his position. "J-P's hit, not bad, we're gonna try to break contact, and find our way back down."

I heard Grady's voice in my headset. "Get out of there quick, it looks like the shit's starting down here again."

I had a sudden scary thought. "Moira, where's Lem?"

"He went up the trail behind Jerry and J-P, so he could protect their retreat, he said, when they came back. He must still be up there."

"Okay, he'll come back with them. He stays up here with you, Jerry and J-P come down to help us if J-P can still do it, if not then just Jerry, but have him give Dito a quick look. Have Jerry leave the radio with you."

I could hear the sounds of a firefight swelling down the trail, machine guns, AKs, the grenade launcher again. It was clear now that the first probe had been meant to set us up for the move to our rear. Whoever was doing their tactical planning had assumed that all of us were down below on the firing line. They must have figured out that something had gone wrong. They were obviously no longer worried about hitting their own people coming down behind us.

I remembered that Grady still had no idea what had happened at the cave. I called him up and gave him a sitrep. When I finished I asked what was happening down there.

"We're up to our ass in alligators," he replied. "Kees has been hit. You and Lorayne, you gotta hustle your asses back down here."

I relayed this to Moira.

"What if they try this again?" asked Moira.

"Looks like you guys did okay," I said. "Just keep your eyes open, watch out for Jerry and J-P and Lem coming back, don't shoot them. How's Peter?"

"Was feverish, Jerry gave him something before he left, now he's out."

The volume of fire from below grew louder.

Lorayne gave me a nudge. "C'mon, Hair Doctor. Sounds like they need us bad. We better boogie on down." She took a pinch of tobacco and stuffed it between her cheek and gum.

We took off at a trot, pain shooting through my hip every time I landed on my right foot. I fell behind Lorayne, two steps, then three steps. I couldn't keep up, and then she was shooting from the hip at three gomers who were right on top of us, and one of them bowled her over, and they went down in a heap. I snap-shot the second one, and the third one was down, caught by Lorayne's initial burst, and she was trapped under the one she was wrestling with, and I couldn't shoot for fear of hitting her. So, I picked up a rock and when he reared back to club her in the face with his fist, I bashed in the back of his head. Then I went light-headed, and my knees buckled.

CHAPTER 19

AT FIRST, I didn't know where I was. My head hurt and my back hurt and hard things poked my soft flesh. It seemed dark, but narrow shafts of light reached out from the floor to the walls: shadows around me kept moving. I drifted in and out, but realized that I was in the cave. I rose up on my elbows, saw a heavily bandaged Jean-Paul lying across from me. It seemed as if others lay around me, but I couldn't be sure. The nearest upright person I could see was Moira. She was kneeling with her back to me. When I called out to her, she turned around.

"Welcome back, Harry. How 'ya feeling?"

"Like shit," I answered truthfully.

"We thought at first you were dead. There was blood on your hands and the front of your shirt and you were unconscious. Jerry checked you quick, found some cuts on your face, and what looked like some more on your chest, little things, he said, like spent fragments, not enough to kill you, though. I started worrying that you'd had a stroke or something. But your breathing and heart rate were okay. So, Jerry said 'To hell with it,' we'll treat the things we understand. We just let you lie there. I'm sorry. We've been kinda overwhelmed."

"No apology needed. I'm all right. My head is very sore." I reached up, explored a large bump on the side of my head, above my hairline. "Maybe the blast, or whatever, knocked me against something hard, knocked me out. I've got this place on my head, it feels like it."

I tried to sit up. This made my head hurt worse, but I stayed with it. My stomach also felt strange. I thought about this, recognized the feeling.

"I'm hungry," I said.

"Our supplies are all jumbled up in a pile near the mouth of the cave. I moved things around to make room at the back when we started bringing everyone in. I can find you a candy bar, I know that's all everybody's been eating, but that's the quickest thing I can come up with."

I forced myself into a more upright position and looked around. Peter was against one wall, Jean-Paul was lying next to him. I didn't see anyone else. "Who else is hurt?" I asked.

"Dito's over there sleeping," she said, pointing to the shadows, where I could barely make out a recumbent form, "He can't walk so good, but Jerry bandaged up that big wound across his stomach—he said it wasn't deep enough to waste sutures on, but it'd probably hurt a lot. Still, he doesn't think Dito's in too bad shape. Everybody else is down the trail just a little ways, about halfway from the position you guys held most of the day. Grady and Kip decided we didn't have enough people left to hold down below, they said we needed a narrower front. Right now, it doesn't seem to matter much. After that last attack the gomers seem to have called it a day."

"Who's left?"

"Kees and Tommy are dead. Colin and Lem and Lorayne are banged up, but functional. Grady and Kip seem okay. Jerry had me give morphine to Jean-Paul. He doesn't think he's going to make it through the night."

"I didn't think he was hit that bad. How did Jerry get him down here from up above?"

"He wasn't hit that bad up there, and Jerry and Lem lowered him down on the gomer's rope. But just about the time they got down, the gomers started shooting those grenade things at us again, and one of them chewed him up really badly."

"Bad luck."

"I think that's all the luck we have left," said Moira.

She handed me a candy bar and a cup of water. I took a couple of bites and a big sip of water.

"How much water do we have left?"

"Enough, Harry. Enough to make it through 'til morning. By morning there may not be many left to drink it."

Her tone was flat, inflectionless. Still, I wanted to contradict her. Instead, I took another sip of water and finished the candy bar. I sat and watched Moira as she checked Jean-Paul's bandages and the tourniquet round his leg. Her hair was tangled, her face grimy, her flying coveralls torn and blood-spattered. She moved from one task to the next, slowly but purposefully, as if one task at a time was the most she could manage.

I could feel a small measure of strength returning. I forced myself to stand, discovered in the process that it wasn't just my head and back that were aching—I hurt all over. I staggered up to the mouth of the cave and then sat down on a conveniently shaped rock. From this position I stared into the deepening twilight. Here there was no protection from the damp wind off the lake, which had freshened notably since the afternoon. Someone had dragged the bodies of the two gomers away from the mouth of the cave, but the third one still dangled from his rope, swaying slowly with the breeze, pieces of his equipment clanking like some macabre wind chime. I got up again and crossed the few feet that separated the mouth of the cave from the lip of rock that, like a parapet, served as a barrier to stepping off into the ocean. I felt very tired and very much alone.

I considered going back into the cave to look for my rifle, then noticed that one of the dead gomers had a holstered pistol on his hip. I opened the flap, saw that it was a little Makarov, and decided that this was weapon enough for the moment. After checking the magazine and the chamber to make sure it was ready to shoot, I levered the hammer down to safe and dropped it into my pocket. Armed once again, I walked down the trail to look for the others. This didn't take long. The position they now held, not much more than twenty meters from the cave, was a jumble of rocks which, like our former position, offered partial compensation for the fact that we couldn't dig in. Colin and Lem and Jerry were on the left side of the trail; Grady, Kip, and Lorayne on the right. Only Grady and Colin were awake.

"That you, Harry?" Grady whispered over his shoulder, not taking his eyes from the trail below.

"Yeah, Grady, it's me."

"Figured it had to be. Too light-footed and stealthy to be Moira, and I don't reckon either Peter or Jean-Paul or Dito is likely to take a stroll anytime soon. I expected it wouldn't take too long for you to come around."

"I guess not."

"Helluva thing the way you old guys just up and take a nap in the middle of a firefight."

"Yeah—I missed my nap time after lunch today."

"We're both getting too old for this shit, Harry."

"What happened after I conked out?"

"Not a whole helluva lot. They started grenading us pretty bad about the time you and Lorayne went up to the cave. We're not exactly the best grenade target up here, a lot of rounds dropped straight down into the lake or hit up on the cliff, but when you shoot enough of 'em, well, some of the shit's gonna stick. They don't seem to have any shortage of them. Grenades got Kees, and J-P too. Then they came up the hill hard, and we got overrun. Those guys that you and Lorayne ran into got the farthest. I think that's what got you, one of them had a hand grenade, Lorayne shot him just after he pulled the pin, cut her up a little bit like you but didn't put her out. Once they got in among us, they had to stop lobbing in the rifle grenades, and we managed to push 'em back out. Lem's shot in the leg, just below the knee. Jerry doesn't think it's so bad, flesh wound, but it's got to hurt, he wouldn't take any morphine, says we still need him as a shooter. He's right. We found one of those pints of whiskey you were carrying earlier, liquored him up a little. Things kinda died down, and we took up here."

"Sounds lively," I said.

"Was, for a bit. Couldn't get back for Kees and Tommy, though."

"If you can't, you can't."

"Yeah, but it still fries my ass. You're s'posed to bring out your dead."

"Nothing you could do, Grady."

"Maybe we can get 'em back tomorrow."

"Sure—maybe somebody will helo in a Mike force company to reinforce us, and then we'll counterattack right down the hill."

I didn't mean it to sound as sarcastic as it came out, but I could see immediately that I had wounded him. "I'm sorry, Grady. I didn't mean it the way I said it."

"Forget it, Harry. You always were a hard-headed old sonuvabitch, anyway."

At least he hadn't said "hard-hearted." But maybe that was true, too.

"Would be nice to have a little help right now, wouldn't it though?"

Grady thought about that one for a few seconds. "Not too fucking likely, is it? That's what you were just saying."

"I guess so."

"Moira okay?"

"Yeah, enough so. She seems a little overwhelmed, but she's hanging in there, taking care of everyone up in the cave. The wounded would be lost without her."

"She's a helluva lady. This sure wasn't what she signed on for."

"Not what any of them signed on for, is it?" My thoughts went once again to Tommy. I should never have let him join the team, never mind that he wanted somehow to avenge Bobby. I'd allowed myself too much confidence in our plan, quick in, quick out, to think as hard as I should have about casualties.

We were both quiet for a while after that. Occasionally, I heard voices down the trail and from the top of the cliff, enemy voices, reminders of the depth of the fix we were in.

Kip stirred and opened his eyes. "Hi, there, Major. Welcome back to the land of the living."

"Good to be back."

He stretched for a moment and then stood up beside us. "How are we doing?"

"About the same as when you went to sleep," said Grady.

"Shit's pretty deep, isn't it?"

"Gets any deeper, it'll be over our heads."

Kip looked down at Lorayne, still sleeping peacefully. "The kids did pretty good today."

"Yes, they did," I responded. "They gave us everything we could ask for, and then some."

"Good enough to be Marines," said Grady.

"Or Legionnaires," said Kip.

I thought about this, and I felt a huge lump growing in my throat. My eyes started to water, not so much from pain as from pride and love, pride in the way the kids had performed, love for the heart and grace under fire they had shown. Being a warrior is about the will to win and the skill to prevail. Being an infantryman—or woman, I thought, looking down at Lorayne—is also about the capacity to endure suffering, to endure and to continue the fight. These are the things that make the wearers of the Combat Infantry Badge a special fraternity among veterans of the U.S. Army. The CIB testifies that the wearer has proved himself at the shit end of war. Today had been our St. Crispin's Day, and each of the kids, Tommy, Jerry, Lem, and Lorayne, had earned a CIB they would never receive.

Grady seemed to read my thoughts. "We owe the ones who're left a chance to make it out alive."

"Yes, we do." I didn't have complete control of my voice.

"Our options sort of narrowed as the day went on, didn't they?" said Kip.

"Our options just had the shit narrowed out of 'em—yeah," said Grady.

"Not much room left for exfiltrating," said Kip.

"No."

He then asked, "Are those ropes still hanging up by the cave?"

"They are," I replied, "but going up them is a whole lot harder than coming down. You and Grady might have the upper-body strength for it, Colin would for sure, maybe Lem, before he got hit, maybe Lorayne. Light as she is, she doesn't have all that much weight to pull up. I looked at it this morning,"—as I said these words, morning seemed like a dozen years rather than a dozen hours ago— "and there aren't any real hand or foot holds. It would be a straight muscle climb. I don't think the rest of us would have a prayer, and we'd have to leave the wounded behind."

"Besides," said Grady, "we know they've got troops up there. They'd eat us alive comin' off the ropes, just like we ate them up comin' down."

Kip smiled. "I don't expect, then, that either of you thinks much of doing a 'Butch and Sundance' over the cliff and down to the lake."

"Fuck that shit," said Grady. "If the drop didn't kill you, our wounded would all drown, and probably the rest of us. I'm not seeing anyone here who's up for a serious swim."

"Nor do I like their other tactical solution," I said.

"Which one?"

"A frontal assault on the whole Bolivian army."

"No Camerone, then?" asked Kip, referring to the 19th Century suicide charge that is the defining event in the ethos of the French Foreign Legion. As a former Legionnaire, Kip had been thoroughly indoctrinated in the spirit of Camerone.

"No, Kip—no Camerone. We accomplished our mission. There isn't going to be any killer virus hitting the world just yet, not from here, at least not for a while. We did what we came to do. We're not in that kind of war, and dying gloriously isn't going to inspire other units to carry on the fight. Even the Legion doesn't always do Camerone. They didn't do Camerone when Dien Bien Phu fell, either. There wasn't any point."

Kip smiled again, and I understood what lay behind the apparent fatuousness of his suggestions. Kip's gently ironic approach to leading us through our remaining options.

"It's surrender or die," I said.

"That's the way I see it, Major."

"Might not be given any choice," said Grady. "Might be just 'die,' no surrender about it. We hurt this bunch of gomers pretty bad today. They might not be in any surrender-takin' mood."

He was right. I had no idea how many we'd killed today, but the number had to be substantial, and to that number would be added the ones we'd killed back at the laboratory, including those slaughtered in their beds when we blew up the guard barracks. No, they had no reason to feel kindly towards us. Moreover, I couldn't even begin to guess at the attitude of those in charge. Why would they want us as prisoners? My original arguments against surrender had not lost their logic. Why had those jets not just shot us out of the sky? And now? Wouldn't it be more convenient just to shoot us outright? But if we continued to fight, we would certainly die. I pondered that one for a minute, surprised to realize that the prospect of death didn't bother me especially.

"How much ammunition do we have left?" I asked Grady.

"Not a whole bunch, about twenty rounds a man for the 416s, whatever people have for the handguns they brought along. No grenades for the M203, but we got no M203 anymore either. It got all fucked up same time Kees was hit. I thought about gathering up weapons and ammo from the dead gomers, got an AK and a couple of mags off of the nearest one, but the others are lying too much out in the open."

The only point in fighting it out had been to buy time and see if time brought any opportunities for escape. That remained true, but we no longer had the means to even buy time. Grady summed it up.

"We've got just enough ammo left to really piss 'em off, but that's it."

"No point in kicking it around any further. This isn't the kind of decision we can make for anyone else. Each member of the team deserves a say."

"Yeah," said Grady, "and there's no rush to put it to 'em. Trying to surrender in the dark is another good way of getting our asses shot off. Morning's soon enough."

"Either of you guys feel like getting some sleep?" asked Kip.

Grady and I both said no. Those who were sleeping might as well continue to sleep. We would have a stand-to just before first light. There would be time enough then to put the choices to surviving members of the team.

"Colin's still covering the other side of the trail," said Kip. "I'll go relieve him, send him over here to you. You can see if he has any bright ideas."

Grady and I laid it out for Colin when he came over.

"I wondered what you lot were nattering about over here," he said. "It's dead simple. We find ourselves a set of white knickers, if there's anybody here who's not crapped his full, then we tie 'em to a stick and wave it about and hope for the bleedin' best. You don't have to be a Fellow of fuckin' All Souls College to figure it out. Now I've got better question. Do we have anything besides those fuckin' Milky Way bars left to eat? I'm right knackered, ready for something good, and friend gomer down there may not want to feed us for a bit. I'd love a nice big fish and chips, mushy peas on the side."

"Nothing like that, but there are MREs left," I said, offering to go get them. By that time our conversation had awakened Lorayne, who said she'd help me. We went back to the cave and gathered all but one of the remaining MREs. Moira said that one would be enough for her to share with Dito and Peter. We both tacitly acknowledged that Jean-Paul would not likely eat another meal. I briefly shared with her the gist of our discussion down below.

"There's not much choice, is there?" was her only response.

When we returned, everyone was awake. We shared out the brown packages. I had stew, with cheese spread for my crackers, coffee and cocoa, and a couple of cigarettes afterward. Colin finished his meal, cadged the uneaten portions that Lorayne and Lem left, talked Jerry out of a small swig of the medicinal whiskey, and sat back, obviously content.

"And the condemned had a right hearty last meal," he said, to no one in particular. Then he curled up next to Lorayne and promptly went to sleep. Grady hiked up the trail to be with Moira—there was no longer any reason for him not to—while Kip and I continued to stand watch. As I stared into the darkness, my thoughts made for dreary company. I didn't want to surrender. I was too tired to think about what we might suffer afterwards, but the very idea of it just stuck in my throat.

"Major," said Kip, breaking in to my reverie.

"Yes, Kip."

"I just had a funny thought. I was trying to tote up how many gomers we put away, and then I was thinking about how many I took down, and I got to thinking—you know, the thoughts you think when you think too much. I never really thought about it before, but it dawns on me that I've killed more men in my life than I've fucked women."

I'd never thought about it quite that way, either. "Well, Kip, if that's the measure of a man's life, then you and I are both hopelessly in arrears. But when we get out of this, maybe you can work on redrawing the balance."

"When we get out of this? Maybe 'if's' the better word."

In twenty years, I'd never heard Kip express such a thought.

"We'll get out. Somehow, we'll pull it off. Even surrendering now, well, the guys we're surrendering to, they're out at the end of a pretty long string themselves. We'll come up with something, but now we've got to buy some more time." Kip gave me a long hard questioning look, about as close to challenging an opinion of mine as he'd ever come. Then again, I'd probably never before packed so much wishful thinking into a single sentence.

Grady came down from the cave just before dawn. Jean-Paul,

miraculously, had made it through the night. Peter, on the other hand, had taken a turn for the worse, showing obvious signs of a serious fever. Still, he'd managed to discuss our options sufficiently to add his voice to our surrender decision. Dito had simply shrugged his shoulders when asked. Our greatest difficulty had been coming up with something white to use as a flag, because we had done such a thorough job of ensuring that our clothing and equipment were of an appropriately subdued hue. Moira eventually produced a faded pink handkerchief, which looked almost white.

As dawn approached we awakened all the members of the team, checked our weapons, and went back over our options one last time. After some discussion, we all came around to where we had begun, facing the end with a resigned acceptance. I checked the battery on our satellite phone, decided that a final message to Parks couldn't hurt. If nothing else, he needed to know that a shitstorm might be brewing, one big enough to reach back to him. Mission success had always assumed a clean exit, but that assumption was shot all to hell.

Now all we could do was wait for sufficient light to render our surrender signal visible. We stood by our weapons in case the gomers were of no mind to accept it. We wouldn't allow ourselves to simply be slaughtered like cattle.

It was Colin who first noticed the approaching catastrophe. "Bloody hell—we're about to get fucked. Grady, Harry—get over here."

We darted across the trail to Colin's position and looked where he pointed out to the lake. The pre-dawn light revealed an unmistakable shape.

"Good sized power boat out there, and whoever's at the wheel is maneuvering it to line up with our position," said Colin. As a Royal Marine he knew about these things.

"Setting up to watch our position?" I asked.

"Not bloody likely. He's anglin' in towards us, closing the range. If they wanted to just watch us, they could stay in the middle of the lake."

Grady hurried away, returning with our surviving pair of binoculars. On his return trip he'd drawn fire from down the hill, a couple of AK rounds by the sound of it. Clearly the gomers were awake. Wordlessly, Grady passed the binoculars to Colin, who took them and focused in on the ship.

"Old booger, that one, looks pretty ratty. Not built for speed, probably just for truckin' stuff up and down the lake. Right now, oh man, it's truckin' some nasty shit. Aft there's another of those big machine guns, a 12.7 or a 14.5. Forrard, something like a Carl Gustaf on a tripod, but with a long tail."

"Let me see," I asked, reaching for the binoculars. I studied the weapon carefully. "It could be a French LRAC, but more likely it's Chinese, probably a PF-98."

"And that means what?" asked Grady.

"Well, I left my copy of *Jane's Weapons Systems* at home, but I think it means 120mm, so half again as big as our Carl Gustaf, pretty quick reload time."

"Shit, that's like a tank cannon, we are well and truly fucked."

"He's coming about," said Colin. Even without the binoculars, I could see that the ship was turning to run a course parallel to the shoreline. I raised the binoculars to my eyes once again and studied the boat more closely.

"The gomers on the guns aren't Wiangaran militia, they're oriental. Assuming they're Chinese military, whoever's running this show isn't taking any more chances."

"They're backing away a little bit," said Grady.

I thought about this. "We're too high up for them to elevate that recoilless rifle from close range, they have to be at a shallow angle so the back blast goes over the side, not into the deck." Even as I spoke, I could see the adjustments being made at the tripod of the weapon. "They're getting ready to shoot."

Colin spoke up. "Bastard was just waiting for sun up. "Even fancy electronic sights don't work too fuckin' good when your target's a crease in a hundred-meter-high wall of rock. With the sun, ol' Gomer-the-Sailor-Man can see what he wants to shoot." He paused and aimed a rude gesture out to sea. "We're about to get boogered right up the arse."

I found myself wondering why. Why hadn't they shot us down two mornings ago? Why, then had they come after us so hard yesterday and were now were they preparing to shell us into oblivion?

"Everybody run for the cave," said Grady. "He's about to shoot and he ain't lookin' for any fuckin' white flag."

Even as he spoke a muzzle flashed white-orange and dirty brown, followed almost instantly by a sharp report, and then the explosion of the first shell, high and well off to our right. The second one, though still high, sent us diving under a shower of rocks, and the third and fourth, in quick succession, hit as the last of us made it back into the cave. Now the big missiles came steadily, roughly twenty seconds apart, each vibrating the cliff face like the pounding of a giant jackhammer. The mouth of the cave was a small and obscure target, difficult to hit, but eventually they would hit it, and, when they did, we would all be dead.

The silence. A minute passed, two minutes, three. Then the big machine gun opened fire, methodically pounding the overhang above the entrance to the cave. I looked at the others. If they were feeling fear, as well they should have been, then they were doing a very good job of concealing it. Then one more missile struck, carving a chunk from the rock face just above the cave entrance, spitting a shower of shell fragments and nasty pellet-sized pebbles back into the cave. Too damned close. Would the next one find the opening itself, carry far enough in to collect the lot of us? They'd seen us retreat to the cave, now they'd demonstrated that, when they wanted, they could reach into our last shelter.

Then, abruptly, it all stopped. In the sudden silence, we could hear voices coming up the trail. It was now or never. I nodded to Grady. He snatched up his white flag—his silly little pink flag—and headed for the mouth of the cave. Moira, Kip, and I were right behind. At the cave's entrance we had to step over the torso of the gomer who had been swinging beside the cave entrance. The recent near misses had separated him from his head and legs and from his rope. As we stepped out into the sunlight Grady was already well ahead, carrying the surrender stick at port arms, the dirty pinkish handkerchief half-wrapped around it, over the loose flap partly covering his forearm. And as he ran I realized that, carrying the stick the way he was, it looked just like a rifle in his hands, and I tried to call out to him, get him to start waving it, but it was too late. Straight in front of him, climbing over the clump of rocks that had been our last defensive position, came a dozen or so brown-uniformed men, their AKs at the ready. They reacted quickly.

The first three shots went right through Grady. I could see the gouts of blood, cloth, and tissue expand like flower petals as they exited his back. I don't know how many more hit him. There must have been seven or eight altogether and just as many that missed high. I know, because I heard them ripping over my head. Moira and Kip reached him before I did. Kip snatched our white flag from where it had fallen, unfurled it, and waved it high above his head. Moira knelt beside him, strained to roll him on his back. I knelt at his other side, saw the bright blood spurting from a wound in the side of his neck, splattering on Moira's chest and face. I tried to get a finger on it, couldn't, tried again, failed, tried again and got enough of a grip to slow the flow. I don't know if even a surgeon could have closed that big, jagged tear. I only know that I couldn't. He tried to say something, but I couldn't understand. Then he gathered himself for one more try.

"Hey, Harry," he said.

I leaned forward, trying to hear him better.

"Say again, Grady?"

"Green Beanies eat shit."

I put my mouth close to his ear and whispered, "Semper Fi, jarhead."

He rolled his head into Moira's chest, pressing my hand in between, and pumped out his life's blood between my fingers. When he was gone I withdrew my wet hand and stood up, leaving Moira to cradle him against her bosom.

CHAPTER 20

THE FIRST FEW moments after our surrender proceeded in surreal slow motion. The firing stopped, yielding abruptly to a stillness punctuated only by Moira's soft keening and, astoundingly, the cawing of what sounded like seagulls. Perhaps they'd been with us the whole time, strange wanderers just like ourselves, but it was only in the lengthening silence that I became aware of their presence. Hesitantly, several gomers closed on us, weapons leveled, covering us carefully as they advanced. More appeared, until finally perhaps twenty were circulating close to us, approaching cautiously our location near the mouth of the cave. There they waited, evidently unwilling to press forward. Then a pair of them detached from the others, passing where Moira and I huddled over Grady, stopping at the entrance to the cave. I watched in horror as one of them took a hand grenade from his belt and prepared to arm it. I found my voice and screamed "Non!" Just to make sure, I repeated this in Lingala, glad that I had picked up the basics of the local tongue over the years. Then I continued, fumbling under stress for first the French words, then the Lingalan, then tried Swahili, finally finding the phrases in each language for "our wounded." My antics prompted a brief debate between the soldier with the grenade and one of his compatriots, conducted in an unfamiliar dialect, spoken much too rapidly for me to follow.

The debate ended with the arrival of what appeared to be two officers, one Wiangaran, one a tall and powerfully built oriental. The Wiangaran issued a curt command that sent the two soldiers, weapons ready, to either side of the cave's entrance. Then the oriental officer stepped forward, scanned our faces briefly, and settled his gaze upon me.

"I am Colonel Ma," he said in clear, slightly-accented English. He examined me closely. "But you—you must be Dr. York. I did not expect you to be here."

I was shaken to my depths. How did he know my name?

"I am York." What else was there to say? I scrutinized him closely, remembered the photographs provided in my original briefing folder, which included a picture of the MSS officer in charge of the biological laboratory. This was the same person.

"You say that your wounded are inside the cave?"

"Yes."

"And I take it that you are now ready to surrender?"

"Yes."

"Then call them out, Dr. York."

"Some of them can't walk."

"How many?"

"Several." I wasn't really sure how many. Was Lem capable of walking? Was Jean-Paul still alive?

"Let the others know that they have five minutes to drag the litter cases out."

I did as I was told and, soon the remaining survivors emerged into the open. First came Dito and Jerry, the latter supporting a badly limping Lem with his good arm. Then Colin and Lorayne staggered out carrying Peter.

"Somebody has to go back for Jean-Paul," said Lorayne.

"There is one more," I said, turning to Colonel Ma.

"Only one?" he responded. "We have the black man you left behind at laboratory. We have the two we found last night. We have that one." He jerked a thumb over his shoulder. I followed his gesture, saw Moira rocking slowly, heard her sobbing softly, her arms still clutched tightly around Grady's head and shoulders. "That is fourteen. We had understood you to number eighteen in all. Plus, of course, the traitor Yang, but we found her body near your airplane."

I took his remark in. We had been twelve, plus Moira and Dito, but how had he come up with sixteen plus aircrew. How the hell had he come up with eighteen?

"No, there is only one more, badly hurt."

"Get him, then."

I entered the cave, Kip following close behind. We found Jean-Paul in the shadows at the very back. At first, I thought that he too was dead, but when we lifted him he suddenly moaned, sharply enough to startle us both. We nearly dropped him. He seemed excessively heavy, or maybe I was weaker than I thought. We carried him outside and set him down next to Peter.

"That, now, is everyone?" asked Ma.

"Everyone," I affirmed.

"You will want to be very certain of this," he insisted. "No tricks."

"No tricks," I said.

He turned to the Wiangaran officer.

"Clear the cave," Ma ordered in French.

A quick order was relayed in Kikongon. Two of the troopers tossed grenades deep inside the cave. Five seconds later they went off, the double blast sending a cloud of dust swirling out from the cave. Once the dust settled the same two troopers sprayed the cave with their AKs, firing several long bursts each. Only after this did they enter, returning several minutes later laden with bits and pieces of our gear, reporting that the cave had been secured. In the meantime, the rest of us had been subjected to a cursory search—I think we must have appeared much too battered to be threatening—and were then muscled into a rough semi-circle around Peter and Jean-Paul, and ordered to sit. All except Moira, who Ma seemed content to ignore for the time being.

"I need to perform an inventory," said Ma, standing before. "I only have a few names—Mr. Dawkins, Miss Finnegan, Major Rudd, Mr. Graham—oh, and Dr. York, who was not, I understood, expected to accompany you. Let's see. I believe that we have Mr. Dawkins and Miss Finnegan over there together. Dr. York I have already identified." He paused, took a moment to carefully examine faces. "Ah, Mr. Graham, there you are."

"Wanker," Colin muttered in response. Ma paid no attention.

"And this is Major Rudd, lying here in front of me." He took Peter by the arm, yanked him into a sitting position. "Yes, this is Major Rudd." Although Peter was clearly wide-awake, he seemed understandably disoriented. "Now, "continued Ma, "now the rest of you."

Silence.

"Come, now."

"Fuck off," said Jerry. In spite of all, he'd come up with yet another toothpick.

Without hesitation Ma popped open the flap of his holster, drew out his pistol, extended his arm toward Jerry, and fired four times as rapidly as he could pull the trigger. Four chest hits. Jerry sagged to the ground and lay still.

"Having some of you alive is of great value to me. Having all of you alive means nothing at all. I expect full cooperation. Now, once again. Your names please."

"Do as he says," I said.

The names were given, a few more questions asked. All of Ma's queries revolved around such apparent trivia as the nationalities and backgrounds of the members of the team. Ma had no interest in the things one would have expected to concern him the most—the details of our operation, who was behind it, and so on. More puzzlement. After a few minutes of this he gave up, more, it seemed, from lack of interest than anything else.

"We must be going," he concluded. "I'm afraid we must detach

Miss Finnegan from Mr. Dawkins. Perhaps a couple of you can do this. You," he pointed to Lorayne, "and you," pointing to me.

We stood and walked over to Moira. While Lorayne put her arm around Moira's shoulder and gently pulled, I knelt in front of her, and pressed my arms inside hers, forcing Grady's body out of her grip. Once they were separated, I straightened the corpse and helped Lorayne lift Moira to her feet. She staggered for a moment, and then found her balance. We removed our hands but remained within arm's reach until we were sure that she wouldn't sink to the ground.

"Arrange a litter-bearing detail, Dr. York."

I tried to think this one through. Dito and Lem could assist each other, and Colin and Lorayne, although suffering from minor injuries, could possibly manage Peter. But Moira, although unwounded, seemed scarcely capable of managing herself, much less helping me with Jean-Paul. And I didn't trust my own strength any longer. That left only Kip, and even if I could help him a little, he couldn't manage one litter case and two corpses.

"I will need some of your men," I said to Ma.

He had clearly come to the same conclusion. He turned to his Wiangaran subordinate, who snapped out the necessary orders. Four of his men took the two litters, while others left and returned a few minutes later with several ground sheets. These were passed out to two more teams, who gathered up Jerry and Grady and hauled them away. The rest of us formed up single file between two more pairs of guards, and we started down the trail. When we reached the large boulders, where we had made our original stand, we passed additional Wiangaran troops who fell in behind us.

Our lengthened column continued down the hill, through the evergreen copse from which the gomers had staged their attacks, the tall *Afrocarpus* trees now thoroughly shredded by gunfire. Had it only been yesterday? Just beyond, in a clearing, sat two, no, three helicopters, the last one some kind of small scout, similar in size to one of our OH-58s. Close up they all appeared ill kept, their mottled camouflage paint worn away to bare metal in some places, in other places covered with gray primer, and their national insignia and squadron numbers faded. Still, the fact of their presence here meant that they could fly well enough. We were halted alongside the first of the larger helicopters. Ma, who had struck out ahead of us was talking to the pilots—all Chinese—when we arrived. He broke off his conversation and walked over to me.

"Your people, Dr. York, will be flying in this aircraft. Please have them board now."

I turned to make sure that everyone had understood his message, but he immediately interrupted.

"The bodies will, of course, be slung in a cargo net underneath the helicopter. They will not mind, and it saves my crews a clean-up task. But Miss Finnegan is rather revoltingly soaked in gore. We must do something about that."

He stuck his head inside the open door of the helicopter's cargo compartment, caught the attention of a crewmember inside, and gave an instruction. A moment later the crewmember came to the door with a plastic poncho over his arm.

"Greasy and dirty," commented Ma as he took the poncho, "but not likely to create a stench." He tossed it at Moira, saying "Put this on," but she simply stood there, not reaching for it, letting the garment fall at her feet.

"Dr. York?"

"Moira," I said, trying to achieve a soothing tone. "They want you to put it on."

But she remained still. I was turning to Lorayne to ask her to assist Moira when Ma barked out another command to the Wiangarans. Two of them approached Moira and started removing her gore-saturated flight suit. She neither cooperated nor resisted as they unzipped her coveralls in front and peeled the blood-soaked material from her shoulders. I heard a low, sharp intake of breath from Ma as the flight suit crumpled to her ankles, leaving her clad only in her bra and panties. These too were wet with blood. The two soldiers hesitated momentarily, then responded to a second command by ripping away these flimsy garments and tossing them aside. Moira made no effort to cover herself. Now the Wiangarans were clearly agitated, and two of the pilots sauntered over. Still, it took me a moment to collect myself.

"Lorayne, please help her," I said. "Colonel, stop this before it goes any further. It does you no good." Clearly, he agreed, issuing a sharp rebuke in Chinese that clearly needed no translation into Lingala.

Lorayne elbowed her way past the two Wiangaran soldiers, picked up the poncho, and slipped it over Moira's head, drawing it down until it covered her to her knees. Ever so carefully, she reached through the arm slits and drew Moira's arms through the openings. Then Lorayne pulled the hood from Moira's head freeing her hair from the confining plastic. Lorayne brushed back the errant strands of hair hanging in Moira's face. Finally, she wet her thumb and gently wiped away a splotch of dried blood on Moira's cheek.

Having quietly taken this all in, Ma spoke directly to Lorayne. "Help her on to the aircraft."

Lorayne took her by the upper arm and elbow and guided her toward the helicopter. At the door Moira stopped, frozen by the sight of the bodies bunched in the cargo net. I started toward her, but Kip got there first. Wrapping his arms around her, he boosted her through the doorway in a single powerful motion. He stepped back to allow Lorayne to climb in, then he and the rest of us followed.

The cargo cabin had the drab utilitarian look of all military helicopters, although this one also betrayed signs of poor maintenance. The chromate green paint was flaking and a thin film of what smelled like hydraulic fluid coated the floor. We sat on the floor against the sides of the fuselage. Hearing the engines spooling up, we braced ourselves for take-off. For a moment I thought that we might have the cargo compartment to ourselves, and the thought of overpowering the pilots and breaking away surged through my brain. But even as I came to terms with the absurdity of attempting this in our present state, two Wiangaran troopers clambered through the door. And, just as the helicopter began to lift from the ground, the Chinese crew chief hopped in as well. As we rose he turned and leaned out the door and looked down, probably to make sure that the cargo net had not fouled anything during takeoff. We rose almost vertically. With three helicopters in the cramped landing zone, there had been no room for a rolling take-off. I supposed that it didn't matter much. By my last reckoning, we weren't any great flying distance from the little airfield where the jets had tried to force us to land. That seemed much longer than a day ago. Now it was an eternity ago for Kees and Tommy and Jerry and Grady.

The din inside the cabin was oppressively loud as we transitioned into forward flight. I reviewed the numbers. We had been fourteen to start with, including Moira and Dito. Now there were five dead, with Jean-Paul in a bad way, and Peter—I didn't know about Peter, but I suspected that his condition left much to be desired. But that was already half of our force dead or seriously wounded. Dito had not uttered a word of complaint, but I suspected that his wounds caused him great discomfort. Colin had a superficial cut in his side and a variety of other dings. Lorayne and I had some minor cuts and bruises. Fortunately, the grenade fragments that struck us in the back had largely spent their force. She seemed to be coping well though. Moira was—well, Moira was badly injured in places that did not show. I counted myself among the useless, not because of my wounds, which were merely uncomfortable, but because I felt terribly weak, drained of all energy, hardly capable of functioning.

Only Kip seemed perfectly whole. Gazing across at him, I saw that, unlike the rest of us, he was intently watching our guards and the crew chief, alert to each move, evaluating the situation. I hoped he was finding inspiration somewhere, for it eluded me completely. His eyes flicked toward Colin, settled there thoughtfully. Then Kip turned to me, our eyes met, and he smiled. He spoke, but the words would not carry above the noise, and he turned away, and looked again at toward the cockpit. I followed his eyes, saw nothing that seemed significant, allowed my thoughts to wander again, but this led nowhere. We were prisoners, and that is a hateful thing to be.

The helicopter flight lasted no more than thirty minutes. Seconds after we landed, the doors were thrown open, and we were ordered outside. This was—it had to be—the air base that we had been directed to originally. It appeared to be nothing more than an outstation. It had a single dirt runway, long enough to support the usual varieties of bush aircraft, perhaps even some larger ones, though I wondered how they had expected Moira to put the Catalina down here. To one side stood a single ramshackle hangar, large enough to shelter perhaps one medium sized aircraft. Personnel accommodations consisted of a small barracks and a stubby open-air control tower growing out of the roof of a squat concrete block building, presumably an administrative structure of some sort. Altogether dreary in the manner customary to this impoverished region. The grass was uncut, and the pathways were muddy. As we stood there it started to rain.

A twin-engine propeller-driven cargo plane sat alongside the administrative building. As the sound of the helicopters died away, all that could be heard was the high-pitched sound of a hand drill, coming from the direction of the hangar, the loud voices of the Wiangaran troops getting off of the other helicopter, and, somewhere in the distance, the barking of dogs. We stood by the helicopter, waiting for Ma, waiting to be told what to do next. As we stood, Dito edged over to me and spoke.

"The cargo plane's an older Antonov model, or maybe a Chinese copy—the markings are Chinese. From this distance, it looks in better shape than these helicopters, like it doesn't quite belong here. This little field is, well...."

"A bit shabby, isn't it?"

Although Dito seemed quite fatigued, I noticed that he had regained some of his color.

"I always thought of Cuba as a poor country," he said. "But this makes Cuba look like California."

"I have never been to Cuba."

"We had Batista and then Castro, a criminal followed by a Communist. Here, too, I think, criminals like the "General-President" and now the CCP. It all comes to the same thing, I think. So, it appears, anyway."

Kip joined us.

"We have a problem, Major."

I almost chuckled.

"Just one problem, Kip?"

"One in particular, one right now. Jean-Paul. I don't know how much of a chance he has, but I know he's got no chance if he isn't taken to a hospital soon. And with Jerry gone we've got nobody who knows enough to keep him alive until we can get him to a hospital."

I considered this. For all its run-down quality, this airfield had clearly been set up as a tactical base. It stood to reason that it should have some kind of dispensary and someone with at least a modicum of medical knowledge. There seemed to be no obvious harm in asking for medical help. I looked around for Ma, saw that he had alighted from the smaller helicopter and was standing alongside it issuing orders to several of his men, clearly his men, since they appeared to be Chinese. We might be in the middle of Wiangara, but here the Chinese were running the show.

I started to walk over to Ma, but found myself distracted by a team of workers clad in identical blue driving up to our helicopter in, inevitably, an old Toyota pickup. They dismounted and began removing Grady and the others from the cargo net lying near our aircraft. They rolled them out of the tarps that the soldiers had wrapped them in, and then stuffed them into individual body bags. The body bags were then slung onto the back of the truck and driven over to the cargo plane by the administrative building. There they were off-loaded and laid out at the rear of the plane, just aft of the already-extended cargo ramp. As the body detail unloaded the truck, I noticed that two other body bags already lay in back of the plane. Smitty? And who might the other be? Another question to ask Ma.

I was saved from seeking him out with my questions when he dismissed the last of his subordinates and came over to me.

"We have no time for delay," he said. "I must produce you in Beijing within the next thirty-six hours, and that is a great distance from here. From here to our base in Djibouti, where we meet a long-range jet for the flight home to China. Count yourself fortunate. My masters simply want to put you on display as the criminals who destroyed a medical facility meant to help poor Africans overcome Ebola and other viruses. My friend the "General-President," on the other hand, is very cross with you for slaughtering so many of his palace guards. He wants me to turn you over to him, presumably so he can enjoy watching your women raped and then all of you hacked to death with machetes. As you know, he and his inner circle have a taste for such things." He gave me a hard stare. "You may have temporarily put us out of business here, but rest assured, we know how to extract maximum benefit from having such a nice collection of western criminals in our hands. And don't imagine that you've put us out of business here. Do you think we won't recover? But now, we have little time. The jet will be waiting, and I don't want a tug-of-war with that Wiangaran gang over by the hangar. So, I would be pleased if you would lead your people over to the plane and board through the rear cargo door."

"One of our injured men is in a very bad way. He will likely die soon without medical intervention. Perhaps there are medical personnel at this facility who could provide sufficient treatment to keep him alive until we get to Djibouti. There is nothing we can do for him ourselves. Our medic is the man that you shot after we surrendered."

He glared at me. "I have no time for this!"

He stalked off with an impatient "follow me" gesture. I called to the others, and the same workers who had assisted us earlier picked up Peter and Jean-Paul and carried them to the plane. Ma, hurrying ahead, reached the open cargo doors well before us. There other blue-overalled workers hefted the body bags onto a pallet and pushed it up the cargo ramp while a squad of Ma's soldiers were loading their personal gear. Evidently, they were to be our guards for the flight. As we reached the rear of the aircraft, Ma summoned a pair of the workers and walked briskly over to me.

"Which of your litter cases is the dying man? Not Major Rudd, I hope? We want him in Beijing."

"No," I answered, pointing toward Jean-Paul. "This man."

Ma walked over to him, ordered his men to set down the litter and step away. Then he drew his pistol and fired three rounds. Jean-Paul's body bucked on the litter, then lay still. Ma turned to the workmen and issued a curt order. Then he turned to me.

"I said I needed you all in Beijing within twenty-four hours. I did not say that I needed you all *alive* in Beijing. A representative sample will suffice. Now, please get your people on the plane."

I fought back the impulse to throw myself at him, saw that Kip and Colin and Lorayne were similarly struggling. But no one moved, for which I was very grateful. We didn't need to have anyone else killed. After telling them to head up the ramp, I fell in behind the two workers carrying Peter. As I lingered on the ramp I saw the other workmen hurriedly load Jean-Paul into a body bag and sling him onto the pallet of corpses., which was tied down just inside the ramp. I sat down next to where the workmen had placed Peter. He was conscious, and raised his hand to catch my attention.

"Harry, lean closer," he said.

I did as he asked.

"If it's the last thing you ever do," he said, "you must take that pistol from him and shove it up his arse."

I said nothing, but took his hand and gave it a squeeze. The engines started first one, then the other: soon both were turning over strongly, and I heard the high-pitched whirring sound of an auxiliary motor as the cargo ramp lifted, cutting off most of the outside light. In the shadowy cargo compartment, we sat back and awaited take-off, isolated from each other by the deafening noise, by the guards who hovered over us, by our physical and emotional exhaustion. None of the others looked good. And I couldn't have appeared any better to them. Six of fourteen dead, now—given the size of our little unit, our casualties were comparable to those suffered by the Marines on Tarawa.

Ma and several more troopers entered the aircraft by a personnel door, the latter positioning themselves a comfortable distance from us, but near enough to maintain a close watch. Ma disappeared forward into the cockpit and closed the door behind him. Moments later the plane began taxiing to the runway. At the runway threshhold the pilot wound the engines up to a fuselage-shaking roar, holding the aircraft against the brakes. Then we felt a bump, and a shudder coursed through the aircraft. I pulled myself upright and glanced out the nearest window. Evidently a handful of Wiangaran troopers had tried to prevent the plane from taking off by running out in front of it, but one had gotten too close to the port side engine. I guess he'd only been clipped by the tip of the prop, but that had been enough to leave him headless on the hard-packed clay. The other Wiangarans had retreated to a safe distance, and were aiming their AKs at the plane, hesitating, obviously waiting for an order to shoot. Then the transport leapt forward, raced down the runway, and soon reached lift-off speed. We climbed steadily in the gray light filtering through the overhead clouds, eventually breaking into bright sunlight above. Given our recent flying experiences, it felt strange to be soaring high in broad daylight, well above the nap of the earth.

We leveled off at less than 10,000 feet, an essential concession given the unpressurized and unheated cabin. Even so, it quickly became unpleasantly cold. The Chinese guards broke out blankets from a stack and wrapped themselves in them. After my most recent experience with Ma I hesitated to ask for anything, but finally decided that I had no choice. I stood and started forward. The first Chinese to notice me called out a sharp command. I needed no Mandarin to understand 'Halt!' The others looked up as I stopped and tried, in pantomime, to explain that I wanted blankets. This led to a brief exchange between the several guards, and then they waved me forward. I grabbed up as many blankets as I could carry, and then returned aft, passing them out one by one, finding that in the end I had one for myself and two that I could wrap around Peter. The blankets were not particularly thick, but they made the needed difference.

We scrunched together in twos and threes for added warmth and in this manner made it through the first two hours, the tedium and discomfort compounded by the stench from the non-functioning toilet. By my rough reckoning we were somewhere over Ethiopia, with maybe three more hours to go before landing in Djibouti. I pulled my blanket a bit tighter and tried to recall all I knew about local conditions there, hoping somehow to see a path to freedom. Djibouti had once been a French colony, valued for its strategic location commanding the entrance to the Red Sea. Even post-independence, the French had maintained a military presence there. I seemed to recall that Kip had served there briefly during his Foreign Legion days. But that had been years ago, and, if nothing else, I knew that much had changed recently. The French still had a base there, and the U.S. had a significant presence. Since 2017, however, the Chinese had built upon years of commercial investment—not to say outright bribery—by gaining permission from the locals to build their first naval support base outside the Pacific region. My recollection was that this base had grown by orders of magnitude, with hundreds, perhaps thousands, of PLA Navy personnel stationed permanently. But my further recollection was the more tantalizing. If memory served, the Chinese base concession didn't include a full-sized runway, but only a glorified helipad. The air connection from Djibouti to China still relied upon the one large international airport, which had a civilian terminal on one side and both French and U.S. military facilities on the other. Did this offer a chance of escape during our transfer between aircraft? Looking at our battle worn crew, looking at our Chinese guards, anticipating even more guards between planes, I couldn't be optimistic. Still, a long shot beat no shot at all.

A depressing thought came over me. The last time I'd flown from this part of Africa to Camp Lemonier, the U.S. base in Djibouti, had been following the disastrous 2017 mission that had cost Bobby Naburje his life. But that led exactly nowhere, so I put the thought aside.

I was trying to figure out a way to engage Kip, Colin, and Lorayne in my thinking without drawing the guard's intervention when I was startled by a loud, backfire-like noise from just outside the aircraft, followed by a lurch to the left. After a few seconds the pilot recovered and straightened the aircraft, but almost immediately we began losing altitude. Instinctively, I looked around for Moira, but my eyes found Dito first. He shouted across to me.

"He's lost an engine. I think he's going to put her down."

CHAPTER 21

AFTER ALL THAT we'd been through, the next ten minutes was in some respects the worst. Whatever the book said about flying on one engine, it hardly applied to the pilot in this plane. Again and again he made adjustments, trying to maintain a stable flight attitude as we descended. Our Chinese guards lost all interest in us, compulsively standing up to look out of the window and then rushing to buckle themselves back into their tin seats whenever the plane took another erratic lurch. For our part, we listened and waited and wondered, until we felt the series of hard bounces that signaled the presence of a solid runway beneath our wheels.

After taxiing for a short distance, the aircraft came to a halt, and the pilot killed the remaining engine. Ma immediately emerged from the cockpit and stomped toward our guards, his face contorted in transparent rage. But fortunately, after delivering his orders, he debarked hurriedly without paying any attention to us. It was left to the guard NCO to make the next move. He marched back to where we were sitting and yelled at us, gesturing at the same time with the muzzle of his AK. It seemed that he wanted us to get up, but his flurry of words meant nothing to me. Then another guard approached and, in passable English, ordered us off the plane.

"What about help with my stretcher case?" I asked, but a look at the sergeant's face told me that this was not the time to pose questions. I looked around. Colin seemed to be experiencing more pain. Indeed, he appeared no longer capable of standing straight, but instead listed sharply in the direction of his gashed side. When he saw me staring in his direction, however, he straightened up and gave me a wink. Dito, at least, continued to look and sound better.

"Lorayne, you and I can take the front of Peter's stretcher, Kip you take the rear. Colin, see if you can help Lem. Dito, maybe you and Moira can help each other."

So arranged, we clambered through the passenger door—for whatever reason the pilot had not lowered the ramp—and into achingly bright sunlight, and a brisk dry wind. The airfield was hard clay, although the presence of several pieces of heavy earth moving equipment suggested that a paving operation had begun. To one side lay a small hangar and a couple of sheds, to the other what appeared like nothing less than a small Foreign Legion fort straight out of *Beau Geste*. This gave me pause until I realized that this must be a legacy of the 1930s Italian conquest of Ethiopia, built to cement their occupation. The landscape was high desert, which didn't help me much. I knew we'd landed in Ethiopia, but beyond that I couldn't guess. Still, I could only wonder at the presence of a working Chinese base somewhere in the middle of a country that, to the best of my knowledge, had evaded the Chinese tentacles that stretched across Africa.

Guards all around us, we marched across the tarmac to fort's entrance, simply an open archway through the outer wall—evidently, the gates had disappeared years ago along with the Italian garrison. This gave way to an open courtyard, with doors lining the interior walls on two of the four sides, and arcades supporting what had once been firing positions along the crenellated upper portion of the outer wall. We were deposited into the first set of doors we came to, which proved to be a small barrack room of sorts, with a metal bunkbed against each wall and a wooden table and four chairs between the beds and beneath the window. After freezing on the plane, we luxuriated in the warmth of the room. The guard NCO shut the door behind us, but did not lock it, since the door had no lock. Still, we weren't likely to go anywhere. Kip and I eased Peter off his litter and onto one of the lower bunks, and I urged Lem to stretch out on the other bottom bunk. Moira climbed onto one of the top bunks and lay down, her eyes closed. The rest of us settled down around the table. Then, after hours of withdrawal into ourselves and not speaking, the entire group was suddenly chattering. Where were we? What was going on? What would happen next?

Our frenetic conversations died abruptly when the door flew open and the guard NCO stepped into the room. He glared at us and then beckoned for me to follow him. I noticed that a chair had been placed just opposite the door to our room and that one of the guards had been posted there. He sat slumped back against the wall, his AK lying across his lap, his cap down across his forehead. But, despite this languid pose, his eyes tracked me as I followed the sergeant.

Outside, we exited the fort in the direction of the airfield, and approached a row of three small buildings along a hard-packed dirt path. We entered the first of the buildings, stepping inside an ante-room that had the feel of a company clerk's or first sergeant's office. We crossed this room to an inner door. The sergeant knocked, and a voice responded from within. Turning the doorknob, the sergeant pushed the door open while indicating that I should enter. After I did, he closed the door behind me, leaving me standing across from the desk where Ma was seated, speaking on a satellite phone. A brusque wave of his hand ordered me to take a seat. While waiting, I decided that whoever owned this facility belonged to Ma's circle of conspira-tors, or subordinates. However austere, this was this was clearly the base commander's office, and the owner had placed it at Ma's disposal. Someone had also provided Ma with a bottle of Glenlivet single malt and a glass. Concluding his conversation with an explosive grunt and a laugh, Ma hung up the phone. He poured himself a shot and tossed it down, from the look of the bottle, clearly not his first of the afternoon. Then he turned his attention to me.

"I have had to adjust my plans," he said, but his expression showed little in the way of distress.

"Oh?"

"Well, yes. Our aircraft cannot be readily repaired, the task is beyond this pitiful excuse for an airfield, but tomorrow morning we will have a replacement aircraft and will continue our journey. So, we wait overnight in this shithole. But this is not why I ordered you here. I need to know more about Major Rudd's condition. Is he in a bad way? Does he need medical attention?"

Despite his relaxed demeanor, I feared the reaction my answer might provoke. I hesitated, then finally spoke.

"He's very uncomfortable, and I believe he's got a fever. Pain medication and antibiotics seem like a good idea, but the best thing would be hospitalization."

"There is no doctor here and the nearest hospital is two hours away. We control this little airfield, we're rebuilding it for the Ethiopian government for use against the Oromo rebels, but I can't entrust you to an Ethiopian hospital. I cannot allow that. Until we get to Djibouti, we must not draw attention too much to ourselves. But I can see that such medication is provided. And a doctor will be on the plane that will carry us to Beijing."

"Thank you."

"You are sure that he will survive?"

I thought about this one.

"I think so, but he'll need a doctor soon." I was absolutely mystified by his solicitude for Peter. Still mindful of the risk of igniting an outburst, I continued. "You seemed indifferent to our wounded before."

"And I was, except for those who serve a useful purpose. Arrangements had been made. Representatives of the print and broadcast media will meet us in Beijing, not just Chinese, but the international press, all prepared for a news conference presenting shocking revelations involving NATO-sponsored international thuggery, with complicity from influential persons at the highest levels in Washington. You represent a gigantic turd, and we mean to drop it where it will have the greatest result. Major Rudd, shall we say, helps to internationalize your criminal enterprise. You, Major Rudd, and the beautiful Ms. Finnegan make for a compelling presentation, particularly with her criminal history. We wished to have Mr. Dawkins as well, he has a certain reputation, after all. And we might find a use for that faggot Saumarez. With you four in hand, we can keep the television cameras rolling as we tell our story. The others, well, my masters in Beijing might find a use for them, but I think not. We will see."

"I understand."

"No, I doubt that. Beginning to understand, maybe, but no more. Anyway, you have been provided a room for the night. Make the most of it."

He poured and drank another shot.

"Could we have some food?" I asked. "It's been a long time since we last ate."

"I will see to it."

"Some clothing for Ms. Finnegan—she can't go on naked under that poncho."

He hesitated, evidently pondering the pros and cons of Moira's semi-nakedness, whether for his political purposes or perhaps out of simple prurience, I couldn't tell.

"It will be done."

"Facilities for washing?"

"No—I think you will look just fine in your present state. When we put you before the cameras, we want you all to look like the criminals you are.

At least one more question seemed worth the risk, particularly now that I'd just been told that I was needed alive.

"So, the virus facility was just bait?"

"No—of course not. We had worked for years perfecting the virus, and for the better part of six months to build the lab as the zero point. No, we didn't plan to lose it. You surprised us there. We did not expect you for at least another two days, and we were looking for three helicopters to stage out of Sarh in southern Chad."

And, finally, confirmation of what I'd begun to suspect when helicopters had responded the night of our attack. We'd been betrayed by someone in Washington. I felt a hot rush of anger. Had it been Sandy Sawyer? I would put nothing past her, but blanched at the thought that someone in her position might be tied to China's Ministry of State Security. Someone, though, had compromised our mission. Never mind that I'd at least partly outsmarted Sawyer, or whoever. Their intent had been to betray, to cause the mission to fail and to get us all killed.

"Have a drink, Dr. York," he said, taking a second glass from the cabinet behind him and splashing a shot of whiskey into it. I realized that he was getting drunk.

"I don't think so," I said.

"Take the drink, you sneaky Estonian bastard. I wouldn't have credited the usual dumb American with such subterfuge, but you, you're really someone from the East."

I reached for the glass and drank.

"If you hadn't lied about your plan, I would have my show trial exhibits *and* the lab, intact, our plan ready for execution. Now I have to return to Beijing and beg forgiveness." He paused. "One more thing. I know you've already thought about how you might make a break when we land in Djibouti, getting across to the American facility. Forget it. It's too much trouble to carry you around on stretchers here in the middle of nowhere, but before we land we're going to sedate the lot of you."

I drained my glass, set it down on the table. Ma glared at me. "You've had your drink, now get out of my sight. We'll see how goddamn clever you are when we put you on trial in Beijing."

"Trial?"

"No, Dr. York, no more for now. I am not so drunk that I will elaborate. Now send the sergeant in and wait for him to escort you back. I'll see that your people are fed and that medicine is sent over for Major Rudd."

The sergeant was waiting just outside the door. I pointed towards the doorway to indicate that he was wanted inside. I stood by while he received his instructions from Ma.

The sergeant returned me to the rest of the team and then sent off two of his men to retrieve the food and medicine Ma had ordered. They hurried back with several cardboard cartons filled with odds and ends and then hurried away to rejoin the party developing at the other end of the hut, where the remaining Chinese were quartered. Ma was not the only one who intended to make a long, boring night more bearable with the aid of liquor, though I suspected his troops enjoyed a lesser tipple.

We greatly welcomed having medicine for Peter. The food consisted of some kind of cross between a soup and a porridge, accompanied by a stack of flatbread akin to Indian *naan*. To drink we had water. Under the circumstances, this dull and meager offering took on the dimensions of a great feast. Repeating what Ma had told me to the rest of the team prompted a few ironic comments about 'the Last Supper,' but I could see spirits rising about me as we finished eating. After dinner, Kip produced a pack of cigarettes and we passed it around.

"I'm not a smoker," he'd said, "but I wound up with these, and I figured they would be appreciated sooner or later."

I took a cigarette and lit up, listening to the sounds of revelry from the other end of the building. I wondered if the guard outside our door had abandoned his post to join his friends, and then I wondered what difference it would make if he had.

I was sitting on the bed next to Peter. I'd expected that the pain medication would knock him out; instead, it only seemed to relax him. We talked for a few minutes, idle conversation. But then he grew serious: "Well, Harry, you're the head boy. It's up to you to figure out how we're going to get out of here."

Although he'd caught me off guard, I knew that he was absolutely right. We'd all been existing from moment to moment, reeling from one disaster to the next, with the prospect of execution—sooner or later—looming darkly before us. But now Ma's comments had given me reason to believe that some of us would live—that I would live—but there were no guarantees. What of the others, the ones who had not been singled out as key players in his political friend's media pageant? And even if I lived, could I play the role for which I was being cast? I stood up, waited until the various conversations died and I had everyone's attention.

"We've got something to decide," I said, "and we've got only a little time to do it."

"What do you mean?" asked Kip.

"I mean this: are we going to try to escape tonight?"

"Don't you fancy a bit of a wait?" asked Colin. "Do you know where we are? It looks outside like Tim-buk-fuckin'-tu."

I had to admit that I didn't know where we were. Then Dito spoke up. "I do know where we are," he said. "When we were walking from the plane I looked around, you can see the name of the airfield painted in big block letters above the hangar doors. I've seen the name on flying charts. We're right about the middle of Ethiopia, maybe two hours flying time to Djibouti."

I explained what I'd learned about the handoff in Djibouti and the flight to Beijing.

"So, Major," said Kip. "We're going to Djibouti. I know it some, and I know we might find friendlies there. Are you suggesting that we try to escape there?"

"All I'm saying is that, if it hadn't been for an engine malfunction, we'd have been already there, and already on the jet to Beijing. Some of us Ma wants as circus exhibits, the others he seems pretty indifferent to. We've seen what his indifference means."

"I always wanted to be in the circus," said Lem. This was the closest to a display of spirit I had seen from him in a long while. I hated to squash it.

"I don't think Ma sees you as being a key part of the circus. I'm sorry. The same is true for you, Kip, and for Colin and Lorayne over there. And I don't think there are really any long-term promises for the rest of us. Playing for time's always one option. It just may not be the best one here."

"You have something in mind, Harry?" said Peter.

"Just some thoughts. We can't walk out, nor can we steal a truck and drive out. But maybe we can steal a plane. I guess it'd have to be the plane that's coming in tomorrow morning, since the one we came in on is broken. So, we steal it, and fly it ourselves to Djibouti. Look, it's here or not at all." I explained about Ma's plan to sedate us, and made it clear that the "us" probably only meant the four he wanted in Beijing. "Stealing the plane here means a chance for all of us. Otherwise...." my voice trailed off.

"I'm all for it, Hair Doctor," said Lorayne. "I don't much go for the idea of being shot at dawn. But there's a bunch of big 'ifs' in what you're saying." She tilted her head toward the upper bunk, where Moira still lay, apparently sleeping. "And Dito's not in the greatest shape either. Or maybe Lem—he's a pilot, too."

"But mainly rotary wing; I'm not as good as Moira or Dito on fixed wing," said Lem. "I can try, but I'll probably need one of them to help. And as you can see, I am also not in the best of shape."

"Dito?" I asked.

"Steal the plane and I will fly it. If I need help, I think that Moira'll be able to assist."

"The guards are mostly drunk," said Kip.

"Ma, too," I said, "if he continues at the rate he was going earlier."

"So," said Lem, "we overpower the guard outside the door, sneak past the drunks, steal the plane, and go."

"But there is no plane until tomorrow," said Dito.

"By that time, the drunks may be sober."

"And," added Kip, "we're not exactly in the best shape for over-powering anyone."

This was probably an understatement for, despite our renewed energy and optimism, we were a feeble-looking crew. Of the entire group, only Kip seemed to be in condition to confront an armed guard with his bare hands. Under other circumstances I'd have had no doubt he could do it, but I knew that even Kip was no better than eighty percent.

"Ah," said Peter, "you need something with which to smite the ungodly, right? I may have just the thing. Here, Harry, reach into this pocket for me please."

I unbuttoned the cargo pocket on his good leg, pushed my hand past a wad of rags, felt something cool, metallic, hard—a tiny automatic pistol. I took it out and found that it was one of the little stainless steel Seecamp deep concealment models in .32 caliber. It fit the palm of my hand, but, if memory served, carried six rounds in the magazine plus one—I checked—in the chamber. Not a very authoritative caliber, but, as the saying goes, better than throwing an ashtray.

"It was Jerry's," said Peter. "Just before we surrendered, while he was giving me a pain shot, he slipped it into my pocket." Once more I blessed the casual contempt with which Ma's men had viewed the task of searching us. I reached under my shirt, found the gauze bandage under which I'd concealed Dr. Yang's thumb drive, yet another blessing if we made it back to the world.

I squeezed Peter's hand. "This is perfect. Maybe this gives us a fighting chance."

We discussed striking immediately, while the guards were still in the midst of their party. But we needed the new plane, and we couldn't risk tipping our hand until it was on the ground. So, this meant waiting—if we couldn't benefit from dealing with drunks, at least we could hope that their collective hangover would offer an advantage. Our timing would have to be perfect. Take out the guard outside the door with the little pistol. Steal his AK and confront the other guards down the hall. Grab their AKs and go after the remaining guards, then take over the plane. Well, three of us would—Kip, Lorayne, and myself. The others would make for the plane, the wounded helping each other along. I had my doubts about their collective ability to move Peter, but the very thought of escape seemed to have strengthened them.

In this manner we planned throughout the night. No one was capable of sleeping. About five a.m. the guard was changed outside the door, and, if the new guard seemed to be morosely hung over when he opened the door to check on us, he also appeared wide awake, a tall, chunky man who'd be tough to get the jump on. We debated this prospect until Lorayne came up with the solution. "If Kip tries to go out there, he'll never get a chance to raise the pistol before being shot. But I can do it."

"How?" Kip and I asked together.

"Well, maybe I'm not built as good as Moira, but what I've got ought to be enough to get the job done."

CHAPTER 22

UNDER A LIGHTENING sky, we watched out the window as the little airfield came sluggishly to life. About seven a.m. a cook trundled a cart of what looked like coffee and sandwiches around the courtyard to the troop quarters, as the level of noise indicated that the drunks were awakening. No sign of Colonel Ma, who I hoped was nursing an excruciating hangover. Finally, about two hours into the morning, we heard the sound of an airplane flying over low, and then, moments later, the unmistakable sound of taxiing just outside the walls of the fort, and then the sound trailed off. Our plane had arrived.

"If it's another plane like the one we were on, they won't need to worry about refueling," said Dito. "The crew will likely want a few minutes on the ground, but you said Ma was in a hurry. I suspect they'll be coming for us soon."

"We better get ready, then."

Kip picked up Peter and gently placed him on the litter. Moira positioned herself at the front of the litter and Colin at the rear, ready to pick it up when the moment came. I caught Moira's eye and was rewarded with a wan smile. Dito and Lem leaned against each another. Kip took up a position just inside the door.

"It's time," I said, speaking to Lorayne.

She faced toward the door with her back toward us, took off her shirt and removed her bra. She then put the shirt back on, clutching it closed without buttoning it, and tucked the little automatic under her waistband at the small of her back. I stepped up beside her, ready to open the door.

"Okay, then, ready everyone, ready Lorayne, okay, on three, one, two, THREE!"

I opened the door and Lorayne stepped out, her left hand clutching her lapel, already beginning to pull her shirt open, her right hand free to reach behind her back. I was looking over her shoulder. The guard's eyes went wide as her breasts came into view, he pushed back his chair and started to stand up, and then I heard three quick shots, saw his face open up, and blood spatter brightly on the wall behind his head. Although I was closer to the door, Kip darted past me. By the time I passed the threshhold he was yanking the AK out from under the fallen guard and Lorayne, without bothering to rebutton her shirt, was heading down the hallway with her little pistol. I noticed an automatic pistol at the guard's belt, grabbed it, and went after them, checking the chamber and flicking off the safety as I went. A guard staggered out into the hall, naked from the waist up. Using her last four rounds, Lorayne stitched him neatly from neck to navel.

Stepping over this guard's body, Kip directed a couple of quick bursts through the open barracks-room door, then entered, clearing the room with the balance of a magazine. I took the water closet, flinging open the door. A guard sat on the toilet seat, his pants around his ankles. I shot him twice, once in the chest, once in the head. As I turned, Kip was coming out of the sleeping area, four AKs slung over his shoulder, an armful of magazines clutched to his chest. Lorayne and I each took an AK and stuck a couple of magazines in our cargo pockets. Glancing over my shoulder, I saw Moira and Colin struggling down the hall, Colin with Peter on his shoulder, with Dito and Lem following close behind. I pressed my pistol into Colin's free hand, while Kip gave the last AK to Lem.

"Okay?" I looked from Kip to Lorayne. "Kip, you're out the door first, take the pilots. Lorayne—follow me—we'll head straight for Ma's building."

Then we were quickly out the door, Kip darting left, while Lorayne and I went right. We'd struck so suddenly that all the aircrew were standing bunched together, the new arrivals and the ones from our previous flight, frozen in the open like jacklit deer. Kip cut them down with a succession of short bursts, changed magazines, then took up position to cover the rest of the team.

As Lorayne and I approached the next building Ma and one of his sergeants stepped out the door directly in front of us. We shot them both, and they went down, and we shot them again on the ground as we rushed past them into the building. Inside we found a clerk and a radioman; Lorayne shot them while I pumped a few rounds into the radio. Back outside, I knelt briefly alongside Ma, to satisfy myself that he was truly dead. We'd hit him three times in the chest, once in the neck. When I rolled him over I saw that the round through his neck had exited upward out the back of his skull, taking bits of brain and bone with it. I didn't bother to check for a pulse. From the sergeant lying next to him I took another AK and a couple of hand grenades.

Lorayne arched her eyebrows and said: "You know, Hair Doctor, it looks like we've got this place under control, at least long enough to get on the plane. You think you're going to need all that extra hardware?"

She was right. All the gomers we'd seen were now dead. The entire area was quiet, except for the *clump-clump-clump* of a diesel generator from a shed behind the barracks and the squeaking wheels of the handcart Moira and Colin had commandeered to carry Peter. Still, I decided to keep the extra weapon and the grenades. After all we had been through, no precaution seemed excessive, and we still hadn't accounted for some of the workers we'd seen yesterday—we could only hope that they would be deterred by the raging gunfire.

I saw that the others had reached the aircraft, and Lorayne and

I headed in that direction. As we reached the side of the plane, Kip emerged from inside. "It's clear—no gomers hiding under the bed. And it's a good thing old man Ma wanted to hurry us out of here— check it out." With a sweep of the hand he indicated the pallet laden with body bags. "They had just finished loading them, I think, when the shooting started. We saw a couple of workers hightailing it out of here as we got here."

I offered a short silent prayer. I'd accepted, gut-wrenchingly, the idea that we'd be leaving our dead behind, a sad nod to the need to give priority to the living. Now I wouldn't have that extra burden on my conscience.

"Let's start getting aboard," I said.

Lorayne helped boost Lem into Kip's waiting hands. They disappeared from view and then Kip returned, ready to help with Peter's litter. This took some doing, but soon Peter was safely snugged down inside the troop compartment. I told Kip and Lorayne to scout around for any more gomers. I divested myself of the extra AK and followed Dito and Moira into the cockpit; Dito was already firing up the engines. I noticed that he had taken the left seat—the position of the senior pilot.

"Are we good to go?" I asked.

"I think so," he said. "Looks like enough for Djibouti, but who cares, if it gets us out of here."

"Do you need charts?'

"Yes, and they're probably around here somewhere. We'll worry about that once we're in the air. For now, all I need to do is head northeast."

"Good enough. How long?"

"Five minutes and I start taxiing out."

"All right—I'll get Kip and Lorayne back to the plane."

I went back through the cargo cabin, satisfied myself that all was in order there, and exited the aircraft. I saw Lorayne immediately and waved her over, but I couldn't find Kip. Enveloped by the engine noise, I cupped my hand and yelled into Lorayne's ear, asking where he'd gone. She gestured toward a building across the way, some kind of equipment shack. As I followed her pointing finger I saw Kip emerge from the building. I waved to him, and he started trotting in our direction.

Kip was maybe halfway to the plane, as far from cover as he could possibly be, when a burst of automatic weapons fire rang out. The tarmac erupted in spouts of dust and broken asphalt as the line of bullets tracked towards him. He went down immediately, rolling away from the threat, maybe he'd been hit. I turned and fired in the general direction of the sound of the shots, then Lorayne was beside me with her AK, and we were firing toward the corner of the hangar where it looked like a pair of unaccounted-for guards had rejoined the fight. Then, out of the corner of my eye, I saw that Kip was up and running, running like hell, and Lorayne and I both fired again and again, trying to keep the gomers' heads down. Then another weapon joined in, from above and behind us, killing the two guards. I looked around and saw Colin standing in the open door of the plane, AK in hand, being held upright by Lem. Together they'd compensated for their individual injuries and made the shot.

Dito was pumping his fist through the open cockpit window, urging us to get aboard. Kip climbed into the plane, apparently unhurt. I waved Lorayne back, and she boarded. Glancing around one more time, I followed her through the door. Dito released the brakes, and we rolled forward. But after only a few meters we came to an abrupt stop. I stuck my head out the still-open door and saw why Dito had stopped. A cargo truck, roughly the size of a big pickup truck, raced toward us on the unpaved road that paralleled the runway, kicking up a huge cloud of dust. It was roughly five hundred meters distant and closing fast, and the cargo bed was crammed with gomers. I hopped down onto the tarmac, took cover behind the plane's front wheels, and opened fire—anything to stop their onward rush. The truck halted, and maybe a dozen gomers piled out, returning fire.

Sheltering behind the front wheel had been a bad decision—we couldn't afford the risk of damage to the plane. But neither could I move without getting killed. I was also low on ammunition; I switched the selector on my AK from full auto to semi-auto and squeezed off single shots, trying to keep the gomers' heads down, hoping for help.

Which came from a surprising direction. The gomers had been using the cover of a ditch alongside the runway to advance; I had kept their heads down, but hadn't stopped their forward movement. Suddenly they were up and running, running away from me, toward the truck they'd abandoned, and some were dropping, crumpling into the ditch. Kip and Lorayne had taken up position at the head of the ditch, and were pouring enfilade fire along its length, turning it from a protective trench into a killing zone. I ran over to them, took up a firing position, and added a few carefully aimed rounds.

"They're all back at the truck," Lorayne yelled between shots. We were all conserving ammunition now, firing singles rather than bursts.

"Think they'll bug out?" I asked.

"No way," said Kip. "I don't think there's but two of 'em left, they're at the front, using the engine block and the front wheels as cover. They won't give that up to get in the cab."

Stalemate. We couldn't kill them from where we were, they couldn't kill us, but the airplane would have to taxi past their position to position for takeoff. Then I remembered the grenades. I had stuffed them in my cargo pocket after taking them from Grigoriev's sergeant. I put down my rifle and fished them out.

"We've got to get close enough for these," I said, and, even as I said it, I knew that there was no "we" about it. I was too old and slow to do what needed to be done. I handed the grenades to Kip. "You know what to do. Lorayne and I will cover you, keep their heads down."

Finesse did not figure in the equation. Lorayne and I kept firing, alternating our shots, making sure the gomers stayed tucked in behind the front wheels. Kip ran straight down the ditch until he was about twenty meters away from the truck. His first grenade hit the side of it, was deflected, and rolled yards away where it exploded harmlessly. If he missed with the second one, he'd have to rush them with his AK, and I didn't like his odds for surviving that. But his second throw was perfect. The grenade bounced once on the near side of the truck, rolled underneath, and came to a stop just on the other side, underneath the side-mounted gas tank behind the driver's door. The grenade exploded, followed a microsecond later by an immense "whoosh" as the gas tank erupted into towering flames. One of the gomers, his clothing afire, ran down the runway. Kip shot him twice in the back, a reflex action that served as an act of mercy.

We rushed back to the plane. I climbed into the cockpit and stood between Dito and Moira, as Dito taxied to the end of the tarmac. We made an almost 180-degree pivot and lined up for a takeoff run that would probably take up almost the full length of the runway, past the burning truck, past the hangar and the other buildings, past the handful of gomers who had emerged from God knows where and were milling around among their fallen comrades.

"I know there's probably no alternative," I said, "but those guys are probably going to be shooting at us as we take off."

"How long would it take you and Kip and Lorayne to deal with them?"

"I don't know. A few minutes, but it could take longer. We're not exactly at our best, and I don't think we have enough ammo left."

"So be it. Let's roll."

He opened the throttles wide, running up the engines against the brakes. Then he released them and the aircraft started forward, at first slowly, then gaining speed, but not rapidly enough to suit me. As we drew abreast of the hangar I saw two guards step out into the open and line up their weapons. They fired. Dito flinched, and I realized he had been hit in the side. But he maintained control of the aircraft, and we continued to gain speed as he lifted us gently from the runway. And then, as we climbed steadily, Dito suddenly pitched forward against the controls. The plane lurched abruptly, but then straightened immediately as I heard Moira say softly, but confidently, "I've got the aircraft, Harry. You take care of Dito and then see if you can find me a chart. I'll get us home."

CHAPTER 23

TWO DAYS AFTER Grady's funeral someone blew up my Porsche. At the time of the explosion it was sitting in the parking lot of a grocery store in Ashland, Kentucky. I'd identified myself as the owner to the first responding police officers, called Lorayne—who was the reason for my presence in Ashland—and then called Toby Parks, while the deputies and firefighters looked on bemusedly, and a considerable crowd gathered just beyond the taped barrier. Weirdly, we all found ourselves standing around the wreckage wearing face masks against the threat of Covid. Lorayne's arrival eased their suspicions of me, but particularly when the sheriff himself gave her a big hug. It's nice to have friends in high places.

Evidence of my friends in even higher places appeared a few hours later when a pair of ATF bomb experts arrived by helicopter from D.C., along with a CIA liaison officer. While the ATF guys immediately joined the locals in sifting through the debris for physical evidence, the Agency man took me to, of all places, the Post Office, to a small room that smelled remarkably like an interrogation room.

"Someone seems pretty pissed off at you," he said. "I think that we'd both like to figure out just who that might be."

I like to think I'm not easily shaken, but the sheer cold-blooded 'out of nowhere' quality of the whole thing had me thoroughly spooked. "Yeah," I replied, "I'd like to find them before they find me again."

"Okay," he said. "I'm here because I do domestic stuff some," his grin confirmed what we both knew, that the Agency isn't supposed to 'do domestic.' He looked me over carefully. "I gather you're some super special operator and you're just back from saving the world." His words were vaguely sarcastic, but his friendly expression disarmed my irritation. "I give you a word, okay, and you know it's kosher to talk about what you've been up to. Everyone back at the head shed thinks there's got to be a connection."

"Go ahead." Parks had given me the word over the phone.

"Rosebud, right?"

"Rosebud."

"Okay, so much for *Citizen Kane*. Take me back to the end of your mission, walk me through the steps. Somebody's been following you, or picked up your trail somewhere. The locals and the Feebies will work backward from whatever we find here, but I need you to work me forward from where it all started."

I started with our takedown of the facility and he raised his hand, palm out. "No, not that far back. I've got no need to know for that. Just start when you got back to the world. I have the broad outline, but I need you to walk through it with me so maybe I can find out where the bomber got on to you."

Moira had flown to Djibouti without issue, while I worked out the best way of handling our arrival. Using the plane's satellite phone, I'd relayed a message to Parks, but doubted that he had time to smooth things by the time we landed. With that in mind, I had Moira announce our arrival to Djibouti control as an emergency flight with badly injured aid workers aboard. True enough, if a bit mislead-ing. I'd gotten on the radio and added the same message in French.

The military side of the international airport contained both French and American facilities, and I figured that this couldn't hurt. Kip had explained that the military owned the south side of the airport, so when we put down, I directed Moira to taxi in that direction, away from the civilian terminal and the Djibouti authorities. As I expected, our approach to the military terminal had been blocked by response vehicles, and armed Marines—this is primarily a Navy facility—surrounded the plane as soon as the engines stopped.

At first, no one had a clue what to do with us, so, predictably, they simply locked us up in the brig. Soon Parks had worked through the layers of military bureaucracy, and I'd been given a chance to talk to him directly and, even more importantly, to upload the trove of documents and photos Dr. Yang had provided. By the time local Chinese representatives began to make noises about the hijacked plane, word had come from Washington to simply give it back to them, while explaining that the "hijackers" were in custody and would be dealt with "appropriately." Knowing that they were on shaky ground, the Chinese backed off, while the locals simply watched the byplay between their two wealthy international patrons.

I'd worried about the media fallout, but needlessly. Back home, the presidential election had entered its final days, and, as Grady might have put it, nobody gave a shit about what we'd been doing. Moreover, to the extent that either the current administration or its potential replacement cared, we'd relieved them of a monumental nightmare. We were flown home almost as VIPs, debriefed for days by the CIA—whose main concern seemed to be finding a way of taking credit for what our 'Letter of Reprisal' team had accomplished. Our KIAs went to Dover AFB, I was dragged into D.C. for another round of higher-level debriefings, with many questions regarding Colonel Ma's revelation that our mission's cover story had been betrayed by someone, obviously someone with high level connections in the U.S. government. Many questions, but, frustratingly for me, nothing in the way of answers. Finally, along with the rest of the team, I had basically, been invited to disappear into obscurity once again.

"After D.C., then what," my Agency friend asked. "I'd say you were cool at that point. What happened next? We had you under observation until Camp Peary, but then what?"

"Okay, then, you know that they flew me down by helicopter to Camp Peary, then your guys drove me home to Virginia Beach in an unmarked sedan. Okay, so far, but someone could have been watching for me outside my condo."

"You're an operator. You pick up anything out of the ordinary?"

"No, but I wasn't really looking. I figured it was all over."

"Figured wrong, didn't you? Okay, next."

I'd still been on ice in D.C. when Dover started releasing bodies to the next-of-kin, so Kip and the other surviving team members had taken on the burden of assisting in funeral arrangements and disbursing payments to the families of those who hadn't made it. Peter was still recovering, so Colin and Lem had done this for the Europeans, for Kees and Jean-Paul, but Kip made the rounds of the American families. Smitty's family had seemed mystified, deeply suspicious of the large sum of money he'd earned—but they took it anyway. Jerry's family unquestioningly accepted his mission paycheck and, more grudgingly, Kip's condolences. But they made it clear that his presence at the funeral was unwelcome, perhaps because he was mysteriously connected to their son's death, perhaps simply because he was a black man in a Blue Ridge mountain town that knew black faces only via satellite dish and television. Tommy's family, of course, had paid a bitter price, two sons lost in this little private corner of the war against encroaching tyranny. It seemed to me that it would be all the more bitter to not know what their sacrifice had bought, and so I broke my own secrecy rule and asked Kip to tell them exactly what had happened. The mother seemed mystified still, but the father—yet another soldier like his sons—appeared gratified that their deaths were something more than tragic accidents.

Working through Toby Parks, I'd persuaded the military not to release Grady's body to Mary Anne until I completed my debriefing. Grady had never been very religious, but Mary Anne is, and she wanted him buried properly in the modest graveyard behind the Singing Creek Baptist Church. The minister said the usual feeble things, made all the more feeble by his references to the "aircraft accident" that had taken Grady's life. I'd been prepared to tell Mary Anne the true story, but she made it very clear that she really didn't want to know what had happened. As a military retiree, Grady rated an honor guard that fired a salute over his flag-draped coffin. I watched with quiet satisfaction as the officer in charge supervised the folding of the flag and then presented it to Mary-Anne. The best part was that, in a time when a shortage of honor guards has fostered the widespread use of amateur 'stand-ins,' these were real Marines, from the ceremonial detachment at Marine Headquarters, a special grace note orchestrated by Parks. They did everything right, all the way down to wearing Covid masks that matched the white gloves worn with their dress blues.

There were other special touches. A piper, perfectly kilted and expert, played "Carrickfergus" and "Amazing Grace" and something else, something lovely and moving that I did not recognize. Peter had arranged for this, had literally paid the piper and flown him to the U.S. because he recalled a remark that Grady had once made, that every soldier deserved a piper at his funeral. A trumpeter, a kid from the local high-school band—I think he was a friend of Abby's—played "Taps." And in the echoing silence after the last note, Abby came to me from her mother's side, her eyes full of pain and loss, and gave me a hug, and then drew Kip into her embrace.

Describing all this to my CIA interlocuter brought me to an emotional halt in my narration, one that, thankfully, he had the wit, the sensitivity, to at least momentarily respect before continuing.

"Okay, then, somebody could have made you at your apartment, or maybe when you picked up Kip Bennett to drive to the funeral. I'd say by that point you could've been well and truly blown. What about the car? Could someone have gotten to it?"

"Not likely. My place is, well, like a town house, I've got a garage for it, and I keep it inside. The door's locked and it hooks into my alarm system."

"The funeral?"

"Maybe. Like I said, I wasn't looking for it. But we went straight to the church, then the cemetery, then I dropped Kip off at the airport in Morgantown and headed over here the same afternoon. The only time I was away from the car was at the church and the graveyard."

"Well, probably we can find out if anyone suspicious did anything there. Like as not, every teenager in town was eyeballing your car— not many Porsches out in South Bumfuck, West Virginia. So, you drove here that afternoon."

Before leaving me after her debrief, Lorayne had invited me to come down for a visit. She'd reiterated the offer at the funeral, and, since I was already halfway to Kentucky, it seemed an entirely reasonable thing to do. The following afternoon, having spent the night with Mary-Anne and Abby, I turned west and headed for Ashland. Although Lorayne had invited me to stay at her place, I felt a little awkward about it, so I checked into a motel, ate a solitary dinner, and then called to let her know that I was in town, but very tired. I'd come by in the morning.

After a restless night I got up early and went looking for Lorayne's apartment. She lived in an older part of town, on a street of Victorians converted to apartments. I parked on the street and walked past a couple of cars parked nose to tail in the narrow driveway. She'd said that hers was a second-floor apartment, with an outside stair that had been added when the house was converted. I found this and ascended to what had once been a second-story balcony, now the entrance to her apartment. I pressed the buzzer and stood at the door, trying to peer through the filmy curtain that covered the large oval glass in the center of the door. There was a light on somewhere deep in the apartment, but the closer rooms were dark. I waited for a moment and buzzed again. Soon another light came on, and then another lit up the room just inside the door. I saw a silhouette through the gauze and then heard the rattle of a door chain being detached.

"Well it's about time, Hair Doctor," she said as she opened the door. I saw that her hair was wet and that her face looked fresh scrubbed, and that she was wearing a long white tee-shirt that clung damply to her body. "I'd just gotten out of the shower when I heard the buzzer. Come on in. I'll get some coffee started."

I followed her across the small sitting room and dining area, to a hallway that gave on one side to the kitchen and on the other to the open bedroom door. She stopped, turned and reached out to take both my hands. "The last time we came to a crossroads together was when I was walking point on that God-awful trail. I guess we picked the right fork then."

"I guess we did," I said.

"Well, this is another crossroads, isn't it? Right fork, the kitchen, and left fork…"

"The bedroom…"

She gave my hands a gentle tug, easy to go along with, easy to resist. I went with the tug and then we were together and, after a forever moment she stepped back and led me into the bedroom. "I'm an old man…," I began, but she put a finger to my lips and said, "You're a very dear old man and I've wanted you for a long time now." And then we were somehow undressed and she was helping me past my anticipation and anxiety and, to my wonder and joy, everything suddenly started to go right and we were making love, truly, and, for me, for the first time in a very long time.

Later—a long time later—we finally made it to the kitchen, and after breakfast we talked and held each other. A younger man would've no doubt taken her once again, but she seemed content and so was I. She made a joke when I finally remembered the check I'd brought her, asking if it made her the highest paid whore in history, then shushed me when I became embarrassed about it.

"No, no, Harry, just a bad joke. You'd never've had to pay to make love to me," she said. "I've loved you since way back, but you always seemed hung up on Moira."

And I told her that, yes, maybe I had been, but that all that had passed a long time ago. And even as I said it I knew that it was nothing more, nothing less, than the simple truth.

She suggested that we go out to lunch, claiming that she wanted to go to her favorite restaurant and 'show off her new boyfriend." When we were dressed and ready to leave, she went to the hall closet and took a motorcycle helmet down from the shelf. "You have to ride with me," she said, "I think that one will fit. I borrowed it from my brother." I put it on, found it snug but bearable, and watched as she took down a second one. We went down to the garage, and she took out her bike, a bright purple custom-painted Harley Road Glide. Her downstairs neighbors, fortunately, had long ago left for work and the driveway was clear. I climbed on to the pillion seat and dropped my hands to the passenger grips, but she reached back and took them, placing them firmly around her waist. "There, much better that way," she said, and we rolled out the driveway and blasted down the street. She handled the huge bike masterfully, and I quickly found myself as comfortable trusting her riding skill as I'd come to trust her tactical skills. We pulled up at an old tavern on the riverfront, had thick cheese steak sandwiches with a mountain of French fries, and I had a beer while she stayed, sensibly, with Coke. "I don't drink and drive, and I damn well don't drink and ride." Friends passed through, and I was introduced repeatedly, with the proprietary words and gestures that left no doubt that I belonged to her. Afterward she asked me if I wanted to ride around some more, but to my great astonishment I found that time had worked its wonders and that I was ready for something else once again, and so we hurried back to the apartment.

Later that afternoon we found ourselves standing side-by-side, looking out her front window at the blue hills in the distance, and she remarked that perhaps I'd best pull the Porsche up in to the driveway before the others came home. "Not a car to leave on the street around here, I'm afraid." When I'd dressed again and was ready to go downstairs, she asked me if I wanted to have dinner out or eat in. I looked at her standing there, wearing nothing but a blue silk robe and found that decision particularly easy. "Eat in," I said. "Then since you're firing up the car anyway, why don't you run down to the grocery store and pick up a couple of steaks and some baking potatoes." She gave me directions for what was little more than a five-minute drive, which, in a fit of school boyish exuberance, I made entirely while winding the engine out loudly in first and second gear. I pulled into the parking lot, found a space well away from the other cars and from the threat of an errant shopping cart, and went inside. I was standing in the checkout line when I heard the blast and felt the storefront glass rattle and then give way. I raced past the stunned shoppers, over the broken shards and the twisted metal window framing, out through the uproar and damaged cars, to where I could clearly see the orange flame and black smoke boiling up from what had once been my beautiful car.

When Lorayne arrived at the blast scene, she immediately discovered that one of the first responding officers was a cousin, which considerably eased the suspicion with which I'd been treated since identifying myself as the owner of the car. She stayed with me until the investigators arrived from D.C., then allowed her cousin to follow her home while I went away with the Agency man. I told him all this, while skating over the romantic details.

"Okay, then—I think we can wrap this up. Where are you going to be for the next few days? Here? With your young lady?"

"That's it."

"We'll get you some protection. I doubt if it's necessary. Somebody does a bomb when they don't want to be ID'd, they won't likely force their way into your apartment and shoot you. But protection's good anyway. You've given me some stuff to work on, anyway. Just in case, do you need a weapon?" Having had a glimpse into Lorayne's gun safe, it was easy to answer "no."

He made a couple of phone calls, then took me back to Lorayne's, where local cops kept vigil until some Agency heavies showed up from Camp Peary. For the next two days we stayed to ourselves, opening the door only to the minders and, at various times to Lorayne's brother and two sisters. Her 'momma and daddy' lived several hours away, and she'd made a point of not telling them that someone had tried to blow up the new man in her life.

Toby Parks called about six a.m. on the third morning.

"We've got something," he said. "You need to get back here ASAP. The chopper's coming back for you. The investigators will be staying down there for a few more days, but it's about not to be their investigation anymore. The chopper'll be at the local airport in an hour. You need to be waiting for it."

"What about Lorayne?"

"What about her?"

"I'm not leaving her down here, not when I don't know any more than I do about this thing."

"She's probably okay, but there's room on the bird, so bring her along. I gather she's decided you're something special. Not too bad. You're one lucky SOB."

"Well, aside from the fact that someone wants to kill me."

"Ah, Harry, you've spent your whole life with people trying to kill you. But how often have you been loved?"

As I broke the connection I decided that he had a point, and as I watched Lorayne throwing her woman things into a suitcase I knew that he was right.

CHAPTER 24

A LITTLE LESS than three hours later we touched down at Davison Army Airfield, the small aviation facility associated with Fort Belvoir, near the Potomac River just south of Alexandria. Usefully low profile, compared to helipads closer in to the city. A pair of black Suburbans met us on the field. I passed the briefcase over to the man who identified himself as the team lead, and we got into the first vehicle. Although the windows of both trucks were dark tinted, it was clear that the chase vehicle contained at least four men, and there were two others besides the driver and the team chief in our lead vehicle, all of them armed. Someone, I assumed Parks, was taking absolutely no chances. We exited the post onto U.S. 1, cut across to the George Washington Parkway at Mount Vernon, and headed north along the river, past Alexandria and then across the river, ending our journey, oddly enough, at the Watergate. We were shown into a luxurious apartment—I guess there aren't any crummy apartments at the Watergate—and, after being given a few minutes to get settled, I left Lorayne and followed the team leader to an office in another part of the complex. Inside I was ushered into a conference room and found Parks waiting for me, along with a man roughly my age, who looked vaguely familiar from newspaper photographs, and a much younger man who sat with the now-opened briefcase containing the bomb evidence.

"Good to see you in one piece, Harry," said Parks. "This is Mr. Black," he said, gesturing to the older man, "and this is Mr. Green. Mr. Black's staff has been working on your case pretty much around the clock and, when the investigators reported their find, he arranged to have Mr. Green fly up this morning from North Carolina." He cocked his eyes at me. "You know the place."

I did, in fact. Up from North Carolina, a man with an interest in clandestine bombs. Mr. Green was, quite clearly, a colleague from the CIA's special activities staff, one of the explosives gurus resident at Harvey Point, an old Navy blimp base long ago annexed into the Agency's covert empire.

"I think that it's time we pooled our information," said Parks. "Mr. Green? What have you got?"

"The ATF boys were right on the money." He picked up a piece of mangled metal, fused with molten black plastic. "What we have here is a modular three stage detonation device, or the remains of one. It had a simple toggle switch that served as an initial arming mechanism. As long as the switch's in the 'off' position, nothing can happen. Think of it as sort of like the safety on an automatic pistol. Probably carried the thing taped for extra protection, just like you'd tape the spoon on a grenade. Once the switch is "on," however, two more elements come into play. The first is a simple little mercury switch that serves as a motion sensor. It activates when the mercury is displaced and makes a contact, in this case when a car accelerates or decelerates hard enough to move the mercury back and forth in the tube."

"I did just that," I said, and described my burst of speed on the way to the grocery store.

"Well, Dr. York, that little moment of driving exuberance probably saved your life. The concept behind the second element is to maximize the odds that the person driving the car has set out on a journey of some distance, the theory being that most people don't go racing at a high rate of speed down to the corner grocery. There are other more reliable methods, but all of them involve more extended access to the vehicle. This one is designed to be used with a small charge, attached with magnets to a metal structural member. The idea is to keep the whole thing small, easy to conceal. Charge weight was probably not even a half pound TNT equivalent, my guess is less although I think that we'll find that the chemical analysis will tell us it was Semtex."

"Does that take us anywhere, then?" I asked. Semtex is a Czech-manufactured plastic explosive, once the signature plastic explosive of the Warsaw Pact countries.

"No, not hardly," injected Mr. Black. "Semtex is everywhere. But this firing assembly Mr. Green was describing, that might just tell us everything. Continue, young man."

"Yes, sir. Well, like I was saying, the second sequential element was the motion device. But this thing was designed to work with very small charges. The original concept was to use this thing close to the front suspension with a charge just large enough to blow a good-sized hole in a tire, damage the steering or a suspension link. Thus, the third element, a timer device. It works like this. The bomber has some prior idea of the victim's driving habits. Say for example, the victim leaves his office, drives easily for a few minutes, then accelerates smartly as he goes up an expressway on ramp. Ten minutes along, he's cruising along at 75 mph when "bang," the front tire goes and so does some key suspension element. A great driver maybe saves things, but most of us aren't Mario Andretti, right? The car careens out of control, crashes, the driver's killed. And all with a device that could be daubed with mud and clamped with a magnet inside the wheel well, something anyone could do with no more than ten seconds access to the car. Our little modular system typically remains partially intact, just like you see here, but it doesn't matter, usually the blast separates it from its mounting point and it falls off on the road, well away from where the vehicle finally crashes to a halt. Sweet."

"But wouldn't the accident investigation reveal damage to the tire or to the suspension consistent with an explosion.'

"Probably, if there was a properly-done investigation. But these were designed for use in places that might've had the occasional stretch of freeway, or at least high speed two lane, but weren't likely to have very good accident investigation procedures."

"Or," injected Mr. Black, "places where one needed a kind of damage that would show well for the average untutored journalist, but which wouldn't ever be subjected to a proper official accident investigation."

"So, what the hell happened here? This thing blew my car to bits."

Mr. Green offered a rueful smile. "Whoever did this, they didn't reckon with the fact that a Porsche 911 has the engine in the back and the gas tank in the front, just ahead," he paused, "just ahead of the driver and just a little bit behind the front suspension. You hot-rodded over to the grocery store, which started the timer. Then you went inside, and the timer kept running until 'boom.' The blast ruptured the gas tank, and hot bits of metal created a secondary explosion that blew up the car. It's not like on TV. Modern cars rarely explode as the result of a crash, but the showbiz folks like the visual, so they rig a charge to blow up the gas. Your boy stumbled into the same special effect, and he blew your car all over the parking lot."

I gave all of this some thought. "It sounds as if this whole thing has a signature that you recognize."

"South African." continued Mr. Black. "1980s vintage. BOSS came up with them as a useful means of taking down some of the opposition." The acronym 'BOSS' referred to Bureau of State Security, the secret police unit that served the former Afrikaner *apartheid* regime. "When they used it domestically, they counted on the fact that they could lean on the regular police a bit. As long as it looked good enough to fool the liberal journalists or some nosy Europeans or Americans, it sufficed. When they used it elsewhere, it was usually in places like Namibia, where they weren't likely to encounter much in the way of accident investigation. But after the Mandela and the

ANC came to power, a lot of the BOSS guys scattered. You might say that their prospects were not exactly improved by the regime change. One of them was their best bomb guy, a young man named, I believe, Bernie Croes. He made it to Argentina, and then to Colombia, where he found a worthwhile market for his skills."

"And," now Parks entered the conversation, "a few years later still, he settles in Curacao under another name. The local authorities don't catch on, he's got lots of money by this time, he's got a condo in Willemstad overlooking the harbor, and he becomes a Dutch citizen. Then the stock market tanks at the end of the Nineties, our boy Bernie's a little over-extended in tech stocks, and he needs to start working for a living again."

"But at that point," said Mr. Black, "he moved out of our realm, and into that of domestic criminality. In other words…"

"The Bureau's domain," I finished the sentence for him.

"Exactly. Of course, since 9/11 we work very closely with our FBI brethren when it comes to potential terrorist activities, but I gather that the former Mr. Croes has not been regarded in that light. Merely a criminal and, apparently, one who simply provides a line of electrical devices. He doesn't do the dirty work, he doesn't wire them in to a blasting cap and an explosive charge, and, in fact, I gather it's even been hard to make a case that what he sells is actually illegal. Not for him."

"So?"

"So, we're handing the bomb aspect back over to the Bureau and the ATF to follow up."

Toby stepped in, "But what about the more fundamental question—what's an ex-BOSS hood doing trying to blow Harry to bits?"

"And well you might ask, Mr. Parks," said Mr. Black. "We don't have direct evidence, but circumstantially there are Chinese fingerprints all over this thing. First, the MSS likes to contract out its 'wet-work' to westerners when it has a job away from big cities with large Asian communities. You'd need a microscope to find the Chinatown in Ashland, Kentucky. Second, while your original BOSS crowd has gotten pretty long in the tooth, the ones who made a business of this post-Mandela have brought along a younger generation. And we have pretty good evidence that they've done some work for MSS in the past."

"Still, this seems pretty thin."

"Point taken, Dr. York." He looked again at Parks, who nodded. "Mr. Green, would you leave us alone here for a minute, please? We're about to enter territory where you've no need to know."

Green got up and walked into an adjacent room, closing the door behind him.

"What follows, is going to be a bit vague. You've been in the business long enough to know why. But I'll try to give you enough so that you can have confidence in what we are telling you, so that you'll be okay when I tell you that we need you to leave this alone. I know that you have your own resources, and we can't have you blundering into things. We do have a phone conversation with fingerprints, so to speak. A call to Mr. Croes in Curacao from Los Angeles."

"Los Angeles?"

"Yes, well, Newport Beach to be precise. And we've also got an ID on the caller."

"So, who, what?"

"So, nothing, Dr. York. We have all of the inferential and negative evidence, as you say, and we've got solid positive evidence of a domestic link, a domestic link both to Bernie Croes and, also to a suspected MSS operative. A lot of people have worked very hard for days to establish that link. Now we've got a crime occurring on U.S. soil, a putative link to a U.S. citizen, and a solid counter-intelligence connection. Obviously, we will continue to take an interest, particularly regarding Bernie Croes and the BOSS connection, but, necessarily, the FBI takes the lead."

"And?"

"Well, now, that's something you'll have to put to the Bureau."

"I don't have any good contacts at the FBI."

"Well, then, I suggest that you ask Mr. Parks to help you. He seems to have good contacts everywhere. Mr. Green?" he called out, raising his voice to carry into the other room. "It's time for us to go." Green came out and the two of them left together. I turned to Parks.

"So now what?"

"Like he says, Harry, leave it be. You're all set to stay here for the time being, and there'll be continuing protection for the other team members until this thing settles down. I'll be able to let you know when."

"That's it?"

He leaned forward, his face and voice tense, not a trace of the nonchalance that he wore like an old sweater.

"Harry, please, this time don't ask me for more. This is big, and it's pretty damned murky, and it's not just the Agency respecting the FBI's turf or anything. They want out, and, based on what I know, they have good reason. I'm not wired into the Bureau like I am the other outfits, but I can try to keep enough pressure on to have them finish putting the evidence together. Look, the election's over, a new administration's coming in—forget the damned lawsuits—and a lot of chairs are about to be shuffled. The good news is that everyone who counts is delighted at what your team pulled off in Wiangara. Nobody who matters, incoming or outgoing, wants to question an action that stopped a new super deadly Covid from rolling over all of us. And everybody who matters just loves what you brought out on that thumb drive and the leverage it gives us in dealing with the Chinese regime. But the domestic connection could unravel into something really nasty, and there's no way you and I can solve that one by ourselves. Let the Bureau do its thing. I promise to stay on top of them, and I promise you, your team will get protection until this thing gets put to bed. That should be good enough."

"No, Toby, it's not good enough. It's pretty damned pathetic. We're supposed to just live with this."

"It's going to have to be good enough. I don't think I can make it better, not this time. Maybe something'll come up, but until then…"

"Shit!"

"Precisely."

CHAPTER 25

FOR THREE DAYS our Watergate stay was like a honeymoon. Lorayne and I explored each other, learning each other's bodies and, between episodes of lovemaking, we talked and talked, getting to know one another, sharing our pasts, dreaming of the future, and determinedly avoiding the fact that someone had tried to kill me. But after three days even honeymooners need more than the four walls and each other. I called Parks and insisted on a change of scenery. "We're going to go stir crazy in here before long," I said, "and I'm not going to have the best thing that's ever happened to me go bad because we're locked up together in a gilded jail cell." After some negotiation—I wanted one of the military guest houses on the Marine Corps base at Kaneohe Bay on Oahu, and the Agency's first counter offer was a river front location in North Carolina at Harvey Point—we eventually settled on a Lake Michigan beach house near the town of Sturgeon Bay in Door County, Wisconsin. How the CIA came to own such a property stretched the imagination, and the house itself was pretty bland, but the location was perfect. Door County is a kind of Midwestern Cape Cod, jutting upward from Green Bay and out into Lake Michigan.

Our protection team dialed things back a couple of notches, providing loose protection that allowed us to walk the beach and visit restaurants driving ourselves, rather than being carted around in a Suburban with a chase team. When we'd first arrived, the snow was still heavy on the ground, but the house had a great woodstove and a wood shed filled with well-seasoned splits of oak. Lorayne missed her motorcycle, so, to by way of making it up to her, we rented a couple of snowmobiles and explored the nearby trails, much to the consternation of our protection team. In the meantime, we watched the news, and I checked in with Parks on a regular basis. The headlines told of further Covid surges, but these appeared explicable as mutations of the original virus rather than harbingers of a newly-released super-virus—all well and good. And Parks had nothing to report, on any of the several fronts that mattered.

But while we enjoyed our little idyll, the word filtering back from other members of the team told a story of increasing frustration and anger at their inability to resume their normal lives. Even our extended honeymoon had its fragile moments, particularly with the onset of spring. Honeymooners, after all, do need to dream of the future and, as time passed, our dreams of tomorrow began to curdle in the face of the ongoing uncertainty. Moreover, Lorayne was someone deeply rooted, missing her parents, family, and friends back in Kentucky. What brought things to a boil, however, was a visit from a pair of Bureau agents out of the Milwaukee office who wanted to talk to us about the Witness Protection Program. I hit the ceiling, almost literally shoved them out the door, and called Parks as soon as they were gone. "This is horseshit, Toby!" I yelled into the phone, "not chickenshit, it's too damned big. It's horseshit, and it can't—I repeat, it cannot go on. Clear."

"I'm reading you five-by-five, Harry. So, what do you want to do about it?"

That was the nub. I wanted it to end, but I didn't have a plan for ending it. What I needed was more information, and I hoped Parks now had the information I needed.

"For starters, a face-to-face. Just you and me." I thought about this for a moment. I wanted to pick the place, somewhere where our minders couldn't eavesdrop, even with directional mikes. Then I recalled something I'd seen earlier in the local newspaper. "This is Friday, Toby. Sunday afternoon there's a big sports car race down at Elkhart Lake, first one of the season. It's perfect for a meet. That's about 100 miles south of here. You fly into Milwaukee and drive up. I'll meet you just inside the main entrance."

"Okay, Harry, you've got it."

My minders were not well pleased, but that was the benefit of playing the Parks card. Government employees are conditioned not to piss off Congressmen, unless their superiors direct them to do so, and I was counting on the fact that the Bureau and Agency honchos would see this as an opportunity for Parks to get me back in the box once again. In the end I was also counting on Parks's friendship, because I was about to put it to the ultimate test.

Parks arrived shortly after I did on Sunday afternoon, and, after treating ourselves to a Bratwurst and beer, I pointed to a place along the fence at trackside and told my escorts that we would be there, we would remain there, but that they would have to watch us from where we were currently standing. This made a distance of maybe fifty yards, not really enough for protection from a directional mike, but for that I was counting on the intervening noise of hundreds of other nearby conversations, punctuated by the ear-splitting—and electronics baffling—scream of passing race cars. Besides, although my minders had known that we were meeting at the track, the track is nearly four miles long, and I had the option to pick any place, or a succession of places, along the perimeter. They would've been hard pressed to set up something in advance.

We took up our position and Parks asked, "I'm here now, Harry. What is it that you want? What do you plan to do?"

I'd been thinking hard about this. "Okay, it's like this. You and your friend Mr. Black made it very clear that, even the day after they blew up my car, you had hard evidence that pointed domestically. You also made it pretty clear that you didn't think that this could ever be brought to trial, but that with enough evidence the FBI could, how'd you say it, 'leverage' our safety."

"Yeah, sure."

"All right, then. Like I said, I've been thinking hard about this, and I've realized that, if these clowns are now starting to talk witness protection, then somehow the leverage is lacking. Now I've been around the Army and the government for a long time, and one thing I know is that, if an agency has some kind of hot potato to juggle, and if they're afraid of someone pushing back, then they'll drop the damn potato. The only way they'll do something with it, the only way they'll even keep juggling it, is if someone else is pushing back in the opposite direction. With me thus far?"

"Okay, yeah." He didn't seem very comfortable with where I was heading.

"So, I think what's really going on is that the Bureau doesn't want to push up against whoever it is that they think's behind it, and they just want me and the rest of the team to go away quietly, not rock the boat, not force them into doing something hard. Maybe they've hit a brick wall on the MSS connection, or maybe," I gave him a hard look, "maybe that connection goes so high up in our government that they're afraid to go after it directly. Or maybe they've decided to get cute, leave the leaker in place, and start feeding them disinformation for their MSS handlers."

"I'm following you."

A particularly loud cluster of cars roared past, and I waited for the noise to clear.

"As I see it, there's two ways I can bring this to a conclusion. One is that I go to the press with what I already know, including the bombing, Bernie Croes, Mr. Black, and so on."

"Please, no—that's a bad one."

"You're right, it is a bad one, and I don't want to do it if I don't have to. The second one is that I go after whoever's behind this whole thing. Maybe I can't take them down, but maybe I can hurt them bad enough to reach a quid pro quo, you don't hurt me or my people, I won't hurt you."

"Jesus H. Christ, Harry! You're sounding like Don fucking Corleone. 'Make 'em an offer they can't refuse.' Are you serious?"

"Serious as a heart attack. Look, this has to end. The team did a job for this country, for the world, and paid one helluva price. They don't need a ticker tape parade down Fifth Avenue, but they deserve a whole lot better than spending the rest of their lives ducking in the shadows. So do I. You were the one, after all, who challenged me that day at Antietam to grow up, to be a real player, to stop being Peter Pan. You were right then, but now that I've become one, I can't go back. I delivered on a team and a mission. Now it's time that I delivered for them. That's what players do, Toby, and that's what I'm going to do."

"Okay, Harry, okay…"

"No, you're absolutely right. If I do the press thing it becomes open-ended and messy and the moment I open my mouth, I lose control of where it goes. I'd much rather try for a cleaner solution."

"What do you have in mind?"

"That's just it. Until I know more of what this whole thing is about, until I know at least as much as you know, I can't even begin to make a plan."

"You're putting me in an awful place."

"I know it, Toby, and believe me, I hate to do it. But show me the alternative. You can't because there isn't one."

"You're dead set on this. If I don't share what I know and help you take it on, you're going to the press."

"I'll be so 'Deep Throat' it'll make Linda Lovelace look like Mother Teresa."

"Okay, then…." Another pair of race cars howled by, drowning out his next words. "Hey, Harry, can we get away from the fucking cars a little bit. I can hardly hear myself think."

We walked a ways down the track and up an open hillside, to edge of a small stand of trees.

"Now," I said, "will this do?"

"The thing you have to know," he began, "is that there's really not much. The call to Croes came from a man named Foster Smith. Smith's a business man, but he's got an old-line Mafia connection, his mother's maiden name is something like D'Allesandro, but she married out, her old man didn't want her living out her life like a *Sopranos* episode. Usual pattern in my generation. So, she marries a movie guy, or rather the son of a movie guy, a money man, a producer. Clean, but only Hollywood clean. Her daddy had maybe put a little money behind his daddy's movies. Anyway, time passes, the happy couple prospers, but Smith's not the businessman his daddy was, and he gets overextended, and his father-in-law helps him out a little. In the end, the line between the legit generation and the old crooks becomes fuzzed a little, and Smith winds up knowing some of the hard guys, doing a little business with them directly."

"So?"

"So, Smith fancies himself a big wheel, does the charity balls, the wife likes this and so does her daddy—respectability, right—and this leads him to the political fundraisers, and he gets to know some political types, and he likes them to see him as a hard case, maybe tougher, more powerful than he really is. Maybe even connected, which, of course, in a small way he actually is. And then it gets really, really interesting."

"How so?"

"Well, you already know that MSS has tentacles everywhere these days, our government, big corporations, but they've also made a point of linking into organized crime. Crooks and spies, always something in common. And you don't need to be Hetty fucking Lange to know that MSS is all over Los Angeles these days."

He lost me for a moment before I made the connection to the TV show.

"Okay, I get it, but where's the actual link? What does our mission have to do with an organized crime wannabe from Los Angeles, even one in bed with MSS?"

"I'll get to that, but there what I've got mainly is speculation. You need the hard info first. Anyway, the phone call from Foster Smith to

Bernie Croes asks Croes to run up one of his signature gadgets, and asks if maybe Croes has a friend in the states he can FedEx the gadget to, and maybe the friend can wire plant it and take out one inconvenient old man. And Croes does have couple of friends, but here it starts to get pretty muddy, the friend Croes is talking to is one of these guys whose past life ends about five years ago, nothing older, no credit cards, no driver's license. But we do have one thing of interest."

"What's that?"

"Well, we've got phone records and credit card receipts that put this clown in Ashland, Kentucky the night before your bomb went off."

I was feeling both impatient and excited, sensing that we were about to reach the pay-off.

"You've got to give our friend Mr. Black some credit. Once they had the link to Smith, they were all over Croes, watching, listening, and all over Smith, too. Lot of bullshit stuff, but computers are fast. They know Croes has an MSS connection, and they also manage to link Smith to an MSS player whose day job seems to be watching the Navy sail in and out of San Diego."

"Keep going."

"Okay, here's the payoff. Now that they've come this far, they absolutely blanket Smith and his MSS buddy. Everything. Phone records, internet accounts, anything that even hints at the use of a burner phone. Like it or not, when NSA has a target to focus on, they are very, very good at peeling back every electronic layer in a person's life. Meanwhile, the FBI counter-intel guys are also all over them. So far, so good. And then, while they're doing all this sniffing, somebody farts in their face."

"Dammit, Toby!"

"They pull up a link to guy named Martin Kinkade, and guess what? Kinkade is a congressional staffer, the senior political staffer in the congressman's California headquarters, the one who oversees local liaison and constituent support."

"And"

"And Kinkade's staff counterpart on the Hill, the one who does all the legislative stuff for the congressman is none other than...."

"Sandy Sawyer."

"The very bitch herself."

"I don't know who or how, but someone who knew about the "Letter of Reprisal" deal, who'd gotten the cover version of the plan we cooked up, someone shared it with her, that's pretty clear. Harry, I'm sorry as all hell, this has been burning my conscience ever since I heard what Colonel Ma said to you, but, believe me, it was impossible to line up the political support for the "Letter" without including more folks than I wanted. You know how it goes—tell somebody, and they can't keep themselves from telling somebody, and, well...."

"And, well, we could have walked into a trap and lost everyone for nothing. As it is, we probably lost half the team because Ma's people were leaning forward already." I'd been pretty sure of something like this since that night sitting across the table from Ma, but I just hadn't wanted to face the depths of the betrayal. And Sandy Sawyer, which made it deeply, ineradicably personal. "Goddamnit, Toby! We deserved better than this." I caught my breath. "And we deserve better now, what's left of us."

"No argument, there." I'd known Parks a long time and had never seen him so obviously guilt-stricken. "Harry, I couldn't be more sorry—there just aren't any words. But will you let me add just one more thing, one thing that might make it better somehow, something good from all this sorry mess."

"Okay, I guess."

"Once Sawyer came under the microscope, the Bureau determined that the Chinese had turned her as well. Probably after the mission leak through her buddy Kinkade, they decided to cut out the middle man and run her directly. Maybe her role in the leak gave them a hold on her, maybe she's just another one of those shitbirds who can't see any harm in 'closer relations' with Beijing. It's recent, that much seems certain. The MSS must be thrilled at having such a high value asset. But it also gives our side a good hand to play. Deceive her on something vital, and we deceive them."

"So, what you're telling me is that Sandy Sawyer is now untouchable so long as we're running her against the Chinese. The Chinese will do everything they can to protect her, and so will our guys.

"You're on to something there, Harry. From the time word got round that you guys had pulled off the mission successfully and that you were coming out alive, our girl Sawyer went absolutely bat shit trying to find out where you were. The smart boys think that may have been the first tasking she got from her new MSS handler—the timing was right. We don't think they know about Dr. Yang's thumb drive, so you and your team would be key players if we decided to go public about what they were doing in Africa. But Sawyer—she might have tried going after you anyway, on her own hook. She still hates your guts for making her look bad back in 2017."

"We may not be in declared war with China, but it sure feels like war all the same, and Sawyer smells like a traitor."

"Sucks, for sure."

"Basically, then, the Chinese want me and the team dead, and our side would just like us to disappear quietly down a memory hole. Witness protection my ass. They're less worried about protecting me or the team, and more about keeping us well out of the way and under control."

"Maybe so, Harry, and maybe none of the upright players can see a path forward right now. I sure can't."

"Toby, it has to end, once and for all, it has to end."

"Okay, Harry, you know all that I know. What're you going to do?

"I don't know yet. I've got a lot to sort out, and once I decide, you've got to stay out of my way. You owe me that much. But once I'm sure that everyone on the team is safely out of the line of fire, at least I now know where to start."

"And where's that?"

"You said it yourself a moment ago. You said if I really wanted to end this thing, I'd have to reckon with Sandy Sawyer. I intend to do just that."

CHAPTER 26

FOR STARTERS, I wanted every surviving team member in one safe place where we could see to our own protection. For this purpose, only one location would suffice, and, after I informed the FBI that we would take care of our own 'witness protection,' we received all the cooperation one could ask for. The harder part lay in explaining over the phone to the various team members why I wanted them to assemble in Tallinn, the capital of Estonia, not exactly the center of the universe. But everyone responded positively, even Moira, who'd stayed on the periphery at Grady's funeral and had pretty much isolated herself ever since. They arrived piecemeal over a period of three days, each greeted at the airport by Lem, Lorayne, or myself.

A rambling old beach house near Virtsu on the Gulf of Riga served as our safe house. This was, in fact, the place where my family had spent summer vacations in the years before the war. The house had survived the war intact, and during the years of Russian occupation had been kept up by the government and used for recreational purposes by various local Communist Party functionaries. After Estonia regained its independence, the house had continued in government hands until my sister returned and purchased it in 1997.

For personal security I arranged for each member of the group to be provided with a Makarov pistol. The greater part of our security, however, consisted of the location of the house, on an open spit of land protruding out into the Gulf. That, and the team of twelve former members of the Estonian Army, well-armed, who Lem had recruited to add muscle to our protection. The upper story of the house dominated the terrain for miles in any direction, and I stationed an around-the-clock lookout with NVGs to maintain observation from this location. The neck of land connecting us to the mainland was secured by a roadblock, and the beaches were discreetly patrolled. Nothing short of a rifle platoon could root us out of this location, as I observed to Peter in explaining these arrangements.

"Good on you, Harry, for taking care of us so nicely," he responded. "But y'know, we've just got over standing off one bloody rifle platoon, and my heart's just not into doing it again so soon."

Later that evening, with all the team members finally present, seated around the dining table, I laid out all that I'd learned from Parks and allowed everyone to vent their outrage. I allowed this to continue for a good few minutes, then I reached into my pocket, took out a handful of identical thumb drives, and doled them out across the table.

"Dr. Shih Yang, bless her heart, gave me two thumb drives, each one containing detailed documentation of everything the Chinese government intended to do with the facility we destroyed. It was all there. The deadliness of the new virus, the willingness to murder millions of Africans at the point of release, the expectations for its worldwide spread, the crushing blow to rival economies throughout the world, and then the miraculously timely presentation of a vaccine, earning China the world's gratitude even as Chinese investors combed through the wreckage of western stock markets, in effect, looting the world on their path to hegemony. There's photographic evidence of the live human experimentation in all its horrendous detail. Above all, there's a copy of the directive that Colonel Ma had been given, which summarized the plan and provided him with the authority required to oversee its execution, including the specific authority to command resources from the Chinese Communist Party, the People's Liberation Army, and virtually every agency of the Chinese government. It's signed by the director of MSS, and countersigned by each and every one of the aforementioned agency heads. And, lest anyone miss the point, it has a single attachment, in the form of a letter from the Chairman and President himself." I paused long enough for everyone to digest this. "There were two thumb drives. One I kept in my own possession, one I gave to Peter, just in case. As it happened, we both made it out with them, but I had to surrender mine at the debriefing, for pretty obvious reasons. Peter, however, kept his to himself. For weeks now he's worked with some trusted friends from Oxford, having them create a completely defensible English translation of every document. The drives I've given you contain both the Chinese originals and their corresponding translation. Treat them as a form of life insurance."

I'd expected a buzz of questions at this point in my prepared speech, but instead was greeted with silence. "Okay, then, I continued. Apparently, the U.S. government hasn't yet decided what to do with their copy, and I don't care to speculate. However, as far as I'm concerned, our safety and any assurance of a return to normal life lies in making use of what we have here. Looking around this old house, you may be surprised to learn that we are sitting in arguably the most Internet-savvy country in the world—little Estonia is a serious Internet player. And I have some connections here, some very clever friends of the family, so to speak. When we give the go ahead, and I mean this to be a "we" decision, they will placing the documents, a few at a time, in the internal accounts of key government figures worldwide and with leaders of the international news media. Not everything, not at first, but enough to command attention, and with hints of more to come. We will also make a private communication to the Chinese authorities, promising a complete release of the documents in the event that anything untoward should befall any of us. The governing directive, with the signatures, we will save until last. The Chinese government will, undoubtedly, try to discredit the documents, but every time they think they've discredited one document, we will hit them with another. Maybe this will work, maybe not, but as Peter and I see it, it's time to use the gift Dr. Yang bequeathed us."

"And," Peter spoke up, "it also serves notice to our own governments that we're not to be messed about."

I guess I'd expected a lot of discussion, but the unanimous consent came immediately. Kip summed it up for everyone. "It's the only leverage we've got, and besides, making the bastards squirm is at least some payback for the guys we lost."

"Okay, then. Peter and I figured you'd go for this, so everything is already in place. All I have to do is make one phone call tonight and the documents start to roll out." I looked around the table again, made sure that I had everyone's attention. "Now to the other thing we need to decide—what do we do about Sandy Sawyer?"

Everyone immediately understood the need to confront Sawyer, to press her into admitting what she'd done, to pry from her some explanation of why I'd been targeted for assassination, and, most of all, why she had betrayed us. But then Colin spoke up.

"What happens after she spills her guts to you, boss? I mean, she'll likely do it, you're a right talker, but what then?"

I hesitated to reply, for the simplest of reasons. I had no answer. My father had always been a man of reason and justice and now, back where reminders of him were everywhere around me, I wanted to be no less. I allowed the silence to lengthen, not wanting to influence the others, wanting a true read of their feelings. Finally, Moira stood up from the seat she'd taken in the corner of the room, to one side and away from all the others. I'd been worried about her from the moment she'd arrived. She looked terribly gaunt, she ate little, and had seemed listless; scarcely engaged, more like the woman covered in gore on the hillside than the one who'd taken control of the plane to fly us out. But now she began to pace, becoming more agitated with every step. When she finally stopped and stood squarely in front of me, her shoulders were shaking and her face was contorted in a terrible rictus of rage.

"Kill her, Harry. Kill the bitch. You don't even need to talk to her, you've already figured it out. She sold us out, sold us out for some damned silly political game, or maybe just because you hurt her pride. Look around you, if she'd had her way, not a one of us would be here. And she killed the others, just as sure as if she'd pulled the trigger. All the guys, poor little Shih Yang, Grady, oh God…," and she began to cry and I stood and put my arms around her and she sobbed against my chest, "oh God, God, God, Harry, I couldn't even be there with you when they buried him, oh God, I even went to his little town and parked down the street from the church, but I saw them, saw his wife, saw his daughter, and oh God, Harry, I just couldn't…" and she became incoherent and Lorayne was at my side, lifting Moira's hands from my waist and leading her away into the next room. I sat down, and no one spoke at first. Finally, Peter reached his hand to my shoulder, gave it a squeeze and said, "She's right, you know."

"I'm a soldier, Peter, not a murderer."

"We're not talking murder here, but justice."

"I don't know. I've thought about it, sure, wanted nothing more when Parks told me. But just drop her. I don't know."

Kip spoke up. "This can wait. Get Sawyer alone, make her talk, then's the time to decide. But we have to make it clear to everyone, both sides, that she's no longer anyone's asset. That, and another clear message that we're not to be screwed with."

I looked around the room, saw no one else who seemed ready to press the issue, and turned to outlining the remaining parts of my plan. But if I'd gained a deferred decision on Sawyer's fate, I encountered a near rebellion when I announced my intention of slipping back into the States by myself to confront her.

"Nonsense, Harry," said Peter. "You may not run any physical risk from Sawyer herself, but someone tried to blow you to bits, someone connected directly to her. You need someone to cover your arse."

I resisted this, I'm not quite sure why, and eventually we decided to sleep on it. But later that night, as Lorayne and I lay together in bed, she raised up on one elbow, looked down at me and said, "Your life isn't just your life anymore. It's my life, too. I know that you've got to do this, for all of us, but not alone, not without help. I couldn't bear it if you didn't come back."

So, the next day it was agreed that Kip would follow me back to the States. He'd keep his distance, lying off far enough to not be noticed, but close enough to intervene. We went 'backstreet' through one of my sister's shipping connections in Hamburg to get him a German passport. There are a lot of black Germans these days, so this wouldn't occasion much notice. For my part, I'd continue with my Estonian passport—odd, after nearly a lifetime, to be "Heiki Juuru" once again. I flew from Tallinn to Helsinki, from Helsinki to London, and from London to the States, landing at Dulles, exhausted after all the time spent on airplanes and in layovers.

To recover from the long flight, I took the shuttle to the airport Marriott, slept for twelve hours straight, and then started my preparations. A cab ride into the District to another Marriott, this time the one at near the Metro Center subway station. After checking in, I bought a cheap cell phone with one of those throwaway rate plans, still using the name Heiki Juuru.

My walk had taken me all the way over to 14th, within shouting distance of the White House. I was hungry and thought briefly about walking down the street to the Willard and blowing a hundred dollars on dinner, but that seemed more the kind of thing to do someday when Lorayne was with me. Instead I cut back along H Street toward the hotel and stopped in at the Café Mozart, one of my favorite German restaurants. I had the Rahm Schnitzel and a single small pilsner and then walked back to the hotel. I pulled the shades to block out the afternoon sun, set the alarm, and napped for a couple of hours. I knew that Sawyer was a workaholic, and I'd learned that she kept a workaholic's schedule, going in to work at about four a.m. and staying until about seven p.m. My watch read half past seven. Sawyer lived in an apartment near Folger Park, just southeast of the Capitol itself, and she worked in the Rayburn building, only a short walk away. So, she was probably just getting home, kicking off her shoes, having a drink and whatever she had for an evening meal. I wanted to catch her with her guard down, but I couldn't leave things too late in the evening. I held off another hour, which was as long as I dared if I wanted the plan to work.

As it turned out I got all that I wished for, a sleep-filled voice answering the phone, then fear, then anger, then fear again as I lined out what I might do if she didn't show up when and where I demanded. She agreed and then, just as she was starting to temporize, I broke the connection. I then called Kip, gave him the outline, and, that done, took the elevator down to the ground floor, exiting onto 12th Street. I continued down 12th, past the Barnes & Noble and across Pennsylvania Avenue. I'd counted on the pedestrian traffic beginning to thin out—pre-Covid, this wouldn't have worked, what with crowds around the National Theatre, the Warner, Ford's, or the MCI Center; now, however, the streets quickly became almost ghostly quiet. I glanced up at the statue of Benjamin Franklin as I continued to walk south past the Old Post Office Building—some wag had climbed the statue and fitted old Ben with a face mask. By now Sawyer would have made it to the Capitol South metro station. From there she had four stops to get to the Federal Triangle station, just below my feet. I walked a bit further, stopping finally in the shadows of the colonnade on the 12th Street side of the IRS building. This I knew from my earlier reconnaissance was a designated smoking area for the tax workers, and a place where loiterers might still be found. I'd even purchased a pack of cigarettes and shook one out and lit up, enjoying the rush as I drew the smoke into my lungs. My days as a reformed smoker seemed to be over.

From where I stood I could no longer see Ben Franklin, but I could see the most likely point where someone would emerge from the metro and walk in that direction. As I waited, I found myself wondering yet again what I really hoped to achieve. I'd realized that,

Moira and the others to the contrary notwithstanding, I didn't really want Sawyer dead, just taken out of play, removed from her position of influence and power. Maybe I'd gone soft, or maybe I'd had enough of killing.

A trickle of people began to emerge from the Metro station exit, not the usual evening crowd, but then again, the evidence of a semi-lockdown was everywhere. I watched closely as they passed beneath the street light and there she was, same coal black hair, same faintly gothic black garb. I found myself thinking that she must be very good at her work, just in order to get away with the off-beat attire in the button-down world of Capitol Hill. But maybe like all the other government workers, she spent most of her time working from home these days. I watched her turn and head north toward where Ben awaited, but held my position, still watching the subway exit. Kip had been watching Sawyer's place since our arrival, and the plan called for him to follow her over. I waited until I saw him under the street light, then went after Sawyer.

I lingered in the shadow at the corner of the Old Post Office building until I saw that she was looking away from me, tracking the faces of the handful of walkers on Pennsylvania Avenue. Childish, perhaps, but it seemed worthwhile to put her on the defensive. I strode briskly across the intervening space and tapped her on the shoulder. She jerked and whirled around.

"York? You creepy old sonovabitch. I didn't come out here to play fucking hide-and-seek."

"Of course not," I said, "You came out here to answer all of my questions."

"The hell you say. Maybe we can cut a deal here, but I'm not just going to bend over for a butt fuck."

"It may come as a distinct shock to you, but I can't imagine fucking you. But make no mistake. If it comes to that, I'll fuck you over properly."

"Try me old man—just try me. And don't try pushing that crap you mentioned on the phone about going to the networks. I'll take that one head on, and I'll beat you."

I wasn't surprised at the language, but I was at the self-assuredness. She'd seemed altogether more anxious on the phone a few minutes earlier. Somewhere she'd found a revival of confidence.

"Then maybe there's another reason why you should satisfy me."

"Such as?"

"Such as the fact that I'm the only person standing between you and some very capable people who want to see you dead."

"Oh, let's be melodramatic about it."

I'd been fairly low key, matter-of-fact until then, but that pissed me off, not the patent disbelief, but the sarcasm. "You had someone try to kill me, and you set my whole team up to die in Africa. About half of them did die, and I'm holding you accountable. The survivors of the team want you dead, but I backed them off, at least for now, at least until I get some answers. But make no mistake. Satisfying me is the only thing that stands between you and being killed."

"I don't know anything about trying to kill you, and I most certainly did not set you up to die in Africa. I set you up to be captured, that's all. Captured, that's what they promised me, captured and put on trial. I'm not a murderer like you Special Forces bastards. I don't believe in killing people." She made as if to push past me, back toward the metro station. I reached out, gripped her shoulder hard, and spun her around. "You're not leaving just yet," I said, keeping my grip on her shoulder. "But let's go for a walk." I'd meant to go somewhere else for our talk, and now that we'd made a very public show of our anger, I didn't want some well-meaning passerby to intervene. "We do need to talk."

I pulled her the first step in the direction I wanted to go, north along 12th, and, when it was clear that she was not resisting, I relaxed my grip and then dropped my hand. We waited at the signal, then crossed Pennsylvania. There were only a few cars, and we had the sidewalk virtually to ourselves. We continued in silence halfway up the next block, then she glanced up at me and asked, "Okay, old man, what do you want to know?" Despite the 'old man,' her tone was less shrill, almost thoughtful.

"What was the point? Why did you go to the Chinese and blow the mission? You just confirmed it yourself. Was it just trying to get to me, just because, once upon a time, I'd pissed you off?"

"Don't make too much of yourself, old man. Sure, I was pissed off at you back then, but never mind what you think, you're not that fucking important. You seem to forget that I'm a player, I'm big time, too big to get bogged down going after your piddly old ass. I was playing for much bigger stakes."

"Such as?"

"My congressman is going places, and I'm going with him, straight to the top. And the Chinese are going to help him get there."

We'd reached the corner of 12th and F and I nudged Sawyer to the right along F.

"So, you were prepared to see the whole world torn up by another virus just so your boy could get ahead?"

"I didn't give a flying fuck about the facility. Give me a fucking break. The shit Parks was talking about, when I first heard about your little mission. Fucking fairy tales, just like the fucking WMDs in Iraq. Yeah, I know Parks and his buddies spooked some folks, but that was just more Wuhan lab nonsense. You may have bought it, but I sure as shit didn't."

I thought again about poor Shih Yang, who'd given her life to get the world to pay attention.

"Then…?"

"The Chinese are not the enemy. Even the fucking Pope says so. Once we get a little distance from all the "Chinese virus" crap, we can all get back to doing business again. We need them and they need us. When the time comes, my man will be leading the charge, and he'll have lots of friends behind him, and a big bankroll, too. 2024's going to be wide open, and he's going to be head of the presidential class."

She turned back toward me, smiling, pleased at the chance to display how clever she'd been, any trace of unease in our confrontation totally gone. Or so I thought.

"You're just not a player, York, and you don't understand the rules. You may think you won, with your cowboy mission and everyone thinking you saved the fucking world. 'Letter of fucking Reprisal.' Give me a fucking break. But I couldn't make anyone see that. Even my boss was tiptoeing around bigshot Toby Parks. That really pissed me off."

"So that's when you sold us out?"

"You can call it that. I call it seizing an opportunity. I get the word through to a friend, and he got it through to his friends. They're waiting for you and they capture all of you when you parachute in. They take you to Beijing, make a public display of you, No one here wants to know, the Chinese get big leverage, and they owe me and my boy big time. We're in the driver's seat and you're screwed for life. It would've worked, too, if you and that asshole Parks hadn't lied about your plan."

"You were prepared to see us all die? Just like that?" For all the ugliness I've seen in my 70 years, I couldn't get my head around the sheer matter-of-fact brutality of what she'd revealed.

"No, no, no, you'd have been captured and put on trial, just like I said. Nobody wanted you dead, and after a while maybe we'd have cut some kind of deal to get you back, at least maybe everyone but you. You're the one who got your people killed. My plan would have saved their asses."

What Hannah Arendt had once described as the 'banality of evil,' was something I'd always associated with the great dictators, but now I found myself face to face with it, in someone too clever to be wise. I wondered what she'd have thought watching the casual way Colonel Ma had murdered Jerry and Jean-Paul.

We crossed 9th Street in silence. I knew what I needed to say next, but I wanted to wait, wait for the place I'd marked out earlier for our final confrontation. But Sandy Sawyer wasn't the kind of person who lived with silence for long. "Look, York," she began, "I'm not the bad guy here. I'm just a realist. Right now, just about everyone in this town wants to go after China. Hell, they're even forcing shutdown of the fucking Confucius Centers—how fucking stupid, what a total overreaction. So, don't get all pompous with me about it. I'm for peace and friendship, and what's wrong with that."

A motorcyclist passed us going east as we drew abreast of a construction site, part of a series of major renovations extending along F Street almost to the MCI Center. This was the spot that I'd chosen to shake her. I took her by the arm again, pressed her to the side, off the sidewalk and through an opening in the board wall that the builders had erected to keep passers-by out of the site. She resisted, putting her hand to my chest to push me away. I clutched her thumb with my free hand and rotated her hand sharply, putting enough leverage into it to let her know that I could break her wrist if I chose. It's an old 'come along' grip, one that requires little muscle to generate sharp pain, and almost instant compliance. We stepped off onto gray dirt littered with concrete dust and chunks of mortar, our path lit by strings of bare bulbs running along exposed wires. After a few feet we found a roughly made board stair that took us up into a more intact portion of the original building, bare brick walls, old wooden floors, doorways with no doors, but distinct rooms nonetheless. We passed through two rooms, then stopped at the doorway leading into the third room, a doorway marked in yellow chalk by a European style 7, with a slash across the upright.

"Kip?' I called out softly.

"Right here, Major," he responded, stepping through the doorway. He was wearing rough clothes, the stubbly beginnings of a beard, and he smelled a bit sour, nothing like the usual Kip, but in keeping with the 'street person' role he'd assumed for the purpose of watching Sawyer's apartment. I shoved Sawyer toward him. "She's all yours," I said. He caught her, spun her round, and, wrapping his big arms around her, pulled her backside against his chest. The effect would have been enhanced if he'd taken hold of her breasts, given them a rough squeeze, but that just wasn't Kip. But if the look of terror that had come over her was any indication, we'd scared her enough to accomplish my purpose.

"Take her arm," I said. "If she doesn't give me the answers I want, break it."

Controlling her with his right arm, he used his left to wrench her arm behind her back and hitch it up halfway to her shoulder blades. I heard a motorcycle go past, slowly, just puttering down the street. Were we deep enough into the construction site? Too late, now, we couldn't just go dragging her around.

"Let's talk about how you tried to have me killed," I said. I waited for a response, but she'd lost her smart mouthedness. Instead I got a weakly muttered, "I never tried to have you killed, not ever, never." Her voice trailed off, and I made a motion to Kip, and he brought her arm up a little tighter. I glimpsed real pain in her expression. "Okay, let's try again. Tell me about what you told your MSS contact, what you asked him to do." No answer. I stepped forward and slapped her face, hard. It felt very unnatural, but I couldn't leave all the physical pressure to Kip. Somehow the very fact of hitting her made me more angry, not less, and, when I repeated the question, I realized that I sounded—and was—really pissed off. Even so, I only got a shake of the head. "Okay, Kip, I'm going to ask her one more time. If I get no answer, break her arm." I repeated the question, waited a moment, and then motioned yet again.

"No, wait, no—okay, I talked to her about you."

"And?"

"Yeah, well, we were talking and I told her about you and told her that when you turned up, you might have a hard-on for the Congressman, and that she might need to take that into account."

"And?"

"And? Hey, what kind of shit is that? And? That's it! That's all! I just said they needed to do something about you."

Pivotal moment. I knew that there had to be more, and also knew that it would be hard to get it out of her. I knew Kip would actually break her arm if I told him to. I knew, too, that he was physically capable of breaking her neck, if it came to that, but I didn't want that. I hadn't come prepared to kill her myself, and I couldn't ask a friend to do it. I hadn't planned this out, not the actual business of making Sawyer talk.

"So, it was just a warning, then. Nobody wanted me killed?"

"Well, no, you're a mean old bastard, but kill—I can't imagine."

And that was the real core of things. She couldn't imagine, never could have imagined, for all her intellectual capacity she lacked the simple humanity to imagine. I thought that I already knew the answer to my next question, but still, it had to be asked.

A figure materialized out of the shadows behind Kip, armed raised, something black in his hand, and as he swept it down against the back of Kip's head I realized it was a pistol. I heard the sound of metal against bone and saw Kip relax his grip on Sawyer and start to sag to his knees. I seemed to be reacting in slow motion, brushing Sawyer aside, trying to reach past Kip to the man with the gun.

"Halt! Halt! Now or I shoot you!"

The voice came from behind me, arresting my forward motion. I turned and a second man stepped into view, through the door, and into the room. It had been an unusually mild day for early spring, and he was wearing khaki shorts and a lemon-yellow golf shirt, and a fanny pack around his waist, plus what appeared to be a cell phone in a carrier on his belt, a long cord connecting it to an earpiece and throat mike. He also wielded a very large unfamiliar-looking automatic pistol, a Star, maybe or an Astra in his right hand, a bulbous suppressor protruding at its muzzle. He waved it carelessly in my direction, motioning for me to back away from his partner.

"You are, I know, a good soldier, Major York, but you and your friend are not so good as spies. We have been watching her apartment, and he was there watching, and so we followed him and you." Just then Sandy Sawyer started to bolt, but in one smooth motion the man who'd dropped Kip reached out and grabbed her ankle, spilling her on the concrete floor. "No, no, no," he said. "You must stay, missy." I saw that he was dressed very much as the other man, except for wearing a pale blue golf shirt. They looked like tourists in Key West. I also noticed that he spoke with a slight accent, one that I couldn't immediately place, and realized that the first man had spoken in much the same manner.

"We have little time," said yellow shirt. As if to underscore the point, I again heard the sound of a motorcycle, perhaps the one I'd seen earlier, only returning west along F Street, running very slowly. A cop? The District had motorcycle cops, but they worked mainly high traffic areas during rush hour. Not much hope.

"Can I get up now?" asked Sawyer.

"No, you stay, stay right there," said yellow shirt, who seemed to be the senior partner. He said something to blue shirt, a tumble of words in what sounded like Dutch. The partner stuck his pistol into his belt, reached into his fanny pack, and took out a second, much smaller pistol. He ejected the magazine into his free hand, and then pressed a button on the side of the receiver, causing the barrel to flip up against a hinge below the muzzle, exposing the chamber. A Beretta, one of the little .25s or .32s, probably. I didn't know of any other modern pistol with the flip-up feature.

"Watch good," said yellow shirt. His partner shucked a single round out of the top of the magazine, placed that round in the chamber, and pressed the barrel back into alignment with the rest of the receiver. He then pocketed the magazine. "You see, the little pistol, one round only. Klaas will give you the pistol, but we have two bigger pistols, and many rounds. Try to shoot us and you surely die. Give him the pistol."

Blue shirt extended his hand, and I took the pistol from him. Yellow shirt was undoubtedly right, having the pistol and one round didn't do much to even the odds, but it seemed better than nothing at all.

"Now you have the pistol. Now shoot Miss Sawyer, please. In the eye or in the ear, the little bullets don't penetrate so well."

"You want me to kill her?"

"Yes, she is now a bad thing for my boss's friend and he wants her dead."

"Now wait just a goddamned minute!" this was Sawyer, trying to struggle to her feet. Blue shirt had retrieved his pistol from his belt and he backhanded her with it. It didn't knock her out, but it sent her weaving to her knees, a big cut slashed along her cheek.

"Kill her," ordered yellow shirt, "Kill her now." I hesitated. "Kill her now, or Klaas shoots your *kaffir* friend."

I looked from yellow shirt to blue shirt, to Kip, who'd rolled onto his side and appeared to be regaining consciousness, however shakily. Sawyer cowered next to him. I stepped over to her and extended the little Beretta toward her temple.

"It seems that a lot of people want to see you dead," I said gently. "My people wanted me to kill you, and now so do these guys." She turned her head slightly, looking up to me. She was softly sobbing and trembling.

"Do it now, Major York!"

I caught a clump of her hair and rotated her head to the left, bringing the muzzle of the little pistol back in line with her temple. I made a conscious effort to look down at her, to clearly and unmistakably be seen lining the pistol up for a killing shot. And then I yanked her head to one side, brought the muzzle up as I extended my arm, and lined it up with blue shirt's face as I pressed the trigger. Even as his right eye blossomed into a puff of red blood and pink mucous I was diving for him, past Sawyer, over Kip, and under the swaying pistol in his left hand. I grabbed for it with both hands, ripping it from his softening grasp, and diving for the cover of the door behind him, as blue shirt slumped and blocked his partner's line of fire. I'd almost made it and then my toe caught a divot in the concrete, and I went down hard, the pistol skittering out of my grasp as I threw out my hands to break the fall. I rolled onto my back and yellow shirt was standing over me.

"Well, you may be old man, but I give you this, you are fighting man all right," and his pistol looked immense as he pointed it at my face. I lay there waiting for the shot, heard the distinctive cough of a silenced weapon, and wondered how I could have heard the sound before feeling the round, and even as this thought passed I realized that blood was spreading over the yellow shirt, and his pistol clattered next to my ear as he fell on top of me. I heard another silenced report, then another and another, close together. Then footsteps and yellow shirt's body rolled sideways, pulled by an unseen hand, and there stood Colin, a little Walther pistol in hand.

"Are you all in one piece then, Harry? You look a right mess."

I lay there for a moment, just staring up at him, trying to take it all in. Finally, I reached out a hand and said, "Help me up." I took his hand, let him pull me to my feet. "Not that I'm unhappy to see you, but where the hell did you come from?"

"Major Rudd, it was, and your good lady Lorayne. They didn't much like you going off with just Kip to watch, so I took a flight right after the two of you, knocked up an old friend for a motorbike and a cold shooter, and Bob's your uncle. Get on with you, Harry, time's wasting. You want to know why? Well Lorayne said that you were a good man, and the Major said, that's right, but this job wants a hard man, too, and he just looked straight at me. Right he was, too. There's times that good people need a right bastard to do for them. That's me."

I surveyed the carnage. Blue shirt and yellow shirt were both clearly dead, Kip had pulled himself into an upright sitting position, but his expression remained vacant. Sawyer had curled into the fetal position, her arms wrapped around her knees, shaking and crying.

"Let's see if we can get Kip to his feet and help him out of here," I said.

"Good enough," said Colin. "If he's up for holding on to me, I'll get him out on the back of the motorbike."

"Okay, and I can walk, it's not far." In fact, the hotel seemed a million miles away, but I'd have to make it.

He looked at Sawyer and the two dead men. "No harm I'd say leaving this lot right here, we'll be nicely out of it by the time someone shows up for work in the morning." He paused, waved his hand at Sawyer. "But what about her?"

I knew what he meant. "Leave her," I said.

"Lorayne told me to kill her, no matter what."

"I'll square it with Lorayne. It doesn't matter. She thought she was a player, but she's found that she's just another pawn."

He knelt in front of her, cupped her chin with one hand, shoved the pistol in her face with the other. "Fucking brilliant. She's shit her knickers full, she has," he said over his shoulder, then gave her his full attention. "Now listen, you silly little cunt. Harry here's an officer and a gentleman and an intellectual sod to boot. He worries too bloody much about doing the right thing. But me, I'm just a plain lad. So here it is. You get away this time, but just this time. If anything happens to any of my friends, anything, mind, if a pigeon shits on Harry's next car, then that's it, I'll find you and I'll kill you right out, no mistake. Understand?" He pulled her chin up and down, forcing her to nod 'yes.' "Good then, now give us a goodbye kiss," and he kissed her full on the lips, "and we'll let you stay right here with K.C. and the fucking Sunshine Band. Shooters wearing pastel shirts, Harry—it's right insulting. Now, give me a hand with Kip."

We got Kip to his feet, got his arm draped over Colin's shoulder, and they disappeared through the shadowed doorway. I started to follow them, looked back one last time, and walked back over to Sandy Sawyer. She was curled up into a ball and was crying hard, her whole body shaking. I stood over her for a moment, then turned and walked away.

EPILOGUE

IT'S BEEN A few months since we left Sandy Sawyer sitting in her own waste on the streets of D.C. The incident itself prompted a brief flurry of news coverage, then nothing but silence. Draw your own conclusions. Shortly afterward, Sawyer resigned quietly from her congressional staff position and, from what I've read, accepted a teaching position at a small college in Ohio. I shudder at her future impact upon students, but I'm grateful that her ability to influence national policy has been hobbled, I hope permanently.

The team's "truce," if one can call it that, with the Chinese government and the MSS appears to be holding. We released enough documents to give them pause, while hinting strongly at our ability, if threatened, to counter with a series of crushing blows to their international image, particularly among the African states they've courted for the last decade. Targeting the western powers might well have gained them a pass in places like the United Nations, but a plan based upon an almost casual genocide in central Africa plays well nowhere, particularly as international concern for the murderous treatment of the Uighurs continues to gain momentum. Moreover, I gather from

Toby Parks that our own new administration has quietly reinforced the message, supported by the governments of the United Kingdom—thank you, Peter Rudd—and France and a number of other countries around the world. Only the Germans have stood aside, testimony, perhaps, to how deeply the Chinese have already sunk their hooks into the German economy. I don't honestly know how much the Chinese government was really to blame for Covid, and I suspect none of us will ever know. But in trying to exploit, hellishly, the already awakened fears with a deliberate virus release, and then being stopped and, worse for them, exposed, they overreached themselves badly, as tyrants often do. Our little team paid an awful price for stopping them, but I'm deeply proud of what we did.

Deeply, but quietly proud. In the preceding pages, while the memories were still fresh, I've tried to capture what we did and to memorialize the price we paid. My immediate audience is the team, and, to the extent they choose to share, their loved ones. I include Toby Parks in this, with the understanding that doing so, almost inevitably, opens the door to wider circulation within the government. Maybe that's a good thing, and maybe, at some point, there will be value in a wider circulation still, but for right now I want things quiet. Someday, I might take it further, but likely by presenting it as fiction. The story, I would like to think, has its inspirational aspects, and those who know the truth don't need me to insist upon it for a wider public.

And what of the team members? Ever so gradually, we've started to build our new lives, inevitably gaining a bit of distance from each other, but comfortable with a bond forged in blood and fire, a bond that will last forever. Peter has fully recovered physically and, unsurprisingly, has, in his own subtle way, built on what we achieved. After helping to godfather our document release, he found himself invited into the councils of his own government, specifically, the British intelligence community. They are, apparently, fascinated with what we did and how we did it, and see it as a model for sending a message to bad international actors without risking open confrontation. It's too early to know where this might lead, or what impact Peter might have on the process, but he's becoming a player. For better or worse, he's moved beyond vegetating once again in the comforts of Surrey. I like to think he might stay the course, perhaps even one day emerging as "C," the head of MI-6. They could do much worse.

Dito returned to his partner in Las Vegas, and resumed the quiet life they'd been sharing before the mission. He calls from time to time, and I'm always delighted to hear from him. I don't need to belabor the point beyond what I've already chronicled, but I regard him as a true hero, and I'm proud to call him my friend.

Lem now resides full time in Tallinn, where he manages those aspects of my Estonian business that I haven't shared with my sister. Chiefly, these are a nexus of cyber security connections that arose out of our post-mission activities. Lem continues to surprise, not just a good pilot, or a better tactical operator than I had dreamed, but also someone quite comfortable in the world of computers, and their power to shape the world. A remarkable young man. Then again, I don't know why I should expect any less—I knew his father.

I'm not quite sure what to say about the partnership formed between Kip and Colin. In the weeks after Colin rescued us in D.C., the two of them spent a lot of time together, a lot of time sharing their respective outlooks, a lot of time converging on what they wanted to do next. Two seemingly unconnected events gave me at least a glimpse of where this has led. Some time back, I got a call from Parks, who asked if I heard about Bernie Croes. After I convinced him of my cluelessness, he told me that Croes's body had drifted ashore on Aruba, victim of an apparent drowning. Still, the body showed some signs of a struggle, inconclusive, but consistent with someone who'd been held, struggling, underwater. The Aruban authorities had ultimately decided to write it off as accidental, but there had been some interest in two tourists who'd been seen with Croes, a black American and a white Englishman.

Not long after that, the assassination of the Wiangaran "General-President" made world headlines—briefly, given the sad lack of international interest in African affairs. Details were few, but the killing round was identified as coming from a .338 Lapua Magnum, a round much favored by militarily trained snipers for very long-range shooting, and indications were that the shot had been taken from somewhere around 1500 meters. Governments lined up quickly to deny any role in the shooting, although clearly no one mourned much, even in Wiangara. Soon thereafter, the U.N. peacekeeping force in the eastern Congo extended its reach into Wiangara, to the benefit of its long-suffering villagers.

I knew someone capable of making such a shot, given the assistance of a cool and competent observer on the spotting scope next to him. I knew, too, that he had all the motivation in the world for doing it. But none of this truly came together until a few weeks later, when Kip and Colin showed up unexpectedly at our doorstep. I'd decided to step back from the Naburje Foundation and its work in central Africa, but, when I'd asked Kip if he wanted to take charge, he'd turned me down, saying he'd been working on something else. Instead, I'd turned to Bobby and Tommy Naburje's parents in Kenya, and had been delighted at their willingness to take it on. So, as Kip and Colin and I sat down in our living room—Lorayne was visiting her parents that morning—I was genuinely puzzled at what obviously wasn't purely a social call. They were there to ask me to underwrite a new enterprise, something that, as they looked to the future, seemed beyond the bankrolls they shared from their mission payout. When they mentioned the size of the investment they had in mind, I was given pause. Not that I couldn't easily afford it, but it exceeded any obvious venture I would have attributed to them, maybe something akin to setting up a little tactical training academy like the one Grady had once managed. And so, I had to ask the question.

"Would you forgive a vague response?" asked Kip. "You know us, and you know we mean to do something good with the money. Will that suffice?"

I must have looked dubious.

"How about if I say that we're setting up a project, not unlike what you did with the 'Letter of Reprisal,' but aimed at surgically removing certain cancerous growths."

I looked from one of them to the other. Not a medical degree between the two of them.

Colin spoke up. "Sort of like 'Doctors without Borders,' but more in our skill set."

And then I remembered a remark he'd made when we'd met with Peter in that little park in Godalming, the moment when I'd laid our mission before them, and I knew exactly what they'd been up to, and exactly what they had in mind. I wished that Lorayne had been sitting next to me, helping me to check my moral compass, even though I pretty well knew what she would have said, what, in fact, she had said when we'd opened our hearts to each other about the mission: "Harry, foxes may be pretty little animals, but sometimes you have to shoot one to protect the chickens." In any case, I'd crossed this particular moral threshold that long-ago morning at the Antietam battlefield with Parks. So, I wrote the check, and wished them well, wondering, in a small corner of my heart, at the possibility of offering them more of myself than money.

Moira, I'm happy to say, has emerged whole, or, at least, apparently beginning to put Grady in that same silent place she's carried Larry Beale. Two loves, dead in one's arms—I can't even begin to wrap my head around it. Ironically, Mary-Anne Dawkins seems to have been the key. Sometime after Grady's funeral Moira took the bit between her teeth and went to the cabin on Singing Creek. I don't know what was initially said, I've never asked either one of them, but I gather that many tears were shed and shared. And out of shared loss they found a kind of odd friendship—there's no accounting, in the end, for the vagaries of the human heart.

Moira gave up on San Francisco, and now, also improbably, she's our—relatively—near neighbor, one county over across the river in Ohio. She's given up on contract flying since it involves too much exposure to strangers, and she feels more secure, she says, in the heartland. She's taken her mission money, bought a couple of small airplanes, and set up a flying school, training at no charge young women who dream of a future in aviation. Delightfully, one of her first students was Abby Dawkins, who is going to Annapolis next year with plans for a career in Marine Corps aviation. That way she can fly, fight if it comes to that, and honor the memory of her dad, who, I can't help but believe, never shared with her the story of his first wife.

That leaves Lorayne, which means me and Lorayne. We're just married now, only a few months ago. I've kept my condo in Virginia Beach for ocean getaways, but bought a small, disused farm not too far from her parents. I could say that this was about our security, and, nestled among her siblings, cousins, and friends—many in local law enforcement—we make more unenticing targets than we would most anywhere else in the world. But above all we're here because her roots are here, and that matters deeply to her and is welcoming to this sadly rootless old man. I'm blessed that what I thought might be challenges have proven not to be. My new mother-and father-in-law are both younger than I am—just—but we got past that quickly, for my part because they are lovely people, for theirs because I make their baby girl happy.

We don't get out much these days, nesting away our days as we supervise the workmen—more cousins—who are here every day to work on the house and the barns. Will we have livestock? Lorayne wants horses, and I doubt if I'll ever say "no" to her about anything, at least anything that matters. For now, we have a dog, rescued from the local shelter, an older pit bull mix named Santana, improbably ugly and improbably sweet-tempered. Almost overnight he became "daddy's" dog, so much so that Lorayne now insists on another rescue who will spend more time with "mom." Two-legged children? Probably not. As young as Lorayne seems to me, she's in her mid-thirties, and, when we talked about it, suggested that maybe her window had closed. Maybe she recognizes that fatherhood at my age is, frankly, terrifying, and maybe, too, we both recognize that there are lingering threats to our happiness. Children are always hostages to fortune, but most parents don't have a pissed-off nation-state to worry about.

Instead, we've resolved to be the best uncle and aunt we can possibly be, for all her nieces and nephews. And we spend a lot of time just quietly enjoying the day to day. I replaced the Porsche with a pickup truck, one of those with four-wheel drive and all the fancy extras, and, yes, it has a gun rack. We have lots of guns, just in case. I treated Lorayne to a truck just like it, identical except for color—mine is green, hers lavender, a nod, she says, to her feminine side. And she's bought me a motorcycle and is teaching me to ride.

We're happy, then, as happy as she deserves to be, and probably happier than I deserve. We're good talking together, and we're good sharing quiet times together. Now that I've written our story, I spend some of our quiet times trying to find a larger meaning. Ironically, I've increasingly come around to something Sandy Sawyer said. We do need to get along with China. It's a big world, and there should be plenty of room for sharing its good things among nations. The ordinary folk of China may speak differently and look differently, but I doubt if, in the things that matter, there's really much difference between them and my new neighbors and relations in this hard-scrabble corner of Appalachia. We all want and need pretty much the same things. It only falls apart when tyrants get in the way. Unconstrained power feeds on itself, until someone rises up to stop it.

I'll mourn Jean-Paul and Jerry, Tommy and Kees for all the days that are left to me. Bobby from back when. And Grady. I'll let Grady have the last word. A long time ago, sharing a drink, he told me that he'd only ever learned how to pray, really pray, one prayer: "I've fought the good fight. I've finished my course. I've kept the faith. Now, Lord, bring me home."

Semper fi, jarhead.

Author's Note

I started this novel almost thirty years ago, at a time when I'd just come to the end of a four-year stint working with a group of people not unlike the mission team it depicts, a mix of eager youngsters and grizzled veterans working on the fringes of the 'official' special operations community. I thought then that I'd come to the end of a unique chapter of my life and that I'd never again know the likes of this grand team. I wanted to capture something of what had made them so extraordinary, the dreams, the fire, and the heart—the love and passion that made them all special individuals and which had created such a special bond between us.

But life plays funny tricks, sometimes, and, even as I closed the page on that chapter, I found myself opening a new chapter, one filled on a much broader scale, with people of similar ilk. This new phase offered very little time for writing, and meant that the story I started in the early 1990s would be finished, a paragraph here and there, on airplanes and in hotel rooms, in the margins, so to speak, of an even more intense involvement with the overlapping worlds of counter-ter-rorism and national security. Still, the very work that made finding time to write so difficult also opened the door to the special operations community a good deal wider, offering opportunities to get to know its personalities—including one authentically legendary figure and several near legends—on close terms. And it made me want even more badly to carry the story forward, while enriching my insights into the human dimension of special operations, which is what had drawn me to the idea in the first place.

Now understand very clearly. I am not a special operations veteran and would never pretend to be. The common coin of the community is that it despises 'wannabes,' and I'm perfectly content with my own more humble national security contributions. But for nearly twenty years my world overlapped with many such veterans. I've been trained by them and worked with them and even, in recent years, had several of them work for me. I've been fortunate enough to listen to them, to get to know them, and to admire them unreservedly without, I hope, romanticizing their calling or seeing them as other than they are. This novel is a work of fiction, and the characters are fictional because, as any novelist knows, characters, whatever their origins, soon begin to take on a life of their own; none of the characters represents a real person, living or dead. Still, if it is not explicitly about real people and a real mission, it is absolutely meant to be a tribute to some very real people and to the real missions they've performed.

Readers wise in the legends of the special operations community will, however, find traces in the story of one of the most legendary figures in U.S. Army Special Forces history. Years ago, I was captivated with the story of Captain Larry Thorne, who served as the original inspiration for this novel's Harry York. Larry Allan Thorne—really, Lauri Allan Torni—was a Finn who'd fought the Russians in the Winter War and again after 1941 alongside the Germans—the Finns, like the Estonians of this novel, didn't much like the Germans, but they hated the Russians more. Lauri Torni was, one might say, the Audie Murphy of the Finnish Army, winner of the Mannerheim Cross and many more medals. His fame was so great that, after 1945, the Russians wouldn't leave him in peace, and they basically pushed the Finnish government to run him out of the country.

He wound up in the U.S., under the auspices of the Lodge Act, and became a Special Forces soldier, maybe the quintessential Special Forces soldier. And then one day, early in the Vietnam War, he flew off in a helicopter and disappeared, and for nearly forty years he belonged to the world of legend, everyone knowing that he had to be dead, and yet somehow thinking that, somewhere, somehow, he continued his own private war against the Communists. Thus, the original inspiration for this story—what if Larry Thorne (or a fictional character inspired by him) was called upon to mount a private counterterrorist mission, using a team composed of characters inspired by the 'pick-up' squad of individuals that I'd come to know and love.

As might be expected, a thirty-year gestation meant that the story grew distant from its original inspiration and, along the way, sadly, the legend of Larry Thorne was resolved. In 2003 the U.S. government positively identified remains recovered in 1999 as those of Larry Thorne, and later that same year, he was interred at Arlington National Cemetery in a ceremony that paid due respect to his service both to his homeland and to his adopted country. Only traces remain in the novel of this original inspiration, but I hope that these traces pay appropriate tribute to Larry Thorne and to his 'Foreign Legion' comrades who were, in many respects, the founding fathers of the modern U.S. Special Forces. And, precisely because writing this novel became a sometime thing, the timelines necessarily changed as the years went by. The Larry Thorne influence was recrafted to fit Harry's father and his mentor, since Harry had to lose some twenty years along the way. I also chose to translate this character biography from Finland to its near neighbor, Estonia, a small country with a fascinating history, one that has punched way above its weight in the fight against tyranny.

I hope that it will also serve as a tribute to a second source of inspiration, albeit one I didn't recognize until a few years ago. The very first 'grown-up' book I ever read, some sixty years ago, was Gordon Landsborough's (undeservedly almost forgotten) *Tobruk Commando*, the true story of a once famous—and famously disastrous—British commando raid on Rommel's supply facilities at Tobruk. My original paperback copy had disintegrated under the impact of many re-readings by the time I finished high school, and it was only some thirty-five years later that I found an intact version in a used book store. Reading it again, with this novel very nearly complete, I realized for the first time how deeply the themes of the Tobruk raid had sub-consciously informed the story I had written, and how much the raid's central figure stood, alongside Larry Thorne, as the inspiration for Harry York. *Letter of Reprisal* is thus a tribute also to Lt. Colonel John Haselden of the British Army and to the men of 'Operation Agreement,' sacrificed on the altar of the best of strategic intentions and the worst of bureaucratic bungling.

This brings us full circle to the world we now live in. To answer an obvious question, I know of no instance where a **Letter of Marque and Reprisal** has been issued by anyone, official or semi-official, in connection with the war against terrorism—but there was a time, shortly after 9/11, when the concept itself received very lively discussion in certain quarters. Later, as the Somali pirates became an international problem, the concept once again gained currency as a means of protecting our merchant ships. Congressman Ron Paul even introduced legislation to implement it. Moreover, the 1856 *Declaration of Paris* only applies between signatories—conspicuously absent among them are China, the United States, and, of course, all the modern nations of Africa.

As Colin Graham suggests in the novel, perhaps we sometimes need 'Killers without Borders' in order to ensure that the NGOs—the non-governmental aid organizations—have a fighting chance of performing their humanitarian missions. People die in droves in Africa and elsewhere because the world insists on sending doctors and nurses to places where they cannot succeed without first sending soldiers to prepare a place for them. Moreover, it is undoubtedly true that, in the current climate in Washington, doing things 'by the book' usually means getting nothing worthwhile done at all—the "book," after all, seems to be rewritten daily, and without reference to anything more than the most selfish domestic political agendas.

I've updated the story to reflect current political realities, at least as I see them. "Wiangara" may be a convenient fiction, but chronic dysfunction and persistent cruelty mock the aspirations of millions of poor Africans who yearn for a better life. These people deserve better than intermittent attention from the world community and weak-kneed protection from politically-hobbled UN peacekeepers. I've also tried to account for the challenges that might arise in mounting a special operation in the world of Covid-19.

Finally, a word about casting the Chinese government and Communist Party in the role of villains. I trust that any thoughtful reader will appreciate the distinction draw here between them and the people of China. The character of Shih Yang is meant to speak for the goodness that is China, a goodness manifested every day in small ways throughout China, and, more visibly to outsiders, in the Hong Kong protests, the efforts to smuggle out the stories of the Uighur genocide, and the similar courageous efforts by Chinese scientists to shine a light on the original Covid cover-ups. One can yearn for the day when the regime in power embodies all the best that is China. For now, however, we must not allow our respect for the Chinese people to close our eyes to their govern ment's malfeasance. The Chinese Ministry of State Security appears quite frequently these days in books, movies, and TV shows as the "bad guys." One can only say that they have earned it.

Over the thirty-year gestation of this story, I've accumulated a long series of debts. A special "thank you" goes to "the team," the friends who read and re-read the manuscript, offering suggestions, both great and small, that I've gratefully adopted. Roger Lewis, Dave Dietz, Geoff Northridge, and Diane Wineinger represent the core members of "the team," and, without their insight and encouragement, *Letter of Reprisal* would have been stillborn; a late, but highly-valued member of "the team" is my daughter Camara, a child when I started, now an insightful grown woman. Through Roger Lewis, I came to know Bruce J. Berger, author of two wonderful novels, *The Flight of the Veil* and *The Music Stalker*, among others. In addition to being a great writer, Bruce is also a sharp-eyed editor, whose insights and sage advice have helped me past many obstacles. Any flaws that remain are entirely my own responsibility.

The core characters of the story were inspired by my old friends at IPS, and, while they've evolved beyond recognition, it remains a debt I'm honored to acknowledge. We did great things together, guys, greater than we ever could have imagined at the time. If this story should come your way, I trust you'll see it as a tribute.

Finally, and above all, I am profoundly indebted to my wife, Jan. She stayed the course when my head was in the African jungles. She lifted my heart when the disappointments piled up. She served as my first and most dedicated editor, but even more, she believed in me and in *Letter of Reprisal*, at every stage in its tortuous course to publication. For more than three decades, she has been my greatest support and my highest inspiration, not just in writing this novel, but in everything I've done or dreamed of doing.

Printed in Great Britain
by Amazon